Learn Container Basics In An Hour!

Container gardening was very hard for me when I first started. I kept buying book after book, and failing at most of the projects I attempted. Then I bought a video that taught me more in thirty minutes than I had learned in the previous ten years. I decided then and there to include a DVD/Movie with this book so that the learning process would be easy for you.

Watch the DVD/Movie (sold separately) for thirty minutes and skim chapters 1,2, and 15 in this book. Include chapter 4 if you are ready to try a hanging basket. You will be ready to design and plant container gardens like the pros!

The DVD/Movie is designed to show you container design and planting basics. The book is the reference back-up, with everything you ever wanted to know about container gardens in Florida!

I would love to see your masterpieces! Email me your photos at info@easygardencolor.com.

Pamela Crawford

During the course of writing this book, we planted over 10,000 plants in hundreds of containers to see which worked best in Florida. I have come to the conclusion that Florida is one of the best places on earth to plant container gardens. I hope you enjoy reading this book - and learning its lessons - as much as I did writing it!

CONTAINER GARDENS FOR FLORIDA

Pamela Crawford

Color Garden, Inc.

Purchasing Information

The book and companion DVD are available through most booksellers and many garden centers in Florida. It is also available through Amazon.com for orders from out of state. To locate your nearest source or place an order with the publisher, contact us at:

Color Garden Publishing
5596 Western Way
Lake Worth, FL 33463
Phone: 561-964-6500   Fax: 561-967-6205
Web site: www.easygardencolor.com
Email: info@easygardencolor.com

Credits

Author: Pamela Crawford
Research Assistant: Barbara Hadsell
Managing Editor and Additional Text: Kaki Holt, kakiholt@bellsouth.net
Cover Design and Graphic Design Assistance: Elaine Weber (www.ewdlogos.com)
Proofreader: Barbara Iderosa, Best Editing Service, Wellington, Florida
Container Design: Pamela Crawford, Barbara Hadsell, Miguel Olivares-Popoca and Proven Winners unless otherwise noted.
Garden Construction: Tim Hadsell and Miguel Olivares-Popoca
Computer Consulting: Roger Rosenthal, Affordable Computer Training, Palm Beach Gardens, Florida
Landscape Design: Pamela Crawford, Color Garden Inc., Lake Worth, Florida, unless otherwise noted
All photos by Pamela Crawford unless otherwise noted, except for:
    Balazara: Pages 12-14, 136-137, 145 (white bird), 210, 238-239, 253, 278 (agave),
          329 (eugenia).
    gina: Dragon wing begonia in cast stone container on page 175
    Kaki Holt: Page 31
    Kinsman: Pages 113, 118
    Lechuza: Pages 145 (corn plant, lady palm, peace lily, snake plant, zz plant), 152-159, 164-167, 288 (corn
          plant), 292 (dieffenbachia), 294 (ficus), 313 (both photos), and 323 (snake plant) .
    Sanchez and Maddux: Pages 114-115, 131, 134-135, 230-231, 240-241, and 255
    Suzanne Williams: Azalea photo on pages 148, 200, 201, 328

Contents

Contributors

A & W Annuals, a wholesale nursery in Lake Worth, Florida, contributed many plants, test ideas, and general information concerning container plants. They were particularly helpful with coleus.

Anamese (www.anamese.com) from Welsh, Louisiana, contributed beautiful, glazed pots for us to test for this book. See their containers on pages 18-19, 33, 53, 60-61, 123, 192 (top photo), 242, and 256.

Balazara (www.balazara.com) from Wellington, Florida contributed many photographs and much information about Impruneta terra cotta. See their containers on pages 12-14, 136-137, 145 (white bird), 210, 238-239, 253, 278 (agave), and 329 (eugenia).

Bodger Botanicals (www.bodger.com) is a seed company that provided many plants to test through their broker, Michell's (and Michell's representative, Carol Troendle). We were quite successful with many of their plants. See the index for the page numbers that show their plants.

Lloyd Singleton and Danny Miller from the **Breakers Hotel** (www.thebreakers.com) in Palm Beach provided a wealth of information on container plants, especially salt-tolerant plants. See their work on pages 176 (top, right), 189 (top), 195 (top), 222 (two bottom photos), 247, 268-269, 272, 310 (areca palm), and 311 (zamia).

Joe Parr, Ann Pidgeon, and Robin Menino (left to right) from Tampa generously shared their expertise on container gardening. They taught me how to make the huge hanging baskets shown in Chapter 4.

Campania International (www.campaniainternational.com) from Pennsylvania contributed some wonderful containers for us to test. See their products on pages 16-17, 48, 68, 140-141, 183, and 225.

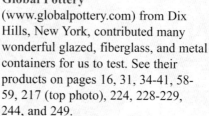

Garden Tender (email address: wob111@hotmail.com) owner Karen O'Brien worked for me for many years in my landscape design business and now runs her own garden business. See her handiwork on pages 150-151.

Giverney Gardens, a garden center in Jupiter, Florida, was the site for the photographs on pages 30 and 31. They also designed many of the containers in chapters about low-water and salt-tolerant containers.

Global Pottery (www.globalpottery.com) from Dix Hills, New York, contributed many wonderful glazed, fiberglass, and metal containers for us to test. See their products on pages 16, 31, 34-41, 58-59, 217 (top photo), 224, 228-229, 244, and 249.

Impact Marketing (www.impactmarketing.com) helps garden writers learn about garden product companies. They coordinated our work with Campania.

International Pottery Alliance (www.potteryalliance.com) contributed many beautiful pots to our trials. See their products on pages 32, 42-43, 46-47, 50-51, 54-55, 57, 138, 193, and 226.

   For container sources, go to www.easygardencolor.com

Contributors with information regarding orchids are listed on page 161 under "Great places to Shop and Learn."

Kurt Crist, Landscape Architect from Sarasota, Florida, shared some of his clients' unique containers. See one of them on page 13.

Lechuza (www.lechuza.de) is a German company that produces very unique and useful self-watering containers that were provided for us to test. See their containers on pages 145 (corn plant, lady palm, peace lily, snake plant, zz plant), 152-159, 164-167, 288 (corn plant), 292 (dieffenbachia), 294 (ficus), 313 (both photos), and 323 (snake plant).

Lotus International from Athens, Georgia (www.lotus-intl.com), provided many containers for us to try. Special thanks to their sales rep, Rhonda James, who came to visit our trial gardens. See their products on pages 45, 56, 62-63, and 245.

Masart (www.masart.com) from Hollywood, Florida, provided the wonderful, hand-painted, Mexican pots shown on pages 26, 48, 52, 66-67, 108-109, and 270. Special thanks to Arturo Bustamonte for visiting our trial gardens and helping us with photo shoots.

Ore (www.orecontainers.com) from Salt Lake City, Utah, provided the wonderful, hand-crafted, iron containers shown on pages 20 and 21.

Pinder's Nursery, from Palm City, Florida, is a grower that sells many container plants to garden centers. Terry Pinder brought us some fabulous plants to test. See some of them on pages 23 and 52-53.

Planter Technology (www.plantertechnology.com) from Hayward, California, provided some great, self-watering containers. See their products on page 259.

Proven Winners (www.provenwinners.com) provided plants and container designs for us to test. We were thrilled with quality of their plants, which are shown throughout this book. Special thanks to Kerry Strope and Nicole Jackson. See the index for the page numbers that show their plants.

Sabu, a pottery wholesaler from Palm City, Florida, provided the containers shown on pages 15, 64-65, 142, 174, 192 (bottom photo), and 248.

Sanchez and Maddux, Landscape architects from Palm Beach, Florida, provided us with photographs of their elegant container designs. See pages 114-115, 131, 134-135, 230-231, 240-241, and 255. Pictured here is Phil Maddux, left, and Jorge Sanchez, right.

Sunlight (www.sunlightflorida.com), a wholesale pot distributor in Ft. Lauderdale, Florida, allowed us to photograph the showroom (left, and on page 25) and gave us lots of information. Also see their products on pages 257, 260-261, and 296 (blue container with fiber optic grass).

Universal Orlando Resort (www.universalorlando.com) Special thanks to Barry McKently, the director, Universal Orlando Horticulture, and to his staff for the gorgeous containers on pages 180-181, 211, 212-213, 246, 283 (white bird), and 314 (Xmas palm). See page 181 for a larger photo of the staff.

Glossary

Annual: A plant that lasts for only one season.

Central Florida: The part of Florida located in zone 9. See map, opposite.

Growth Rate: The growth rate depends on the plant's environment. More water and fertilizer, for example, cause plants to grow faster, so the categories are estimates only. *Slow* refers to a plant that increases its size by less than 20 percent the first year. *Medium* refers to a plant that increases its size by 20 to 50 percent the first year. *Fast* refers to a plant that grows more than 50 percent during its first year.

North Florida: The part of Florida located in zone 8. See map, opposite.

Perennial: Perennials are plants that last more than one season. Some people differentiate between woody perennials (plants with woody stems) and herbaceous perennials (plants with soft stems). This book defines perennials as all herbaceous perennials, bulbs, groundcovers, shrubs, vines, and trees that last for more than one season.

Salt Tolerance: *Low* refers to plants that do not tolerate salt spray on their leaves. *Medium* refers to plants that take some salt on their leaves. *High* refers to plants that take direct oceanfront conditions, provided they are somewhat back from the shoreline. Chapter 11 (*Salt and Wind Gardens*) in this book's companion, "Easy Gardens for Florida," gives much more detail.

South Florida: The part of Florida located in zones 10 and 11. See map, opposite.

Subtropical: Areas that do not routinely have freezing temperatures.

Wind Tolerance: *Low* refers to plants that like fairly protected locations. *Medium* refers to plants that take winds produced in more open locations but not extreme sites, like oceanfront or in a wind tunnel created by buildings. *High* refers to plants that are the most wind-tolerant available. In storms where winds reach 30 to 40 miles per hour for more than a few hours, even plants with high-wind tolerance suffer leaf burn. However, the plants with high-wind tolerance obviously sustain less damage than the ones with low-wind tolerance. The leaf burn does not heal. New leaves grow and eventually replace the ones that are damaged. None of the plants in this book can sustain severe tropical storm or hurricane-force winds without damage.

Above: Many thanks to my primary helpers in researching, and writing this book. From left to right, Miguel Olivares-Popoca, Kaki Holt, and Barbara and Tim Hadsell. See page nine for their specific contributions.

Climate and Zone Information

Range of this book: This book covers the state of Florida, which includes zones 8, 9, 10, and 11. "South Florida" refers to zones 10 and 11. "Central Florida" is zone 9, and "North Florida" is zone 8. **The Truth about Zone Hardiness Maps:** I used to think that the zone maps were always right. Not so! **The Zone Hardiness Maps are more of a 'be careful' than a 'do not plant in your zone or it will quickly die.'** And, it's not as easy as the zone map makes it look. Technically, a zone map would look like a Doppler Radar screen, with zones 9 and 10 being mixed up all over Tampa. Many zone 10 plants are traditionally planted all over central Florida, which is zone 9. Bromeliads and Hibiscus are good examples. Both are quite common in Tampa and Orlando, which is zone 9. The Bromeliad Society was even founded in Orlando, where Bromeliads are not supposed to survive the winters! (Since Bromeliads like shade, most are planted under trees, which usually gives the necessary protection from the cold.) **The individual plants in this book are classed by USDA zone** _as well as local use patterns._

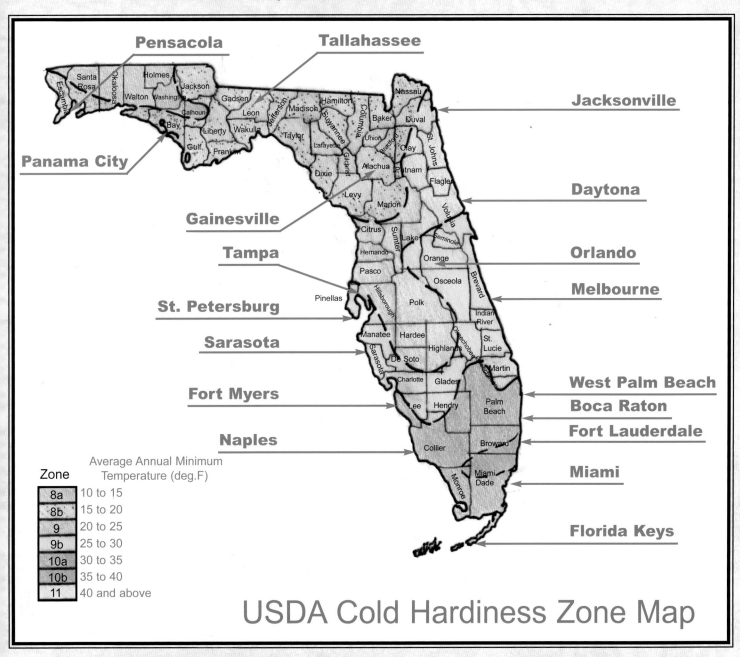

Zone	Average Annual Minimum Temperature (deg.F)
8a	10 to 15
8b	15 to 20
9	20 to 25
9b	25 to 30
10a	30 to 35
10b	35 to 40
11	40 and above

USDA Cold Hardiness Zone Map

Microclimates

Microclimates: A few degrees make a big difference in a light freeze. Learn to judge the following:

1. Areas closer to salt water are warmer than inland areas. For example, St. Petersburg is warmer than Tampa. Boca Raton is warmer than Homestead (which is further inland but much further south).

2. Sheltered areas are warmer than open areas. Plants under trees suffer less cold damage than plants in the open.

3. Areas open to winds from the northwest are colder than areas sheltered from these winds. Eva Pabon of the Osceola County Extension office told me that, when she worked at Disney, they planted lantana around a lake. When the temperatures froze, the lantana that received the cold wind from the northwest died, while the rest of it lived.

4. Areas close to buildings are warmer than more open areas, particularly those located on the south side of the building.

If you are new to the area and want to test your garden microclimates, buy several high-low thermometers from your local home improvement store. When a freeze is forecast, place them in different areas of your garden. They will record the low temperatures without you staying up all night to watch them.

Look around your neighborhood to see which plants have thrived over the years. You can also call your county extension office for local expertise.

Containers are great places for plants that might be damaged by freezes since you can move them inside whenever a freeze threatens. I have very heavy containers that are difficult to move, so I bought a small dolly at a home improvement store and was amazed at how much weight I could easily move with it. It comes in quite handy for freeze or hurricane warnings.

Containers provide a wonderful opportunity for people in central and north Florida to grow tropical plants that might die if they weren't mobile. Our climate is warming considerably, so the number of freezes is decreasing in Florida. Tampa, for example, had 32 freezes in the 1980's and only 4 during the 1990's. For more information about Florida climate change and how it should affect your planting decisions, see "Best Garden Color for Florida," pages 13 to 17.

Areas close to houses are warmer than open areas.

Areas open to winds are colder than protected spots.

Container gardens can be moved inside if a freeze threatens.

For container sources, go to www.easygardencolor.com

Author's Notes

Background: I began gardening at age 3 with my English mother in Mississippi. I moved to Florida in the 70's, planning to have a gorgeous garden filled with color. The next few years brought more blunders than blooms, as I made every gardening mistake in the book! These early errors started a three-decade saga to learn everything I could about Florida gardening. I received a Master's Degree in Landscape Architecture from Florida International University, followed by starting a nursery and garden design business. While designing 1500 gardens, I also started my own trial gardens (on the eight acres where I live and work) to determine which Florida plants gave the highest performance with the least amount of care. Of the thousands of plants tested to date, only about 300 lived through my difficult trials in my low-maintenance gardens. These are truly tough plants!

I am now writing a series of books called the "Florida Gardening Series" about my trial garden experiences. The first volume, "Easy Gardens for South Florida," was published in 2001and features 100 easy plants as well as all you ever needed to know about how to plant and maintain your Florida garden. It will be revised soon to cover all of Florida, and the title will change to "Easy Gardens for Florida.." "Best Garden Color for Florida" is the second volume. It covers everything you ever wanted to know about Florida garden color. "Stormscaping" is the third volume, which covers landscaping to minimize wind damage in Florida. This book, "Container Gardens for Florida," is the fourth volume.

Writing this Book: I've spent the last two years researching and writing this book. Since I had 10 years' experience designing gardens that included containers, I thought I knew quite a bit when I started. That was not the case. The more I researched, the more I realized what I didn't know. Container gardening is the fastest growing part of gardening, and the innovations in plants, containers, and creativity are staggering. So I threw myself in with both feet - collecting the best new containers and testing over 10,000 plants in over 300 containers, as well as researching what to plant in the garden to accentuate the containers. And I traveled around Florida, meeting with many top professionals in the business.

I really appreciate the luxury of gardening space that my trial gardens afford me. I was able to actually plant most of the containers photographed in this book. And since I had the space, I watched each one grow to maturity, giving me the ability to report first-hand on their long-term performance.

I have especially looked for methods of using containers for maximum design impact, like the huge hanging baskets I've seen in England. After my usual number of early failures, I have had some great successes and am very excited about sharing them with you in this book. It not only covers the best plants and containers but also great methods of designing your garden with these containers.

When I began my research, I used many different books to learn how to plant successful, spectacular, hanging baskets. None of these ideas worked well for me. It was as if each description left out some critical element for success. Then, I discovered a video that gave me more knowledge in 45 minutes than I had learned in the previous six months of reading. Because of this experience, my book has a companion DVD with a general overview of container gardening as well as a a variety of planting demos. Watch the DVD first; then, start reading the book. Within an hour, you will be an expert in container gardens for Florida!

Thank You: Many people helped me with this project. Barbara Hadsell located many of the plants and containers. She also designed and planted quite a few of the cool-season containers and hanging baskets. Barbara has experience with flower arranging, which taught me a lot about container design. She also knew a lot about container plants that are popular up north and untested in Florida. We had great success tracking them down for our trial gardens. Luckily, a lot of them did very well in our Florida trials. Barbara's positive attitude and enthusiasm were really appreciated. Her husband, Tim Hadsell, constructed many of the garden accents in my trial gardens, including the pergola on pages 126-127. He also figured out how to install the baskets on posts shown in the hanging basket chapter.

Miguel Olivares-Popoca, my only full-time employee, worked tirelessly throughout this project by planting and maintaining the containers and trial gardens. He never complained, not even after a seventy-hour work week when we filmed the DVD.

Kaki Holt was also invaluable to this project. She planned the DVD, locating the wonderful people who produced it and assisted me in writing the script and making the DVD. Her experience in television and free-lance writing also contributed to researching, editing, and writing portions of the book. The fact that she is an avid gardener helped considerably. Kaki's knowledge of graphic design and computers was also a plus.

I would also like to thank the professionals who helped me with the DVD. This was my first experience with moving pictures, and I owe a lot to the professional know-how of this crew. Bill Baxter, the producer, Mark Thorn, the director, Chris Bush and Kerry Strawn, the cameramen, and all the others who performed over and above the call of duty for this project. I had expected something that looked like a home movie, but they produced a very professional show.

Chapter 1

Start with Great Containers

Thanks to all the fabulous containers now on the market, successful container gardening has never been more exciting. In fact, containers can now rival plants for attention-getting appeal. Since interest in container gardening is growing rapidly, more terrific container designs come on the market every day.

We searched the world for the best, top-quality containers that are well-adapted to the Florida environment. After testing more than 300 different products in our trial gardens, we are proud to present you with the best-of-the-best. Throughout this book, you will see these wonderful pots filled with plants that are the highest performers of our trials. Each pot has ordering information so you can purchase it through your local garden center or internet supplier. See our web site at www.easygardencolor.com for sources.

This chapter covers the types and styles of containers available. Here are a few easy tips for maximum container impact:
- Collect great pots. The large ones look good even when empty. Store the smaller ones in your garage or closet when not in use.

- Don't plan on keeping your pots filled with plants all the time. Keep them empty until you find just the right plant and the perfect spot in your garden to showcase your combination.

- Don't distract from a fabulous pot with too busy a planting; keep it simple.

Left: The pool pavilion in our trial gardens. This was a great spot for me to learn how to mix different containers. Notice how nice cobalt blue looks mixed with many different brown pots. Some of the pots have mixed flowers, and others feature just one plant.

Easy Container Impact: Collect great pots.

I have been collecting beautiful pots for years. An explosion of new designs, materials, and glazes has hit the markets in recent years as the world's gardeners have become more interested in container gardens. The current choices at garden centers are staggering. In fact, many of the dramatic, large containers are strong enough to be garden focal points even when empty.

Don't plan to keep your smaller pots filled with plants all the time, or your hobby could become a chore. Store your small pots in a garage or closet when they are not in use. If you start collecting, be sure to let your family know, so they can give you gifts you would really appreciate.

that look good even when empty.

Left: Two urns by Balazara (*Orcio con Manici,* 36"H x 28"W) grace either side of this fountain. The terra cotta pots pick up the colors from the barrel tile roof.

Right: A large, clay urn among the sea oats at the beach. Since the beach is a difficult environment for plants, it makes sense to use containers that stand alone. Whenever the gardening urge hits you, fill it with beach-loving plants. Leave it empty the rest of the time.

Below: A huge, antique urn from Balazara punctuates the end of a garden pathway. A pot this fabulous looks good filled or empty. Garden designed by Krent Wieland, landscape architect, Lake Worth, Florida.

Easy Container Impact: Great pots...

Single plantings work especially well in pots that make a strong design statement on their own. They are also the easiest arrangements to design.

Above: Balazara terra cotta pots with bromeliads. These plants don't shed their leaves on the pool deck; moreover, they look good all year and are full from the moment you plant them.

Light: Light to medium shade. Many bromeliads take full sun in winter, some in summer.

Season: The plants last all year but protect them from frost. They flower for about four months every year or two.

Lifespan: Indefinitely, if occasionally separated.

Care: Very easy. Bromeliads can stay in the same containers for many years. To learn how to separate bromeliads, see page 342. Fertilize when planting, and repeat every three months with a slow-release mix. Do not get the fertilizer in the leaf cups in the center of the plants. When the soil feels dry, water the top evenly and thoroughly, about once a week in this size pot in medium shade, more in light shade.

Pot: Balazara *Greek Pots*, foreground *Bala* (28"H) & *Pithos* (20" H), background are *Minoiko* (52"H) and *Pithari* (30"H).

Right: This is the largest pot I have, measuring a full three feet tall. It is large enough to provide significant impact in this pavilion, even though it's simply planted with one 'Red Spot' croton from a seven-gallon pot. The photo was taken right after planting.

Light: Sun to medium shade.

Season: All year. Protect from freezes.

Lifespan: Crotons planted in pots this large will thrive for many years without re-potting.

Care: Very easy. One of the advantages of large pots is that they require water less frequently than smaller pots. When the soil feels dry, water thoroughly. In sun, crotons in pots this large require water every few days, less in shade. Trim the crotons to about half their size every summer if they look leggy. Fertilize when planting, and repeat every three months with a slow-release mix.

Pot: Sabu *Kieu Urn* in rustic clay (35"H x 31" W).

For container sources, go to www.easygardencolor.com

need simple plantings.

Easy Container Impact: Bromeliads...

Bromeliads are one of the easiest plant choices for instant impact. These pots on pedestals are good spots for bromeliads because they raise the flowers to eye level, where everyone can easily see them. The pots on this page are actually synthetic, but the quality is so high that they look like cast stone. The fabulous pot (opposite page) is handmade of terra cotta and kiln-fired to last longer.

Above: Bromeliad surrounded by seven New Guinea impatiens. Plant it so that it looks full on planting day.

Light: Sun or shade in winter; light to medium shade in spring and fall.

Season: The bromeliad lasts all year, flowering for about four months. The impatiens bloom best in winter and spring.

Lifespan: Bromeliads last indefinitely, if occasionally separated (see page 342). New Guinea impatiens last about five to six months.

Care: No trimming necessary for the New Guinea impatiens. Fertilize when planting, and repeat every three months with a slow-release mix. Water thoroughly when the soil feels dry to the touch, or the impatiens show signs of wilt. This arrangement needs more water - sometimes daily - in sun than in shade.

Pot: Campania Fiberglass Collection, *Round Leaf Planter* (22"W x 14.25"H) on *Square Frame Pedestal* (16"W x 21"H).

For container sources, go to www.easygardencolor.com

mean instant drama.

Bottom, Left: This pot and pedestal look and feel like cast stone, but are made of Fiberstone - lightweight fiberglass combined with crushed limestone. It is planted with one bromeliad surrounded by seven impatiens and looked full the day it was planted. This photograph was taken six weeks after planting.
Light: Sun or shade in winter; light to medium shade in spring and fall.
Season: The bromeliads last all year, flowering for about four months. The impatiens bloom best in winter and spring.
Lifespan: Bromeliads last indefinitely, if occasionally separated (see page 342). Impatiens last about six months.
Care: Trim the impatiens if they get leggy. It takes about a month for them to bloom again. Fertilize when planting, and repeat every three months with a slow-release mix. Water thoroughly (see pages 338-339) when the soil feels dry to the touch or the impatiens show signs of wilt. This container needs more water - sometimes daily - in sun.
Pot: Global Pottery's Fiberstone Collection *Squat Pompeii Planter* (19"W x 15"H) on *Squat Column* (14"W x 18"H).

Right: A show-stopping terra cotta pot and pedestal that never fail to draw 'oohs' and 'aahs' in my garden. It is planted with a bromeliad and regular impatiens. This Campania terra cotta is handmade in Vietnam and stays remarkably clean. It has been in the same spot in the shade for twenty months looking just like new.
Light: Sun or shade in winter; light to medium shade in spring and fall.
Season: The bromeliads last all year, flowering for about four months. The impatiens bloom best in winter and spring.
Lifespan: Bromeliads last indefinitely, if occasionally separated (see page 342). New Guinea impatiens last about 6 months.
Care: Trim the impatiens if they get leggy. It takes about a month for them to bloom again. Fertilize when planting, and repeat every three months with a slow-release mix. Water thoroughly (see pages 338-339) when the soil feels dry to the touch or the impatiens show signs of wilt. This arrangement needs more water - sometimes daily - in sun.
Pot: Campania Terra Cotta Classics Collection, *Vandisto Urn* (23.75"W x 17"H) on *Presco Pedestal* (17"W x 29.25"H).

Easy Container Impact: Collect simple...

Like the pots on pedestals shown on the previous pages, tall columnar pots also raise plants to eye level. This height makes it easier to appreciate both the plants and the fabulous glazes on the pots. The glaze on the aqua pot is accented with gold, as shown, right. These containers look best when planted simply.

For container sources, go to www.easygardencolor.com

yet elegant containers.

Tall columns planted with dieffenbachia:

Light: Dense, medium, or light shade.

Season: Spring, summer, or fall. Dieffenbachia won't tolerate temperatures under 40 degrees. Does quite well indoors.

Lifespan: Dieffenbachia lasts for many years in a pot this large.

Care: Trim about once a year or as needed if plant becomes leggy. This plant can take drastic trimming in the warm months. Fertilize when planting, and repeat every three months with a slow-release mix. Water when soil feels dry (see page 338-339), about once a week in dense shade, more frequently in more light.

Pot: Anamese *Tall Milan* pots in aqua, blue, and green (36.5"H x 15.5" W).

Easy Container Impact: Great pots...

For container sources, go to www.easygardencolor.com

simple plantings

These handcrafted iron containers combine unique container material with terrific contemporary designs that resemble sculpture. They come in either a natural rust or powder coat finish. We tested the natural rust and are thrilled with their appearance after eighteen months outside. During their five-to-ten year Florida lifespan, they continue to oxidize, becoming quite rustic in appearance.

Left: Bromeliads and New Guinea impatiens accent this dramatic, two piece container - an urn on top of a column. See page 16-17 for care information of the plants.
Source: Ore #112 *Urn*, (28"W x 28"D x 12"H) on a #106 *Column* (12"W x 32"H).

This page, both pots: Fountain grass in two more Ore containers. See page 297 for information about fountain grass.
Source: Ore #119 *Horizontal Window Box* (33"W x 10"D x 22"H). Ore #117 *Vertical Window Box* (33"L x 14"D x 40"H).

Six Useful Containers to Collect

Low bowls

- Useful on tables because you can see over them.
- Work well as garden accents and floor pots.
- Great for instant plantings, as shown on the companion DVD.
- See pages 28, 32, 44, 45, 130, 140, 175, 209, 255, and 258-259 for more examples.

Sets of three - Many pots are sold in sets of three different sizes.

- Useful as garden accents, as shown.
- Work well next to pools, chairs or benches.
- Good way to mark entries of informal gardens.
- See pages 24, 51, 53, 123, 142, and 177 for more examples.

Tall columns or pots on pedestals

- Very useful because they bring the plantings closer to eye level.
- The most photographed pot types in this book!
- See pages 16-20, 25-26, 114-115, 120, 131, 152, 154, 158, 183, 189, 194-195, 203, a
205 for more examples of tall columns or pots on pedestals.

Hanging baskets

- Hang from any overhang.
- Work especially well to disguise a blank wall.
- Create vertical interest.
- See pages 29, 70-101, 127, 129 and 204 for more examples.

Baskets on posts

- Attach baskets to any type posts.
- Work well to put the flowers at eye level.
- Most popular accessory in our trial gardens.
- See pages 82-83, 89, 92-99, and 214 for examples.

Wall pots

- Hang them from any wall, fence, or lattice.
- Work well but are underused at entry areas.
- Good choice for walls by garage entrances.
- See pages 102-113, 121, 126-127, 128-129, and 141 for more examples.

Container Performance in Florida...

Terra Cotta

Above, left: Machine-made, unglazed, Italian terra cotta has a dull finish. Right: "Made in Italy" stamp.

Above, left: Some inexpensive, unglazed, Mexican terra cotta is quite soft and breaks easily. Right: Glazed Mexican terra cotta (note the slight sheen) is more durable, as are the pots with the thick, black interiors.

Above, left: Top-of-the-line unglazed Impruneta. Right: Excellent-quality Campania required no cleaning in our trials (see page 17).

Advantages:
1. Natural appearance works as a neutral, blending well with any architectural style.
2. Many sizes and shapes are commonly available at almost all garden centers.

Disadvantages:
1. Less-expensive terra cotta is fragile.
2. Most unglazed terra cotta requires cleaning (use Sno Bowl Toilet Cleaner and a stiff brush) at least every six months. Pots kept in shade may need it even more often. Cleaning is hard work. Be sure to rinse it very well, or white blemishes from the cleaning chemical will return quickly. Better quality, handmade terra cotta, such as Campania and Impruneta, is much harder and less porous, so it doesn't need cleaning as often. Many people don't clean their terra cotta, preferring an aged look.
3. Most terra cotta must be taken inside during freezes. Impruneta terra cotta is freeze-resistant.

Buying tips:
1. Many experts say that Italian terra cotta is the best, but we had great success with unglazed Vietnamese terra cotta from Campania (see photo at left and page 17), which required no cleaning at all after being outside in the shade for twenty months. Italian terra cotta is commonly available at most garden centers. Look for identifying marks, like the "Made in Italy" found at the bottom of the pot at left.
2. Georgia puts out a good product as well, but it is not as readily available as the Italian.
3. Some inexpensive, unglazed, Mexican terra cotta is softer and often fired at lower temperatures, which causes it to break easily (see photo at left).
4. Italian, Georgian, Chinese, and Vietnamese terra cotta are kiln-fired, which make them more durable.
5. The top-of-the-line terra cotta is called Impruneta (www.balazara.com), from the village in Italy where it is made. In Italy, it is considered ceramic because of the high temperatures in which it is fired. It is frost-proof, hard to break, and lasts for hundreds of years. It is also quite expensive.
6. Handmade terra cotta is considered finer than that made by machine. The finish is better, and the pots are more attractive.

Glazed Natural Clay

Although glazed, natural clay shares many of the same characteristics as terra cotta, it has a sheen finish, as opposed to the dull finish of the terra cotta pots in the top left photo. The glaze seals the pot, so that it does not require cleaning. Some consider this a disadvantage because the pots don't get that old-world, mossy look of the unglazed terra cotta. These pots come in a variety of natural, earth-tone shades and are extremely popular. Most Florida garden centers have lots of glazed, natural, clay pots.

For container sources, go to www.easygardencolor.com

Results of 12 years of trials

Antique pots

Antique pots are a great choice to add a classical look to more formal gardens. They are often more expensive than new containers, but one would expect that from antiques. Look in antique shops and salvage shops. Some sources include www.balazara.com, www.gardenantiques.com, and Proler Garden Antiques at 310-459-0477. If the prices scare you, reproductions of many of the classics are available for much less money.

Clay Pots with Ceramic Glazes

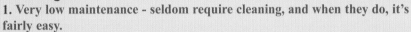

These pots have revolutionized the use of color on pots for Florida. Prior to their entrance to this market (in the mid-90's), it was very difficult to find colored pots that lasted in Florida. Many of the finishes were painted onto clay pots, and most of them peeled off. The ceramic glazes are baked onto the clay at very high temperatures. They hold up well in the tough, Florida climate, although some of them have to be moved inside during freezes. Ask your supplier for more information.

Advantages:
1. Very low maintenance - seldom require cleaning, and when they do, it's fairly easy.
2. The variety of colors is wonderful. Collect many so that you can always find the perfect one for a new plant purchase.
3. More and more garden centers are stocking them.

Disadvantages:
1. Large ones are heavy.
2. Finishes are rustic - you'll find small imperfections in almost all of them. People who like it natural would love them, but perfectionists might not be satisfied.
3. Fairly expensive, although the prices are coming down a bit. Prices vary considerably by size. Small ones are quite affordable.

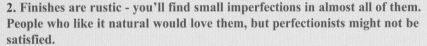

Buying tips:
1. Most garden centers don't stock too many different manufacturers' pots because the minimum order per supplier is quite high. So don't go to one place and expect to see all of the glazed pots in this book! Go to our Web site (www.easygardencolor.com) for lists of who has what.
2. If you see a pot you love, don't hesitate to buy it. Many of these pots are made by small pottery makers in tropical Asia and China. They might not make the same one again.
3. Don't worry about small imperfections in the glazes. Since they are hand-glazed, they all have them - and they add to the charm of the pot.
4. Most of these pots are handmade, so no two will be exactly alike.
5. When I first started using these pots in the mid 90's, there was quite a quality difference from company to company. I haven't seen that lately. I even bought some glazed pots from a man who was selling them out of the back of a truck, and they have lasted quite well.

Above: Glazed pots from a Sunlight, a wholesaler in Fort Lauderdale (www.sunlightflorida.com)

Container Performance in Florida...

Hand-Painted

Employees of a garden center in Sarasota tell me that hand-painted pots are their best sellers. It makes sense, because these pots suit Florida, and the bright colors make container design easy. Since these pots have impact on their own, simple plantings work well. We tested pots from Masart (left) with great success. The quality is excellent. Although they are quite lightweight, we didn't experience any breakage. Each one is hand-painted, so no two are exactly alike. The pots are made in Mexico. Even though some Mexican terra cotta is not of the highest quality, Masart pots are top-of-the-line.

Cast Stone

Above: Campania cast stone pot. This Pennsylvania company has top-quality, cast stone containers.

Above: I spent several days visiting companies in southeast Florida that make cast stone containers. Although some were awful, Artistic Statuary in Pompano is an example of good quality, cast stone that is available locally. Joanne Harrold is pictured above with some of the cast stone containers available there.

Cast stone pots are made from a mold filled with concrete. The poured concrete ages gracefully as it cures. They come in a variety of finishes - like antique, moss, and patina. These finishes give the look of antique containers at a fraction of the cost.

Advantages:
1. They look great, last forever, and require little care.

Disadvantages:
1. They are extremely heavy.
2. Cast stone pots do not tolerate freezes.

What to look for:
1. Good, cast stone pots require good molds. Look for crisp, clear designs. If a detail looks blurry, don't buy it!
2. Look for pots that resemble stone instead of concrete.

Where to shop:
Haddonstone, an English company, is generally considered top-of-the-line. But, of course, it is very expensive. Campania's quality is great, and its prices are a fraction of Haddonstone's.

Be sure to check out local manufacturers. Since these pots are heavy, you pay quite a price for freight to bring them into Florida from elsewhere. Look in your yellow pages under "Stone - cast," and call the companies to see if they make pots. Many cast stone companies specialize in columns or fountains and might not make pots.

I spent a few days checking out suppliers in three counties in southeast Florida that make their own cast stone pots. About half the locations had really awful pots - they looked like white concrete, with very visible seams and blurry designs. But, some of the rest were good. And, I met some nice people to boot!

For container sources, go to www.easygardencolor.com

Results of 12 years of trials

Fiberglass

Above, left: Global Pottery 'Fiberstone' combines crushed limestone with fiberglass. It looks and feels like cast stone (page 16). Right: Global Pottery fiberglass that looks just like rusted iron (page 249).

Above, left: Campania fiberglass has an old-stone finish that looks authentic (page 16). Right: Global Pottery grey fiberglass that looks great (page 229).

I am generally a fan of natural materials, so I resisted testing synthetic containers. My positive experiences with fiberglass over a twelve year period changed my mind. Think about it - fiberglass is used to make boats, so it must hold up well in Florida's heat, humidity, and salt.

Fiberglass comes in a variety of finishes. Check out the simple, white window boxes on pages 116-117, which can easily be painted to coordinate with your house. Fiberglass also features faux finishes, as shown left, to mimic stone and metal.

Advantages:
1. Fiberglass is very low maintenance - seldom requires cleaning; and when it does, it's fairly easy.
2. Lasts a long time - probably as long as you will!
3. Lightweight, which is a big advantage when you are moving them, but a disadvantage if the pot is in a windy location.
4. Looks great! Even experts could not tell fiberglass made to look like cast stone from the real thing in my trial gardens.
5. Good-quality fiberglass is not cheap, but it is worth every penny.

Disadvantages:
1. Since they are lightweight, do not use them in windy locations unless they are weighted down or otherwise secured.

Metal

Above, left: Aluminum does not rust. This one has been outside in Florida for six years. But aluminum doesn't give the old world look of cast iron. Right: The rusted finish of a cast iron pot I bought, not knowing that it would rust.

Above, left: Campania cast iron. Apply a Rustoleum clear coat annually to inhibit rusting. Right: Ore handcrafted iron is supposed to look rusted.

Be careful when buying metal for outdoor use in Florida. Many of the metal pots on the market now are meant for indoor use and quickly rust outdoors. Aluminum doesn't rust, but most metal containers are made of iron, which does rust, or brass, which oxidizes and eventually turns black. I bought a beautiful, black, cast iron pot, and it started rusting within a week! Here's how some other metal containers did in our trials:

Campania cast iron with a wax rust patina is left outside to establish the desired rustic look. Then, a wax finish is applied to delay the rusting process. We tested one for eight months, and the rust started after six months. To continue delaying the rusting process, the company recommends applying a Rustoleum clear coat annually.

Global Pottery brass is meant for indoor use, but I tried the one shown on page 224 outside to see what would happen. In six months, it has shown no signs of oxidation. The company attributes this short-term success to the fact that they dip it in acid to form a reacted finish. They don't know how long it lasts outdoors and still recommend it for indoor use only.

Ore iron containers are supposed to rust. They are one of our most popular containers in our trial gardens. People comment that they look like pieces of art ! See pages 20-21 for more info.

Chapter 2

Petunias

Snapdragons

Violas

Mixed Plantings

Tall snapdragons form the centerpieces of both of these cool-season containers. They look great when all the flowers bloom at once, like the white ones below. One caution: The snapdragons all stop blooming at once while new buds are forming. The flowers re-appear in about another month.

The hanging basket (right) is so large that it still looks great without the snapdragon flowers. It lasted about six months during the cool season.

The bowl, below, was planted with large plants shortly before this photo was taken. The plants were so large compared with the size of the pot that the arrangement only lasted about six weeks. But the low cost, coupled with the ease of planting, made it well worth the time.

My first attempts at mixed plantings were mediocre at best. I found the planting part easy but the designing difficult. However, I kept trying, and along the way, I discovered these ten secrets to designing beautiful, mixed container gardens. But be careful! Once you try a few and see how easy and creatively fulfilling it is, you may get addicted! I've found container gardens so much fun that I can seldom pass a garden center without turning in to see what kind of masterpiece I can put together! These plantings are easy and instant. All of the examples shown in this chapter were photographed shortly after planting.

Ten easy tips for designing mixed plantings:

1. Choose your combinations at the garden center.

2. Trust your eyes and instincts.

3. Start with your centerpiece.

4. Choose companion plants that like the same growing conditions.

5. Choose mounding or trailing plants for the edges.

6. Arrange the edge plantings around the centerpiece.

7. Choose different sizes and shapes of flowers.

8. Use leaf color.

9. Vary textures.

10. Group pots effectively.

When I was learning about container gardening, I didn't make much progress from reading books. Then, I found a video that taught me more in 30 minutes than I had learned from the prior six months' readings. So, I made a DVD companion (see www.easy-gardencolor.com for buying info) for this book to help you learn like I did. Watch it before reading this chapter and mastering mixed plantings will be a piece of cake for you!

Tip 1: Choose your combinations at.....

I design my containers at garden centers like this one - Giverney Gardens in Jupiter, Florida. It is much easier to work with available plants than to design on paper at home, only to find that the garden center doesn't have what you want. I shop at many different garden centers for my plants and have found excellent selections at most of them. My garden center trips have became design adventures that I anticipate with pleasure.

Be adventurous with your selections. Plants are inexpensive in Florida, and container gardening gives you an opportunity to try many different looks, which is often difficult in a structured garden.

Learn to trust your eyes and instincts when putting your combinations together. Pick the plants that make you smile!

Left: Kaki Holt, our managing editor, shops for plants at Giverney. Right: Judy Traver from Giverney Gardens helps the author choose plants.

your garden center.

An Easy Method for Choosing Plants for a Mixed Planting

1. Choose your centerpiece first, which will be the tallest plant in your arrangement. Look for something you really like, such as this golden dewdrop.

2. Put your centerpiece on a cart and push it around the garden center. Look for smaller plants that look good with it.

3. Be sure your next plant shares the same growing conditions - like water, light, and fertilizer - with your centerpiece.

4. Choose another small plant that looks good with the others. Again, be sure it shares the same growing conditions with the other plants you have chosen.

5. Arrange the smaller plants around the larger one, as you would in your container. This is a way of guesstimating how many plants you'll need.

6. Go home and plant it! The plants I chose looked fabulous in the Global Pottery French Yellow *Elegante* container from their Classico Collection.

Tip 2: Trust your eyes and instincts.

Above: A bromeliad used as the centerpiece is surrounded by alternating blue torenia and pink dragon wing begonias.
Light: Light shade.
Season: April until October because the upright torenia is a warm-weather plant. The other two plants will do well for most of the year.
Lifespan: Torenia lasts about two to three months, the begonia for about six months. The bromeliad will last for years in a pot this size, but only blooms for a few months each year.
Care: Fertilize every two months with a slow-release mix. Water when dry to the touch, about every three days. If any plant becomes untidy, trim it slightly. See page 342 for keeping the bromeliad after the other plants have died.
Pot: International Pottery Alliance's Dynasty Collection *Shenzhen Lined Planter* in Sesame Blue (19" W).

Choosing the right plants for containers is a lot like the color coordination you do with your interior design or your wardrobe. Trust your eyes and instincts! I took these throw pillows with me to the garden center when I was buying these plants and pots. That way, I could be sure the plants and containers would coordinate with the fabric in this gazebo.

Left: The bromeliad is the centerpiece surrounded by pink polka dot plants. Notice how the colors in the flowers coordinate with the throw pillows.
Light: Light to medium shade. This arrangement takes more light in the cool months than it will in the summer.
Season: All year, provided it is protected from frost.
Lifespan: The polka dot plants lasts six to eight months. The bromeliad lasts for years in a pot this size, flowering for a few months each year or two. See page 342 for information about separating bromeliads.
Care: Pinch back the polka dot plant monthly. Water when the soil is dry to the touch, about every three days if kept in this much shade (see pages 338-340 for more watering info). Fertilize with a slow-release product every two months.
Pot: Source unknown.

For container sources, go to www.easygardencolor.com

Learning to design containers is much easier after you have watched the DVD companion to this book. For buying info, see www.easygardencolor.com.

Above: The same bromeliad used on the table arrangement forms the centerpiece of this strawberry jar. Pink dragon wing begonias and blue torenias fill the side pockets. While many strawberry jars are too small for plants sold at garden centers, the side pockets on this one fit plants in 4.5" pots, which are commonly available.

Light: Light shade.

Lifespan: The upright torenia lasts about three months, the begonia lasts for about six months (may require pinching back), and the bromeliad lasts for years in a pot this size.

Care: Fertilize every two months with a slow-release mix. Water the top and individual pouches when dry to the touch (see pages 338-340 for more watering info), about every three days. If any plant becomes untidy, trim it slightly. See page 342 to learn how to keep the bromeliad after the other plants have died.

Season: April until October because the upright torenia is a warm-weather plant. The other two plants do well for most of the year if they are protected from frost.

Pot: Anamese Strawberry Jar in sand (24"H x 20"W).

Tip 3: Start with the centerpiece.

One easy design method is to plant a tall plant in the center of the pot (the centerpiece) and surround it with lower-growing plants.

Above: The pink pentas form the centerpiece, surrounded by blue torenia. This pot is so attractive that plantings can be very simple and still form a great composition. This arrangement was planted with three pentas and two torenia, so it would look full on planting day, when it was photographed. We soaked the root balls in water so that we could squeeze them to reduce their size prior to planting (see page 342). The pentas were in full bloom but went out of bloom a few weeks later, all at the same time. The penta plant stayed green for two more weeks while new buds were forming. That is one disadvantage of the butterfly pentas - when they all bloom at once, they all stop at once for a rest.

Light: Light shade to sun.

Season: April until October because the upright torenia does better in the warm months.

Lifespan: About two or three months. The lifespan is short because the pot is so small.

Care: Because the lifespan is so short, not much care is needed. The pentas bloom more if the old blooms are removed. Water when the soil feels dry, about every other day in light shade, up to every day in full sun (see pages 338-340 for more watering info).

Pot: Global Pottery *Oval Fleur De Lis* in French Yellow (16"L x 11"W x 9"H).

For container sources, go to www.easygardencolor.com

Learning the centerpiece concept is much easier after you have watched the DVD companion to this book. For buying info, see www.easygardencolor.com.

Choosing the centerpiece is an easy way to start your mixed arrangement. Any type of plant can be a centerpiece as long as it has an upright growth habit. The only other requirement is for it to be taller than the surrounding plants.

Left: Blue salvia forms the centerpiece, which is planted in the center, touching the back. Golden shrimp plants and red butterfly pentas accent the salvia. We soaked the root balls in water so that we could squeeze them to reduce their size prior to planting (see page 342). The plants were placed very close together and this pot was photographed on planting day. The pentas were completely filled with flowers, which went out of bloom a few weeks later, all at the same time. The penta plants stayed green for two more weeks while new buds were forming. That is one disadvantage of the butterfly pentas - when they all bloom at once, they all stop at once. The salvias and shrimp plants bloomed beautifully for the life of the container.

Light: Light shade to sun.

Season: October through June. Protect from frost.

Lifespan: About two to three months. The lifespan is short due to the number of plants in a small pot. Fewer plants increase the lifespan, but the arrangement would take longer to fill out. Transplant the shrimp plants to the garden after they outgrow the pot if you live in zones 9-11.

Care: Since the lifespan is so short, not much care is needed. The pentas bloom more if the old blooms are removed. Water when the soil feels dry, about every other day in light shade up to every day in full sun (see pages 338-340).

Pot: Global Pottery *Fleur De Lis* in Antique Crackle (16"H x 13"W).

Centerpiece: Blue Salvia
(1 full plant from a one-gallon pot)
Plant profile: Page 321

Golden Shrimp Plant
(2 full plants from 6" pots)
Plant Profile: Page 322

Red Butterfly Pentas
(5 plants from 4.5" pots)
Plant Profile: Page 315

Tip 4: Choose companions that need...

Plumbago
(1 plant from a
three-gallon pot)
Plant Profile: Page 318

Butterfly Pentas
(3 plants from 4.5" pots)
Plant Profile: Page 315

For container sources, go to www.easygardencolor.com

the same growing conditions as the centerpiece.

Plant sun-loving plants together, as shown with the plumbago and pentas to the left. The plants on the right all thrive in light shade.

Left: Blue plumbago forms the centerpiece of this arrangement, surrounded by pink butterfly pentas. It was photographed shortly after planting.
Light: Full sun.
Season: April until October.
Lifespan: About four months, but neither plant stays in bloom the whole time. Plant the plumbago in a larger pot or in the garden (zones 9-11) after it has outgrown this container.
Care: The pentas bloom more if the old blooms are removed. Water when the soil feels dry, about every other day in light shade, up to every day in full sun (see pages 338-340 for more watering info).
Pot: Global Pottery *Fleur De Lis* in French Yellow (16"H x 13"W).

Above: The golden shrimp plant forms the centerpiece, surrounded by blue torenia and a pink dragon wing begonia. This pot is so attractive that plantings can be this simple and still form a great composition. The arrangement was planted to be full immediately by dipping the root balls in water to reduce their size. See page 343 to learn this technique.
Light: Light shade.
Season: April until October. The upright torenia is a summer plant.
Lifespan: About two to three months because the pot is small.
Care: Water when the soil feels dry, about every other day in light shade. The shrimp plant blooms more if the old blooms are removed. And since the shrimp plant lives much longer than the other two, plant it in a larger pot or in the garden (zones 9-11) after the other plants have died.
Pot: Global Pottery's *Square Planter* from "The Country Home Collection" (10"H x10"W).

Tip 5: Edge plants: Mounding or trailing?

The green ti plant is the centerpiece of this arrangement. It is surrounded by two different mounding plants: caladiums and dragon wing begonias. Mounding plants, like the name implies, are shaped like a mound. Angle them out slightly to cover the rim of the pot.

Left: A ti plant is placed in the center, touching the back. A dragon wing begonia is planted in the center of the front, with one caladium on either side. We soaked the root balls in water so we could squeeze them to reduce their size prior to planting (see page 342). This arrangement was full on planting day.

Season: April until October.

Lifespan: The arrangement lasts about four to six months in this container. The ti plant (zone 10-11) can then be transplanted to the garden or into another pot.

Care: Very easy. Water when the soil feels dry, about every other day in light shade. Pinch back the begonia if it becomes too large.

Pot: Global Pottery 'Daisy Planter' in white (12"H x 11"W).

Ti Plant
(1 plant from a one-gallon pot)
Plant Profile: Page 325

Dragon Wing Begonia
(1 plant from a 4.5" pot)
Plant Profile: Page 280

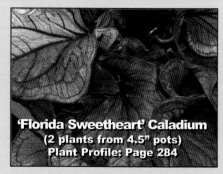

'Florida Sweetheart' Caladium
(2 plants from 4.5" pots)
Plant Profile: Page 284

For container sources, go to www.easygardencolor.com

Learning design concepts is much easier after you have watched the DVD companion to this book. For buying info, see www.easygardencolor.com.

The red 'Madame Chaoul' ti plant is the centerpiece of this arrangement. It is surrounded by mounding caladiums and trailing chenille plants. Trailing plants cascade over the edge of the container. The plant colors coordinate with the pot.

Left: A ti plant is placed in the center, touching the back. A dwarf caladium is planted in the center but up front, with a dwarf chenille on either side. This arrangement was full on planting day.

Light: Light to medium shade.

Season: April until October because the caladiums are warm-weather plants.

Lifespan: The arrangement lasts about four to six months in this container. The ti plant (zones 10-11) and the dwarf chenille (zones 7-11) can then be transplanted to the garden or another pot after the caladium dies.

Care: Very easy. Water when the soil feels dry, about every other day in light shade (see pages 338-340). Pinch back the dwarf chenille if it becomes too large.

Pot: Global Pottery *Handled Planter* in kiwi (12"H x 11"W).

'Madame Chaoul' Ti Plant
(1 plant from a three-gallon pot)
Plant Profile: Page 325

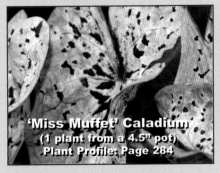

'Miss Muffet' Caladium
(1 plant from a 4.5" pot)
Plant Profile: Page 284

Dwarf Chenille
(2 plants from 6" pots)
Plant Profile: Page 286

Tip 6: Arrange the edge plants...

Red Ann Fittonia
(2 plants from 5" pots)
Plant Profile: Page 330

Anthurium 'Gemini'
(1 plant from a 6" pot)
Plant Profile: Page 279

Bromeliad
(1 plant from a 6" pot)
Plant Profile: Page 284

A 'Gemini' anthurium forms the centerpiece of this easy, long-lasting, shade arrangement. The pink color of the anthurium flower is repeated in the leaves of the red Ann fittonia, which I found in the house plant section of a garden center. I placed this mounding plant on either side of the centerpiece. The bromeliads mark the center of the arrangement and blend well with the other plantings. Notice how great the plants look in this color-coordinated container.

Light: Medium shade.
Season: All year, but protect from temperatures under 45 degrees.
Lifespan: The arrangement lasts about four to six months in this container.
Care: Very easy. Water when the soil feels dry (see page 338-340), about every three days. Pinch back the fittonia if it gets too large.
Pot: Global Pottery *Oval Fleur de Lis* in Tuscan green (16"W x 11"D x 9"H).

For container sources, go to www.easygardencolor.com

around the centerpiece.

Butterfly Pentas
(2 plants from 4.5" pots)
Plant Profile: Page 315

Coleus 'Amora'
(1 plant from a 6" pot)
Plant Profile: Page 287

Sedum
(1 plant from a one-gallon pot)
Plant Profile: Page 322

Coleus 'Amora' (from Proven Winners) is the center-piece of this arrangement. It is surrounded by mound-ing pentas and sedum that coordinate with the leaf color of the coleus. The pentas are placed on either side of the coleus, with the sedum marking the center front. Although the pot is reasonably small, it is very well designed and a good choice for people preferring smaller, lighter-weight pots.

Light: Light shade to full sun.
Season: All year. Protect from frost.
Lifespan: The arrangement lasts about two months in this container because it is so small.
Care: Water when dry to the touch (see pages 338-340), about every day or two in sun. Pentas bloom more if the old blooms are removed. Pinch back the coleus if it becomes leggy or too large.
Pot: Global Pottery *Handled Planter* in kiwi (12"H x 11"W).

Tip 7: Consider leaf color.

Jatropha
(1 plant from a
three-gallon pot)
Plant Profile: Page 301

Mammey Croton
(2 plants from
one-gallon pots)
Plant Profile: Page 288

Coleus 'Dark Star'
(2 plants from
4.5" pots)
Plant Profile: Page 287

'Goldilocks'
(2 plants from
one-gallon pots)
Plant Profile: Page 303

For container sources, go to www.easygardencolor.com

Learning design concepts is much easier after you have watched the DVD companion to this book. For buying info, see www.easygardencolor.com

Leaf color not only frames and defines flowers but also offers constant color in these neon-bright plantings shown in red containers.

Left: This arrangement was planted with large plants and was full on planting day. A lush jatropha was planted in the center, touching the back. Then, 'Goldilocks' were centered on the front rim, angled out. Mammey crotons were planted on either side, with two Proven Winners' 'Dark Star' coleus in the middle.

Light: Light shade to full sun.

Season: All year. Protect from frost.

Lifespan: Four to six months in this container. When the plants outgrow the pot, plant the jatropha and the crotons (zones 10-11) in larger pots or in the garden.

Care: Water when the soil feels dry, as much as once a day in the heat of summer (see pages 338-340).

Pot: International Pottery Alliance *Scallop Rim Planter* in Oxblood (20" D).

Golden Shrimp Plant
(1 plant from a three-gallon pot)
Plant Profile: Page 322

'Defiance' Coleus
(5 plants from 4.5" pots)
Plant Profile: Page 287

'Goldilocks'
(2 plants from one-gallon pots)
Plant Profile: Page 303

Above: This arrangement was planted with large plants so that it would be full on planting day. One, three-gallon shrimp plant was planted in the center, touching the back. Then, two, one-gallon 'Goldilocks' were centered on the front rim, angled out. The middle was filled in with five coleus in 4.5" pots.

Light: Light shade.

Season: All year. Protect from frost.

Lifespan: About four to six months in this container.

Care: Water when the soil feels dry (see pages 338-340), as much as once a day in the heat of summer. When the plants outgrow the pot, plant the shrimp plant (zones 9-11) in larger pots or in the garden.

Pot: International Pottery Alliance *Scallop Rim Planter* in Oxblood (16" D).

Tip 8: Mix sizes and shapes of flowers.

Viola
(2 plants from 6" pots)
Plant Profile: Page 327

Marigold
(2 plants from 4.5" pots)
Plant Profile: Page 305

Snapdragon
(1 plant from an 8" pot)
Plant Profile: Page 323

Lantana
(2 plants from 4.5" pots)
Plant Profile: Page 302

Note the difference in flower size and shape in this arrangement.

Above: Snapdragons form the centerpiece, surrounded by violas, marigolds and lantana. I found these flowers at a single garden center one afternoon. Assembling this arrangement took only ten minutes, and it was full on planting day! Although this arrangement only lasted about a month, its ease of preparation made it well worth the effort. This arrangement is short-lived because of the small size of the container and the fact that the snapdragons stop blooming after about a month. They will re-bloom after a few weeks' rest, but since the bowl is so small, it makes more sense to start over when they stop blooming.

Light: Full sun.
Season: December through April. Protect from frost.
Lifespan: About four to six weeks in this small container.
Care: Fertilize with a slow-release mix on planting day. Water when the soil feels dry, about every other day (see pages 338-340). The marigolds and snapdragons bloom more if the old blooms are removed.
Pot: Source unknown.

Golden Shrimp
(1 plant from a one-gallon pot)
Plant Profile: Page 322

Butterfly Pentas
(4 plants from 4.5" pots)
Plant Profile: Page 315

'Catalina Blue' Trailing Torenia
(1 plant from a one-gallon pot)
Plant Profile: Page 326

Easy flowers with different sizes and shapes complement this bright blue pot.

Above: A one-gallon golden shrimp plant forms the centerpiece and four pink butterfly pentas are planted in the middle. A one-gallon Proven Winners' 'Catalina Blue' torenia is starting to cascade over the front. While the torenia and shrimp plants bloom almost continuously, the butterfly pentas take some short bloom breaks after a peak bloom period.

Light: Light shade to full sun in the cool season; light shade in the hot season.

Season: All year. Trailing torenia, unlike upright torenia, blooms all year in Florida if it is protected from frost.

Lifespan: About two to three months in this container. Plant the shrimp plant in the garden (zones 9-11) after the other plants die.

Care: Fertilize with a slow-release mix on planting day. Water when the soil feels dry, about every other day (see pages 338-340). The pentas and shrimp plants bloom more if the old flowers are removed.

Pot: Lotus International bowl in blue.

Tip 9: Vary leaf textures.

Curly Copperleaf
(1 plant from a
one-gallon pot)
Plant Profile: Page 287

**Coleus 'Crime
Scene'**
(2 plants from 4.5" pots)
Plant Profile: Page 287

Carex 'Frosty Curls'
(2 plants from 4.5" pots)
Plant Profile: Page 297

'Goldilocks'
(2 plants from
one-gallon pots)
Plant Profile: Page 303

For container sources, go to www.easygardencolor.com

Each plant in these arrangements is quite different in texture, which is as important as color in mixed plantings. And the arrangements are not only attractive but also long-lasting and easy to grow. Most of the plants are from Proven Winners.

Left: A Proven Winners' curly copperleaf forms the centerpiece of this textured arrangement. 'Crime Scene' coleus is a striking, front-and-center focal point. Carex 'Frosted Curls' provides a light texture that defines the two plants on either side. 'Goldilocks' trails along the edges. The natural colors in these plants look good with simple, terra cotta pots.
Light: Light shade to full sun.
Season: March to October; the arrangement grows all year if the copper leaf is protected from temperatures under 45 degrees.
Lifespan: The arrangement lasts about six months in this pot. Plant the copperleaf in your garden after the other plants die if you live in zones 10-11.
Care: Pinch back the coleus every month or so. Trim the tips off the copperleaf if it starts looking a bit leggy. Trim the bottom of the 'Goldilocks' before it starts to touch the ground. Fertilize when planting, and repeat every three months with a slow-release mix. Water thoroughly when the soil feels dry to the touch, every few days (see pages 338-340).
Pot: International Pottery Alliance, Old World Terracotta Collection, *Rippled Egg Pot*, 16" W.

Curly Copperleaf
(1 plant from a one-gallon pot)
Plant Profile: Page 287

'Dark Dancer'
(1 plant from a one-gallon pot)
Plant Profile: Page 332

'Fiber Optic Grass'
(2 plants from 4.5" pots)
Plant Profile: Page 296

'Margarita' Sweet Potato
(2 plants from 4.5" pots)
Plant Profile: Page 324

Above: This arrangement is a companion to the one on the opposite page, again featuring curly copperleaf as the centerpiece.
Light: Light shade to full sun.
Season: March to October; the arrangement grows all year if the copper leaf is protected from temperatures under 45 degrees.
Lifespan: The arrangement lasts about six months in a pot.
Care: Trim the tips off the copperleaf if it gets a bit leggy. Trim the fast-growing sweet potato frequently to keep it from taking over the other plants. Fertilize when planting, and repeat every three months with a slow-release mix. Water thoroughly when the soil feels dry to the touch, every few days.
Pot: International Pottery Alliance, Old World Terracotta Collection, *Rippled Egg Pot* (13" W).

Tip 10: Group pots effectively.

A

B

C

For container sources, go to www.easygardencolor.com

Grouping pots is a tricky proposition. It's important for the eye to see the group as a whole rather than individual plants. First, you have to pick pots that look good together. Then, you are better off if you simplify your choice of plants - maybe just one or two different kinds in each pot. Look at the photos of the single pots at the bottom of the opposite page - they look rather non-descript when you view each one by itself. But look at the larger photo to see what happens when you group them together - they look terrific!

The fuchsia really surprised me, lasting a full six months. It is, along with the 'Fiber Optic' grass, from Proven Winners.

Philodendron
(1 plant from a 6" pot)
Plant profile: Page 317

'Fuchsia Autumnale'
2 plants from 6" pots
Plant profile: Page 330

Coleus 'Alabama Sunset'
(1 plant from a 6" pot)
Plant profile: Page 287

Pot A: This new philodendron I picked for the centerpiece coordinates well with the fuchsias.
Light: Light to medium shade.
Season: All year. Protect from frost.
Lifespan: The fuchsia lasted about six months. I planted the philodendron in my garden (zone 10) when it outgrew the pot, and it looks great a year later.
Care: Fertilize when planting, and repeat every three months with a slow-release mix. Water thoroughly (see pages 338-340) when the soil feels dry to the touch, every few days.
Pot: Campania International *Adige Oval* in Garda Green (24"L x 15"W x 9"H).

'Fiber Optic' Grass
(4 plants from 4.5" pots)
Plant profile: Page 296

Pot B: This dieffenbachia has yet to shed the first brown leaf after six months. The 'Fiber Optic' plants on either side add just the right texture.
Light: Light to medium shade.
Season: All year, but protect from temperatures under 45 degrees.
Lifespan: The dieffenbachia lasts for years if it is moved into larger pots about once a year; the grass lived about six months.
Care: Fertilize when planting, and repeat every three months with a slow-release mix. Water thoroughly (see pages 338-340) when the soil feels dry to the touch, every few days.
Pot: Masart M1 *Window Box* (18"L X 11"W X 11"D).

Dieffenbachia 'Starlite'
(1 plant from a 6" pot)
Plant profile: Page 292

Pot C: This simple coleus is all that is needed to set off the grouping. The 'Fiber Optic' plants on either side are repeated.
Light: Light to medium shade.
Season: All year. Protect from frost.
Plants' Lifespan: About six to eight months. Lives longer in the cool months.
Care: Fertilize when planting, and repeat every three months with a slow-release mix. Water thoroughly (see pages 338-340) when the soil feels dry to the touch, every few days.
Pot: Campania International *Adige Oval* in Garda Green (18.5"L X 10"W X 8"H).

Peacock Spike Moss
(1 plant from a 6" pot)
Plant profile: Page 329

Simple or Complex?

Consider these two different plantings in the same type of pot. The one above is about as simple as you can get - one three-gallon penta - while the grouping on the right is much more complex. The one that appeals to you the most will tell you something about the style of arrangement you might want to try first.

Above: This brilliant pink penta shows off amazingly well in this gorgeous pot. Nothing more is needed.
Light: Light shade to full sun.
Season: All year. Protect from frost.
Lifespan: About three months in this pot.
Care: Fertilize when planting, and repeat every three months with a slow-release mix. Water thoroughly (see pages 338-340) when the soil feels dry to the touch, every few days. Pentas will bloom more if you remove the dead flowers. Be prepared because they will go out of bloom for a period before resuming.
Pot: International Pot Alliance, Dynasty Collection, *Senzhen Planter* in sesame green (19" W).

Right: All the plants in this arrangement were chosen to create a study in pinks and purples.
Light: Light shade to full sun.
Season: Winter and spring. Protect from frost.
Lifespan: The cleome only lasts about a month or two, but its pretty blooms are worth the trouble. The rest of the plants last about two to three months.
Care: Fertilize when planting, and repeat every three months with a slow-release mix. Water thoroughly (see pages 338-340) when the soil feels dry to the touch, every few days. Remove the dead blooms from the cleomes and petunias.
Pot: International Pottery Alliance, *Senzhen Planter* in sesame green (12', 15" and 19" W).

For container sources, go to www.easygardencolor.com

Cleome
Plant Profile: Page 328

Petunia
Plant Profile: Page 317

Calibrachoa or Million Bells
Plant Profile: Page 285

Agastache
Plant Profile: Page 278

Mona Lavender
Plant Profile: Page 306

Icicles
Plant Profile: Page 330

Chapter 3

Penta

Torenia

Gaillardia 'Torch Flame'

Gaillardia 'Torch Yellow'

Geranium

Salvia

'Painted Pink' Coleus

Designing with Color

Container gardens offer a wonderful opportunity for self-expression with color - not only from the plants themselves but also from the expanding array of container colors. Collect a variety of container colors, so you can use whatever color works best for the plants you choose.

Color styles change from year to year, more so for interiors and fashion than gardening. However, gardening does have color trends, and it is fun to look at new trends when they emerge. These trends help broaden our horizons to incorporate new looks. But, don't let them rule your decisions. Individuals have their own inner instinct that tells them which colors make them most comfortable. Some people love only white and are quite disturbed by a riot of orange, purple, and red. Others are bored by white and love the bright combinations. Follow your instincts rather than the current style. The style will change next year, anyway.

Above: Butterfly pentas and heliotrope in Anamese containers.

Left: Masart multicolored, hand-painted pots filled with mixed flowers. Special thanks to Pinder's Nursery in Palm City for many of the plants on these pages.

The Cool Serenity of White

'Candidum' Caladium
(1 plant from a one-gallon pot)
Plant Profile: Page 284

Wax Begonia
(2 plants from 4.5" pots)
Plant Profile: Page 282

Variegated Ivy
(1 plant from a one-gallon pot)
Plant Profile: Page 300

The key to the success of mixed plantings in white is variety - large leaves, small leaves, large flowers, small flowers. White arrangements look good in light-hued pots which show up particularly well in shade or evening gardens.

Above: Caladiums form the centerpiece, with wax begonias and variegated ivy planted along the edges. See page 343 to learn how to split ivy root balls.
Light: Medium to light shade.
Season: Spring through fall. Begonias must be in shade in the heat of summer and may fade in August and September.
Lifespan: Four to five months in this container.
Care: Fertilize on planting day, and repeat every three months with a slow-release mix. Trim the ivy if it gets too long. Simply cut away the unwanted portions. Water as needed.
Pot: International Pottery Alliance Terrazzo Collection, *Egg Pot* (15" W).

Right: Cleomes form the centerpiece, with wave petunias and variegated confederate jasmine planted along edges. Polka dot plant fills in the middle.
Light: Light shade because of the polka dot plant; the rest take full sun.
Season: Spring.
Lifespan: About two months because the Cleomes are short-lived.
Care: Fertilize on planting day, and repeat every three months with a slow-release mix. Water as needed. Trim the jasmine if it gets too long. It can be planted in the landscape when the other plants die.
Pot: International Pottery Alliance, *Terrazzo Collection,* Egg Pot (20" W).

For container sources, go to www.easygardencolor.com

Polka Dot Plant
(1 plant from a 5" pot)
Plant Profile: Page 319

Cleome
(1 plant from
a one-gallon pot)
Plant Profile: Page 328

Wave Petunia
(2 plants from 4.5" pots)
Plant Profile: Page 317

**Variegated
Confederate Jasmine**
(2 plants from
one-gallon pots)
Plant Profile: Page 330

Colocasia 'Black Magic'
(1 plant from a one-gallon pot)
Plant Profile: Page 294

Scaevola 'Whirlwind White'
(1 plant from a one-gallon pot)
Plant Profile: Page 332

'Black Heart' Sweet Potato
(2 plants from 4.5" pots)
Plant Profile: Page 324

Black is one of the newest and most dramatic container plant colors. Proven Winners has a "Black Magic and Purple Passion" collection put together by Karen Platt, author of a book by the same name. Proven Winners provided the plants for these two containers and even helped us with the designs.

Above: Notice the difference in leaf sizes and textures of the plants we combined in this pot. Using large leaves like the colocasia (elephant ear) with smaller leaves, like the scaevola, add interest to the arrangement.
Light: Light shade to full sun.
Season: All year. Protect from frost.
Lifespan: About five months in this container.
Care: Trim the sweet potato to keep it from overwhelming the other plants. Water as needed. Fertilize on planting day, and repeat every three months.
Pot: Lotus International *Square Pot* in mustard. (14"W x 14"L x 12.5"H).

Right: What luck! I found a black and lime green pot to go with these plants in the same colors. This combination has been a favorite of many visitors to my gardens.
Light: Light shade to full sun.
Season: All year. Protect from frost
Lifespan: About six months in this container.
Care: Trim the sweet potato to keep it in check. Water as needed. Fertilize on planting day, and repeat every three months.
Pot: International Pottery Alliance, Marco Polo Collection, *Olive Jar* (20" W) in 'Tropical Yellow' (I call it black and lime green!).

Colocasia 'Black Magic'
(1 plant from a one-gallon pot)
Plant Profile: Page 294

'Margarita' Sweet Potato
(2 plants from 4.5" pots)
Plant Profile: Page 324

'Black Heart' Sweet Potato
(2 plants from 4.5" pots)
Plant Profile: Page 324

Sedum 'Angelina'
(2 plants from 4.5" pots)
Plant Profile: Page 332

'Gay's Delight' Coleus
(2 plants from 4.5" pots)
Plant Profile: Page 287

Monochromatic, but Still Stunning!

Perilla 'Magilla'
(1 plant from a one-gallon pot)
Plant Profile: Page 316

Globe Amaranth
(2 plants from 4.5" pots)
Plant Profile: Page 330

Dwarf White Striped Sweet Flag
(2 plants from 4.5" pots)
Plant Profile: Page 329

A new and exciting trend in container garden design is using different shades of the same color. We used purple on these two pages, both leaf color and flower color. For best results, use flower or leaf color that is very different in size and shape. And use a container that sets off the plants well, like these attractive green ones.

Left: The dark leaves of the perilla contrast with the light leaves of the dwarf white striped sweet flag from Proven Winners. Perilla is a new plant for us and one of the best in our container garden trials. The globe amaranth complements the other plants.

Light: Light shade to full sun.

Season: October to June. Protect from frost.

Lifespan: About five months in this container. The perilla will last quite a bit longer if transplanted into another container or into the ground. We don't know its ultimate lifespan, but it has lasted two years so far in our zone 10 gardens.

Care: Easy. Trim the perilla if it gets too large. Fertilize on planting day and repeat every three months with a slow-release mix. Water as needed (see page 338-340 for more watering info).

Pot: Global Pottery *Handled Planter* in kiwi (12"H x 11"W).

For container sources, go to www.easygardencolor.com

Persian Shield
(nt from a one-gallon pot)
nt Profile: Page 316

Globe Amaranth
(2 plants from 4.5" pots)
Plant Profile: Page 330

Ajuga
(1 plant from a 4.5" pot)
Plant Profile: Page 328

Trailing Torenia
(1 plant from a one-gallon
Plant Profile: Page 32

Above: The dark leaves of the Persian shield contrast with the green leaves of the flowering plants. Ajuga marks the center front, repeating the dark-leaf theme. It did surprisingly well in our trials.

Light: Light shade to full sun.

Season: October to June.

Lifespan: About three to four months in this container.

Care: Easy. Trim the Persian shield if it gets too large. Fertilize on planting day, and repeat every three months with a slow-release mix.

New Colors: Copper and Swamp

Pot manufacturers are coming out with new designs and colors all the time. These two are both favorites of mine because they are not only attractive but also different from anything else I've seen.

Above: 'Mardi Gras' copperleaf and pilea combine chartreuse with copper for a stunning look.

Light: Sun.

Season: May through November. The copperleaf can be planted in the ground (if you live in a frost-free area) after it outgrows its container.

Lifespan: Four to six months in this container.

Care: Fertilize on planting day, and repeat every three months with a slow-release mix. Trim the copperleaf if it gets too leggy. Water as needed (see pages 338-340 for more watering info). It needs water at least once a day in summer.

Pot: Anamese *Beehive*, medium (15"W x 15"H), copper.

For container sources, go to www.easygardencolor.com

Above: 'Crime Scene' coleus is all that's needed in this gorgeous, glazed pot with a color called 'Swamp'. The coleus was planted from a three-gallon pot.

Light: Light shade to full sun.

Season: All year. Protect from frost.

Lifespan: Four to six months in this container.

Care: Fertilize on planting day, and repeat every three months with a slow-release mix. Trim the coleus if it gets too leggy. Water when the plant wilts, which can be twice a day in the heat of summer.

Pot: Anamese *Milan Short Square*, medium (18.5"H x 13"W), swamp.

...nca 'Illumination'
...nt Profile: Page 332

New Guinea Impatiens
'Infinity' Dark Pink
Plant Profile: Page 300

Lysimachia
'Outback Sunset'
Plant Profile: Page 304

'Summer Wave'
Amethyst' Toreni...
Plant Profile: Page 32...

These combinations from Proven Winners worked great for five full months.
Notice how well the bright-colored plants work with the rich, dark brown pots.

Above and right: Dark pots bring out the colors of bright flowers, like these New Guinea impatiens and tore-
...nia shown in the arrangements above and on the table opposite. They also contrast well with light leaves, like
...his vinca 'Illumination' and lysimachia 'Outback Sunset.' These easy-to-grow plants combine to form long-last-
...ng, attractive arrangements.
Light: Light shade to full sun during the cool months; light shade when the weather warms up in late spring.
Season: Winter, spring, and early summer. Protect from freezes.
Lifespan: About five months in these containers.
Care: This combination is very easy, seldom requiring trimming. Fertilize on planting day, and repeat in three
...months. Water thoroughly (see page 338-340 for more watering info) when the soil feels dry to the touch or the
...mpatiens wilt. Requires water as often as daily when the temperatures warm up.
Pot: Lotus International, #GRS-1524, 15"W x 12"H (on table) and 12"W x 10.5" H (above). Lotus calls the color
...dark red-orange', but it looks brown to me!

Reverse Impact: Light pots plus...

Easy, two-plant combinations with dark flowers and leaves stand out against light pots. The flower repeats the color of the leaves. These simple combinations show that container gardens do not have to be overly complex to look good.

Left and right: Light pots allow the dark but brilliant foliage and flowers to send the message. The Perilla 'Magilla' (centerpiece of the pot to the left) is a new, high performer that resembles coleus. It is complemented by the trailing geraniums, which took quite a while to bloom profusely but lasted a full five months after they finally got started. The centerpiece of the pot to the right is a 'Painted Lady' coleus that also looks good with the trailing geraniums.

Light: Light shade to full sun. during the cool months.
Season: Winter and spring. Protect from freezes.
Lifespan: About five months in this container.
Care: This combination is very easy, seldom requiring trimming. The geraniums look better if you remove the dead flowers. Fertilize on planting day, and repeat in three months. Water thoroughly when the soil feels dry to the touch or the plants wilt (see pages 338-340 for more watering info). Requires water as often as daily when the temperatures warm up in the summer.
Pot: Sabu *Champa Glazed Diagonal* in cream.

Perilla 'Magilla'
(1 plant from a three-gallon pot)
Plant Profile: Page 316

Trailing Geranium
(2 plants from one-gallon pots)
Plant Profile: Page 295

For container sources, go to www.easygardencolor.com

Coleus 'Painted Lady'
(plants from one-gallon pots)
Plant Profile: Page 287

Trailing Geraniur
(2 plants from one-gallon p
Plant Profile: Page 29

Bright Pots, Bright Flowers

These colorful Mexican pots look good with simple plantings of one plant with bright flowers. Bromeliads work especially well because of their showy shape and often brilliant flowers.

Left: The strong orange of these heliconias complements the brilliant pattern of this large pot.
Light: Light shade to full sun.
Season: Summer and fall.
Lifespan: One summer in this container. It looks straggly after that.
Care: Very easy. Fertilize on planting day, and repeat in three months. Water thoroughly when the soil feels dry to the touch. No trimming.
Pot: Masart *Michoacana,* medium (15"W x 10"H).

Right: A single bromeliad - with its brilliant red inflorescence - provides a counterpoint to the detailed design on this Mexican pot.
Light: The tougher the bromeliad leaf, the more sun it will take. Tender ones like this one take sun in winter but need shade in summer.
Season: The bromeliad lasts all year, flowering for about four months.
Lifespan: The plant lasts for many years in this container, but might not re-bloom.
Care: Fertilize on planting day, and repeat in three months. Water thoroughly when the soil feels dry to the touch, every few days.
Pot: Masart *Belted* (20"W x 20"H).

For container sources, go to www.easygardencolor.com

Colorful Mexican pots group well with other similar pots or with solid-color pots. Placing them with bright blue furniture adds instant color impact to any garden.

Right: This decorative fish planter makes such a strong statement that it needs no plants at all!

Below: This grouping uses bright pots to show off plants with bright-colored flowers. The gerber daisies on the table didn't last too long - about a month or two - but I couldn't resist their beauty. Same situation for the gorgeous yellow lilies shown to the right of the chair. They only flowered for about a month but were quite inexpensive and well-worth the few dollars they cost. Containers give you a place to put those plants you buy on an impulse just because they look good in the garden center. Since the costs are low, the risk is minimal.

Blue Pots, Bright Flowers

Chenille Plant
(1 plant from a 15-gallon pot)
Plant Profile: Page 287

Melampodium
(10 plants from 4.5" pots)
Plant Profile: Page 305

Today's brilliant glazes - like these gorgeous blue ones - almost vibrate with color.

Left: The bright colors of the plants in the pot are repeated in the garden plantings around them. The chenille plant is a shrub that has been trimmed into a small tree or standard.

Light: Light shade to full sun.

Season: Spring to fall. Protect from frost.

Lifespan: The melampodium lasts about four months. The chenille lasts for about two to three years in this container. Transplant it to the garden in frost-free areas.

Care: Trim the chenille hard once a year when the plant is not blooming. Fertilize on planting day, and repeat in three months. Water thoroughly when the soil feels dry to the touch.

Pot: Campania International, *Anduze Urn* (27"W X 31"H).

For container sources, go to www.easygardencolor.com

Kalanchoe
(3 plants from 4.5" pots)
Plant Profile: Page 301

Above: Talk about easy, not only to design but also to maintain! These three kalanchoe provide a dazzling focal point, especially for such a small arrangement. These colorful plants are amazingly tough, easy to propagate, and survive in almost any locale. They also forgive a good bit of neglect.

Light: Dense shade to full sun. This adaptability to different light conditions is a benefit of this kalanchoe, especially its unusual ability to bloom in deep shade.

Season: Winter and spring. Protect from frost.

Lifespan: About three to six months in this container on the average. However, they do not bloom continuously.

Care: This combination could hardly be easier. No trimming required. Fertilize on planting day. Water when the soil feels dry to the touch.

Pot: I bought this 8" pot at Home Depot.

Chapter 4

Hanging Baskets

'Florida Fantasy' Caladium
(3 plants from 4.5" pots)
Plant Profile: Page 284

'Painted Pink' Coleus
(10 plants from 4.5" pots)
Plant Profile: Page 287

Upright Torenia
(10 plants from 4.5" pots)
Plant Profile: Page 326

Dragon Wing Begonia
(10 plants from 4.5" pots)
Plant Profile: Page 280

'Wizard Rose' Coleus
(10 plants from 4.5" pots)
Plant Profile: Page 000

Hanging baskets were the hardest type of container for me to master. When I started this book, I bought every book I could find on hanging baskets, so I could learn how to make huge, beautiful arrangements. All of my initial attempts failed. Then, I found a hanging basket video that taught me more in thirty minutes than I had learned during the previous six months. I decided that planting hanging baskets was easier to learn from watching a demonstration than from reading a book. I immediately decided to include a how-to DVD as a companion to this book.

Joe Parr, Ann Pidgeon, and Robin Menino from Tampa were tremendously helpful to me. They had figured out how to plant the sides of a basket, which solved my biggest problem. And, they were kind enough to take the time to spend almost a whole day showing me their handiwork.

We planted over 3600 plants in 110 baskets to get the information in this chapter. We hope you enjoy them as much as we have!

This chapter covers instant hanging baskets, which are larger baskets that are planted in the sides as well as the top. Traditional baskets are planted in the top only.

Left: This is the hanging basket I made on the DVD about three weeks after planting. It was planted in early May and lasted until September with one cut-back. The torenia disappeared after about a month, but there were so many other plants in the basket that it left no bare spots.
Light: Light shade. Full sun will bleach out the caladiums and too much shade will make the whole basket thin.
Season: April until October.
Lifespan: About four months in this container.
Care: Fertilize with a slow-release mix on planting day. Water when the soil feels dry, about every other day (see page 354). Cut back the coleus and begonias if they look leggy. After trimming mine when it was two months old, it took about three weeks for it to fill out.

Traditional versus Instant...

Traditional Method: Plant the Top Only

This 16" basket was planted in the top only on the same day as the one on the opposite page - which was planted both in the top <u>and</u> through the sides. The plants came from 4.5" containers, which are typical of the sizes you will find at your local garden center. Since you don't want to see the sides of a hanging basket, the cascading plants planted around the edge will need time to grow in order to hide the basket itself. This can take several months. Sweet potato vines are a good choice for quick coverage. (These containers were both photographed the day after they were planted.)

Advantages of planting just the top of the basket:
1. Baskets designed for top-only planting are easier to find because most hanging baskets for sale are not designed for side planting. For side planting, the wires of the basket must be evenly spaced with at least three to five inches of space between them.
2. The rigid, coco-fiber liners (that work well for top planting only) are standards in most garden center.
3. You need fewer plants when planting the top and not the sides.
4. You can plant smaller, lighter baskets.

Disadvantage:
1. It takes time - from a few weeks to a few months, depending on which plants you choose - to cover the sides of the basket when only planting the top.

For container sources, go to www.easygardencolor.com

Two baskets, same plants, different techniques

Instant Method: Plant the Top and Through the Sides

This 16" basket was planted in the top and through the sides on the same day as the one on the opposite page - which was planted in the top only. The plants came from 4.5" containers, which are typical of the sizes you will find at your local garden center. This planting method gives you an instant basket, with the sides nicely covered with plants.

Advantages of planting the top and through the sides:

1. Instant effect, which is particularly important for houses on small lots - each outdoor space is quite important, and you might not want to have an anorexic-looking basket at your entry for two months while it grows in.

Disadvantages:

1. You need a basket with evenly-spaced wires with three to five inches in between them so you can fit a reduced root ball from a 4.5" pot or flat (multipack) through them. These can be hard to find at a garden center. See our Web site at www.easygardencolor.com for suppliers.

2. You need loose coco-fiber to form the sides, which is not normally stocked at garden centers. See our Web site at www.easygardencolor.com for suppliers.

3. You need about twice as many plants - 15 for the one opposite and 33 for the one on this page.

4. The baskets that look good with plants through the sides are large and somewhat heavy.

How do you get a plant through the sides?

Remove the hard coco-fiber liner that comes with the basket. This liner is designed for top planting only. You cannot get a plant through it.

Add a layer of loose coco-fiber to cover the bottom and about one-third of the way up the sides. Add soil and fertilizer up to the edges of the coco-fiber.

Dip the roots of a plant in water to make it easy to squeeze through the sides. Wet root balls are easier to mold - in order to fit them through the smaller openings in the basket - than dry ones.

Slide the roots of the plant through the sides. Position it so that the roots are over the soil and the stem is next to the coco fiber. Pull the coco fiber up around it a bit to keep soil from coming in contact with the stem.

Plant every other square in the bottom layer, alternating two or three different kinds of plants. Add more coco-fiber - to the middle of the top square - and then soil, and fertilizer. Plant the second layer of plants in every square.

Place more coco-fiber around the edges and plant the centerpiece in the middle. Add more soil around the centerpiece and plant the final layer of plants around the edges of the top.

For container sources, go to www.easygardencolor.com

See pages 346-354 to learn how to plant, mount, hang, and water your hanging baskets. And the companion DVD really makes it easy!

Here is the finished basket - 45 minutes after I started it!

When I first began my quest to learn how to make instant baskets, I consulted a lot of books. I attempted to follow their planting directions of about six steps, but my baskets never looked anywhere near as good as theirs did. Once I finally figured out the process, I vowed that I would show you every, tiny, miniscule step so that you don't fail like I did. So, instead of the normal six step process, mine is thirty-one steps that covers six full pages (346 through 351). Maybe I went a little over the top with this one, but you will have the WHOLE story, absolutely nothing left out! And I made a companion DVD that shows the whole process in nine minutes!

However, I don't want you to be intimidated by all those pages of minute instructions. The process is really easy after you have tried it a few times! The opposite page shows the basic steps that will help you understand the layered planting process before reading the detailed instructions.

Basket Basic: Choose the Right Components.

Bad Baskets for Side Planting

This was the first basket we tried for side planting and it didn't work for two reasons. First, the sides were tapered so much that the plants near the bottom of the sides died from lack of light. Second, the spaces between the wires were not large enough to fit the roots of plants that are commonly found at garden centers.

Baskets made of decorative metal are also not appropriate for side planting because you can't fit the plants through the decorations. These baskets are designed for top planting only.

Bad Liner for Side Planting

We not only started with the wrong baskets but also the wrong liners. Since you slide the flowers through the liner, the material must be pliable. Stiff liners that are commonly sold with the baskets don't work for side planting. So I tried spaghnum moss because I had used it successfully to line baskets when I just planted the tops. It is a loose material that you soak in water and then shape it to fit the basket. It didn't work because:

1. Spaghnum moss holds water like a sponge. The stems of the seedlings were in direct contact with the moss. They rotted and all the flowers we planted in the sides died.
2. It is a pain in the neck to work with, requiring about an hour of labor for each of these baskets - just to line them!
3. We attached three sizes of these baskets together, hoping this would give the entire arrangement major design impact. It didn't work. When we watered them, the moss fell from basket to basket, coating the flowers on top with moss. Some of them smothered. Most of them died.
4. I was quite disappointed by the overall effect of this basket set-up. Who would want something that looks like this hanging outside their front door for two months until it fills out? It looked like a three-tiered hair ball to me! Planting seedlings is fine if you have a nursery or green house in which to hide the thing until it fills out, but is not appropriate for many Florida homes with small lots where every nook and cranny of the yard is an important view.

Good Liner for Side Planting

Loose coco-fiber is a terrific liner material. It doesn't hold water, like spaghnum moss, so it doesn't rot the stems of the plants. And it's much easier and quicker to use than spaghnum. See the companion DVD to see how easily it works! The only problem is that most garden centers don't carry it. See our Web site at www.easygardencolor.com for sources and ask your local garden center to bring some in.

For container sources, go to www.easygardencolor.com

See pages 346-354 to learn how to plant, mount, hang, and water your hanging baskets. And the companion DVD really makes it easy!

Good 16-inch Basket

This basket is very well-designed for instant baskets, but we only tested it for about eight months so we don't know how long it lasts. The square bottom attaches well to a post. This is the smallest basket we found that lasted well with side plantings. It measures 16" wide by 8" tall and has a generous 5" between wires. This basket weight about 20 pounds, planted

Centerpiece: Use three plants from 4.5" pots or one <u>full</u> plant from a one-gallon pot. It is important for the center piece to look full.

Edges and sides: Use 30 plants from mulipacks or 4.5" pots. The smaller plants from multipacks are easier to fit in this container.

Great 18" Imperial Planter

This 18" wide Imperial Planter is not only well-designed for instant baskets but also very well-made. The one shown has been outside at my house for ten years, and is just showing its first sign of rust. It also offers the benefit of one-piece construction, so you don't have to worry about hooks coming undone. Don't try mounting it on a post, however, because its round bottom will fall off. It measures 18" wide by 11" tall for the planting area; the entire pot (including hanger) is 24" tall. This basket has 4" between wires and weighs about 40 pounds, planted. Its generous size makes it heavier than the basket above but easier to maintain because it doesn't need water as often. It doesn't have the squares like the one below (which makes positioning your first basket so easy) but the Imperial Planter is my favorite of them all.

Centerpiece: Use three plants from 1-gallon pots or one plant from a three-gallon pot. It is important for the centerpiece to look full.

Edges and sides: Use 40 to 43 plants from mulipacks or 4.5" pots.

Good 20-inch Basket

This 20" wide basket is quite well-designed for instant baskets but rusts after a few months outside. I keep using it, however, because the rust isn't noticeable after the basket is filled with plants. It is ideal for mounting on a post because it has a flat bottom. Be careful with the hooks that hold the chain onto the basket. They need to be closed with pliers to ensure that the basket doesn't fall down. This basket measures 20" wide by 12" tall and has an average of four inches between wires. It weighs 40 pounds, planted. The squares on the sides make positioning plants in your first basket quite easy.

Centerpiece: Used three plants from 1-gallon pots or one plant from a three-gallon pot.

Edges and sides: Use 40 plants from mulipacks or 4.5" pots. This basket looks much fuller on planting day with larger plants.

Basket Basic: Choose the Right Plants.

Most good plants (see "The Top 100 Plants", pages 274-333) work in the top of an instant basket. Not so for the sides. These plants are literally planted sideways, and some like it while others quickly die. Here are the results of our trials for side plantings.

Easiest Plants for Side Planting

Wax Begonia

Coleus

Impatiens

Wax begonias, coleus, and impatiens (all types of impatiens, including singles, doubles, New Guineas, and Little Lizzies) not only thrived in the sides of baskets but also are very easy to find both in flats and the 4.5" pot size appropriate for this use. While other plants listed below did as well as these three, most of them are a bit more difficult to find in the correct pot size for the instant baskets. And you could spend the rest of your life putting together different combinations of just these three plants!

Choose from these three plants for your first basket. One type of coleus and one color of wax begonia may be all you need to fill the sides of your first basket.

Great Performers for the Sides but Harder to Find

Lysimachia 'Outback Sunset' · **Purple Queen**
Trailing Torenia · **Ivy**
Goldilocks · **Dragon Wing Begonia**
Sweet Potato Vines (all) · **Lamium**
Variegated Mint · **'Little Lizzie' Impatiens**

The plants shown (left) performed marvelously in the sides of our baskets - as well as the three shown above them. But they are more difficult to find at the garden centers either in 4.5" pots or in flats. Most are available in larger containers. I have noticed some in 4.5" pots lately but none in flats.

If you would like to try them and cannot find them, be sure to tell the garden center staff. With enough requests, they may bring them in.

Right, top: Dragon wing begonias and coleus are planted in the sides of this 18" Imperial Planter. These begonias were among the highest performers we tested for the sides of hanging baskets.

Right, bottom: Sweet potato, purple queen, and trailing torenia are planted in the sides of this basket.

For container sources, go to www.easygardencolor.com

See pages 346-354 to learn how to plant, mount, hang, and water your hanging baskets. And the companion DVD really makes it easy!

Mixed Performers for the Sides

Upright Torenia

Petunia

Verbena

Pansy

The plants shown (left) rate mixed reviews. The upright torenia, although I used it frequently, didn't live as long as the trailing type. Pansies were very short-lived when planted in the sides, usually under a month, but they thrived in the tops of containers. Trailing verbena did very well sometimes but stopped blooming in others. All of the upright verbena quickly died. Petunias were the most confusing flower we tried - some of them thrived while others quickly died. We had the best luck with Proven Winners' Supertunias, but even a few of them died as well.

Let us know which ones work for you at info@easygardencolor.com

Plants that Died Quickly in the Sides

Marigolds

Viola

Lobelia

Snapdragon

Periwinkle

Marguerite Daisy

The plants shown (left) died quickly in the sides of our baskets. However, most did quite well when planted in the top of the baskets.

We don't know why they died, and it is possible that other cultivars of these same flowers could do well. We will keep testing, and you do the same. If you would like to share any of your experiences, contact us at info@easygardencolor.com

It is important for your first experience with these baskets to be positive, so avoid experimenting with these in the sides when you are just beginning!

I think the reason they died was because of fungus. So, if you are experimenting with plants that we didn't try, avoid those that are quite susceptible to fungus.

Some of Our Favorite Centerpieces

Mona Lavender

Shrimp Plant

Ti Plants, small

Blue Salvia

Grasses

Dracaenas, small

Centerpieces, which are planted in the top of the basket, grow like any other container plant, so there are unlimited choices. Look through this chapter to get some ideas.

We particularly like the ones shown to the left because of their upright growth habit which contrasts well with the mounding or trailing growth habit of the plants we use in the sides and along the edges.

Centerpieces look best when they are quite full on planting day.

In larger baskets, we often used plants from three-gallon pots for centerpieces. In smaller baskets, use one gallon-size plants or three plants from 4.5-inch pots.

Basket Basic: Simple Plants and Other Tips

Limit the Number of Different Plants in the Beginning.

It is easiest to begin with only a few different kinds of plants. Use two or three different plants for the edges and the sides and simply alternate them. Use one more different plant for the centerpiece.

The 16" basket (shown left) features a simple combination of a grass as the centerpiece and three different coleus alternated around the sides and top edge. The edge and side plants were planted from flats into this 16" basket. We used 30 coleus, 10 each color. They came from three flats (multipacks) that contained 18 plants in each, so we had enough left over to fill another container.

Use Coleus, Impatiens, or Wax Begonias for the Sides and Edge.

Your first basket should be fun and successful. If you stick to the easiest plants to locate at your garden center, you will have an easy time of finding them. These three plants do quite well planted through the sides and along the top edge.

This basket (left) features another simple combination - a coleus as the centerpiece surrounded by alternated wax begonias and a different coleus. It is easy to choose three different plants for your first basket. Just use that part of your mind that tells you what shirt to wear with a particular pair of shorts, or what throw pillow to choose for your couch. Let your eyes show you which combinations make you smile!

Learn the Simple Trick of Alternating a Few Different Plants.

This container has only three kinds of coleus alternated in the sides and along the top edge. By alternating, the basket remains balanced. If you use too many different plants around the sides, your basket will not grow evenly. Or, if you plant one kind of plant on one side and another on the opposite side, the same unbalanced look will result.

This 18" Imperial Planter required 13 of each coleus from 4.5-inch pots and one three-gallon shrimp plant for the centerpiece.

For container sources, go to www.easygardencolor.com

See pages 346-354 to learn how to plant, mount, hang, and water your hanging baskets. And the companion DVD really makes it easy!

Size Options for Side Plants

Flats or multipacks

4.5" pots

Leggy plant from a flat

Above: If you plant leggy plants from flats, pinch them back so they will fill out. The basket may not look full on day one, but it will look better in the long run.

Baskets with side plantings require a lot of plants. We recommend either flats that hold multiple plants or the individual plants in 4.5" pots. The size is an important consideration, because the plants in the multipacks cost considerably less.

Plants in flats are smaller than the plants in separate, 4.5" pots. Different garden centers sell different quantities in a flat, from 6 to 18.

Advantages of flats compared with 4.5" pots:
1. Less expensive.
2. Easier to transport.
3. Easier to fit in the sides of most containers.

Disadvantages of flats compared with 4.5" pots:
1. Plants in flats are harder to remove from the container. Don't pull the plant out from the top or you will tear the roots. Cut the container apart with scissors and carefully remove each root ball.
2. You'll need to plant the plants from flats within a few days of bringing them home because the plants are so close together that they will get leggy quickly (see photo, left). Plants in 4.5" pots can be kept for up to a month after buying them, depending on how root-bound they are.
3. Although flats fit well in the 16" baskets shown on page 77, the larger 18" and 20" baskets look fuller on planting day if planted with 4.5" pots.
4. You'll find more variety in 4.5" pots, although the recommended wax begonias, impatiens, and coleus are usually sold in both flats or 4.5" pots.

Important Tips

Above: Large baskets like this 20" one are easier to maintain than smaller ones.

1. **Use large baskets.** Larger baskets weigh more and require more plants than smaller ones. But they are much easier to maintain. They require water less often and allow the plants to grow fuller because there is more room for their roots to spread. My personal favorite is the Imperial 18" basket. The planting area is deep and full, and the basket lasts for at least a decade in Florida.

2. **Avoid these instant baskets in July and August** unless you have a lot of time to water and a great tolerance for being outside in extreme heat. Fall, winter, and spring baskets are great because the plants grow slowly and the weather is cool, so they don't need anywhere near as much water as in the heat of summer. Baskets grow so fast in July and August that the plants quickly get leggy. And the water needs in the sun are huge, as often as twice a day.

3. **Be sure the basket gets enough light.** Baskets that are side planted require more light than traditional containers because the light has to reach down to the sides of the container.

4. **Water wisely.** Overwatering is the major cause of death for plants in baskets that are planted on the sides. The plants on the bottom row are particularly vulnerable to death from overwatering. Learn more about watering on page 354.

5. **Always plant only every other space in the bottom layer.** We leave a little more space between plants on the bottom layer of the sides because they are more susceptible to fungus, which worsens with close planting.

Easiest Plants for Side Planting...

For container sources, go to www.easygardencolor.com

Impatiens, Begonias, and Coleus

All three of these baskets feature coleus, impatiens and begonias planted in the sides and along the top edge - plants that are not only easy to find but also hard to kill! We had very few fatalities with these dependable plants. Although the containers on the left feature dragon wing begonias, they would also do well with the easier-to-find wax begonias. All three of these baskets have croton centerpieces. They are mounted on posts (see pages 352-353 for instructions). We planted 40 plants in the sides and top edge of each basket from 4.5" pots.

Light: Light shade to full sun in winter. Light to medium shade in summer.

Season: The begonias and impatiens do best from October through May, although they are used throughout the country in the summer. Coleus and crotons grow year round. Large baskets are difficult to water in July and August. Protect all of them from freezes.

Lifespan: About four to five months in this container in the cool season. Shorter lifespan in the warm months.

Care: Fertilize with a slow-release mix on planting day, and repeat every two or three months. Water when the soil feels dry - about every two to four days in cooler weather. These baskets are hard to maintain in July and August because they need water up to twice a day. The dragon wing begonias grow faster than the coleus in cool weather. You can pinch them back if they begin to overtake the coleus.

Pot: 20" hanging basket (page 77).

Mammey Croton
(1 plant from a three-gallon pot)
Plant Profile: Page 288

Orange Impatiens
(13 plants from 4.5" pots)
Plant Profile: Page 298

Coleus 'Wizard Golden'
(14 plants from 4.5" pots)
Plant Profile: Page 287

Lavender Impatiens
(13 plants from 4.5" pots)
Plant Profile: Page 298

Easiest Plants for Side Planting...

Mammey Croton
(1 plant from a three-gallon pot)
Plant Profile: Page 288

Dragon Wing Begonia
(18 plants from 4.5" pots)
Plant Profile: Page 280

Coleus 'Mardi Gras'
(18 plants from 4.5" pots)
Plant Profile: Page 287

Both of these baskets feature coleus and begonias planted in the sides. These plants, along with impatiens, are the easiest to find of the plants that do well in the sides of baskets. We had very few fatalities with these dependable plants. Although these containers feature dragon wing begonias, they would also do well with the easier-to-find wax begonias. The baskets are Imperial Planters described on page 77. They are eighteen inches in diameter and look new after ten years of use in Florida.

For container sources, go to www.easygardencolor.com

Impatiens, Begonias, and Coleus

Dragon Wing Begonia
(18 plants from 4.5" pots)
Plant Profile: Page 280

Perilla 'Magilla'
(1 plant from a one-gallon pot)
Plant Profile: Page 316

Coleus 'Wizard Golden'
(18 plants from 4.5" pots)
Plant Profile: Page 287

Light: Light shade to full sun in winter. Light to medium shade in summer.
Season: The begonias do best from October through May, although they are used throughout the country in the summer. Coleus and crotons grow year round. Protect all of them from frost.
Lifespan: About four to five months in this container.
Care: Fertilize with a slow-release mix on planting day, and repeat every two or three months. Water when the soil feels dry, about every other day in summer and every three or four days in cooler weather (see page 354). The dragon wing begonias grow faster than the coleus in cool weather. You can pinch them back if they begin to overtake the coleus.
Pot: Imperial Planter, 18" diameter. This container has spent 10 years outside in Florida and still looks brand new!

Coleus Baskets

Coleus 'Crime Scene'
(1 plant from a one-gallon pot)
Plant Profile: Page 285

Coleus 'Red Trailing Queen'
(13 plants from 4.5" pots)
Plant Profile: Page 285

Coleus 'Wizard Golden'
(13 plants from 4.5" pots)
Plant Profile: Page 285

Coleus 'Freckles'
(14 plants from 4.5" pots)
Plant Profile: Page 285

Both of these baskets feature only coleus - both in the sides and along the top edge as well as in the center. We had very few fatalities with these dependable plants, which are rapidly becoming one of the most popular container plants in the world. Although traditionally used only in summer in Florida, we found they did very well in winter as well, if they were protected from temperatures under forty degrees. And the range of leaf colors and patterns is endless!

For container sources, go to www.easygardencolor.com

See pages 346-354 to learn how to plant, mount, hang, and water your hanging baskets. And the companion DVD really makes it easy!

Coleus 'Saturn'
(1 plant from a one-gallon pot)
Plant Profile: Page 285

Coleus 'Mardi Gras'
(20 plants from 4.5" pots)
Plant Profile: Page 285

Coleus 'Mrs. Harding'
(20 plants from 4.5" pots)
Plant Profile: Page 285

Light: Light shade to full sun in winter. Light to medium shade in summer.
Season: All year, if protected from temperatures under 40 degrees. Difficult to handle in July and August because they need so much water.
Lifespan: About four to five months in this container except for July and August, when they grow so fast they only last for about two to three months.
Care: Fertilize with a slow-release mix on planting day, and repeat every two or three months. Water when the soil feels dry, about every day in early summer and every three or four days in cooler weather. Water twice a day in sun in July and August. Pinch back if they get leggy.
Pot: Imperial Planter, 18" diameter. This container has spent 10 years outside in Florida and still looks brand new!

Add More Variety...

Golden Shrimp Plant
(1 plant from a one-gallon pot)
Plant Profile: Page 322

Red Pentas
(6 plants from 4.5" pots)
Plant Profile: Page 315

Coleus 'Defiance'
(10 plants from a 4.5" pots)
Plant Profile: Page 287

Trailing Torenia
(10 plants from 4.5" pots)
Plant Profile: Page 326

Wax Begonia
(10 plants from 4.5" p
**Plant Profile: Page 2

This basket has a double centerpiece: shrimp plants surrounded by red pentas. I don't know which variety of pentas they are, but they didn't bloom much. The rest of the basket did pretty well, but it would have lasted longer in a container larger than this 16" one.

Light: Light shade to full sun.

Season: This group of plants all do well from October through June. Although most of them do well in the ground in the heat of summer, they grow too fast and require too much water to be easy in these instant hanging baskets during this time, making them difficult to maintain.

Lifespan: About two to three months in this container during the cooler months. Shorter lifespan in more heat. These plants would live longer in a larger basket, like the 18" Imperial Planter.

Care: Fertilize with a slow-release mix on planting day, and repeat every two or three months. Water when the soil feels dry, about every other day in spring and fall and every three or four days in cooler weather.

Pot: 16" basket (see page 77).

For container sources, go to www.easygardencolor.com

as you get more experience.

We call this basket a leftover. We loaded it up with plants that were left over from other baskets. It contains dragon wing begonias, sweet potato vines, lantana, two varieties of coleus, ivy, new guinea impatiens, a croton, and a dracaena - too many plants to show all their photos on this page! It grew a bit lopsided, as shown under 'Trimming' on page 341. Baskets grow better with fewer plant varieties so that they are even on all sides. Another disadvantage of this many plants is that some start to die long before the rest. But it was fun mixing up all these plants nonetheless!

Light: Light shade to full sun.

Season: This group of plants all do well from October through June. Although some of them, like coleus, do well when planted in the ground in July and August, they grow so quickly in these baskets that they get leggy too fast. It is a lot easier to keep these large baskets looking good from September through June.

Lifespan: About three to four months in this container during the cooler months. Shorter lifespan in more heat.

Care: Fertilize with a slow-release mix on planting day, and repeat every two or three months. Water when the soil feels dry, about every other day in spring and fall and every three or four days in cooler weather. It is hard to keep up with the watering requirements in July and August, when it can easily require two waterings a day.

Pot: 20" basket mounted on a post (see page 352-353 for mounting instructions).

For container sources, go to www.easygardencolor.com

See pages 346-354 to learn how to plant, mount, hang, and water your hanging baskets. And our companion DVD really makes it easy!

Mona Lavender
(1 plant from a one-gallon pot)
Plant Profile: Page 306

Melampodium
(10 plants from 4.5" pots)
Plant Profile: Page 305

Supertunia
'Mini Rose Veined'
(10 plants from 4.5" pots)
Plant Profile: Page 317

Petunia
(10 plants from 4.5" pots)
Plant Profile: Page 317

Plectranthus Variegata
or Variegated Mint
(10 plants from 4.5" pots)
Plant Profile: Page 306

Supertunia 'Royal Velvet'
(10 plants from 4.5" pots)
Plant Profile: Page 317

These bright-colored basket have been some of the most popular ones in our trail gardens - they stop visitors in their tracks. We tried regular petunias in side plantings and most died. Finally, we found these Proven Winners' 'Supertunias', most of which did phenomenally well planted on the sides. This variegated mint is another good find as it's proving to be a summer survivor.

Left and above: These lovely baskets were created with Mona lavender as our top centerpiece and melampodium, petunias and variegated mint around the sides.

Light: Light shade to full sun.

Season: Winter through spring, but protect them from freezes.

Lifespan: About five months in this container.

Care: Fertilize with a slow-release mix on planting day. Water when the soil feels dry, about every other day (see pages 354 for more watering info). No trimming required on these plants.

Basket: 20" diameter basket described on page 77.

Note: Each of the containers has 10 purple petunias - one the lighter color and the other the darker.

Great Idea: Baskets on Posts!

We made so many hanging baskets while writing this book that we ran out of space to hang them. So, we mounted them on wooden posts and placed them in otherwise bland spots throughout the garden. The topiary-like effect is beautiful and especially attention-getting, with so many flowers at eye level. Our baskets on posts quickly became one of our favorite container ideas. They create a real focal point wherever they're placed, add an interesting vertical element, and offer a unique way to show off these fabulous arrangements. See page 352-353 for instructions on this fairly easy project.

For container sources, go to www.easygardencolor.com

See pages 346-354 to learn how to plant, mount, hang, and water your hanging baskets. And our companion DVD really makes it easy!

Baskets on Posts for the Cool Season

Supertunia (Petunia) 'Blushing Princess'
(14 plants from 4.5" pots)
Plant Profile: Page 317

Coleus 'Amora'
(14 plants from 4.5" pots)
Plant Profile: Page 287

Supertunia (Petunia) 'Double Pink'
(14 plants from 4.5" pots)
Plant Profile: Page 317

Although these two baskets are displayed together, their color schemes are quite different. They blend rather than match. All plants, except the Mona lavender, are from Proven Winners.

Most plants don't really like being planted on their sides, so we eliminated many through our trials. Most petunias we tested quickly died of fungus. The exceptions were the Prover Winners' 'Supertunias,' most of which did beautifully, as you can see in these baskets.

Above: This brightly colored basket uses only two species of plants - petunias and coleus. We planted both the sides and top.
Light: Light shade to full sun.
Season: February through May. Protect them from frost.
Lifespan: About three to five months in this basket.
Care: Fertilize with a slow-release mix on planting day. Water when the soil feels dry, about every other day (see page 354). No trimming required on these plants but removing dead blooms will yield more flowers.
Pot: 20-inch basket described on page 77.

Right: This lovely basket was created using Mona lavender as our top centerpiece, with verbena, 'Supertunias' and lamium alternated around the sides and top rim. The lamium did quite well despite the fact that it is typically used in more northern zones.
Light: Light shade to full sun.
Season: Winter through spring. Protect them from frost.
Lifespan: About five months in this container.
Care: Fertilize with a slow-release mix on planting day. Water when the soil feels dry, about every other day (see page 354). The flowers bloom more if you remove the dead ones. Groom as needed.
Pot: 20-inch basket described on page 77.

For container sources, go to www.easygardencolor.com

See pages 346-354 to learn how to plant, mount, hang, and water your hanging baskets. And our companion DVD really makes it easy!

Supertunia (Petunia) 'Mini Rose Veined'
(10 plants from 4.5" pots)
Plant Profile: Page 317

Lamium 'White Nancy'
(10 plants from 4.5" pots)
Plant Profile: Page 302

Mona Lavender
(1 plant from a one-gallon pot)
Plant Profile: Page 306

Superbena (Verbena) 'Large Lilac Blue'
(10 plants from 4.5" pots)
Plant Profile: Page 327

Supertunia (Petunia) 'Royal Velvet'
(10 plants from 4.5" pots)
Plant Profile: Page 317

Salvia
(3 plants from 4.5" pots)
Plant Profile: Page 321

'Margarita' Sweet Potato
(3 plants from 4.5" pots)
Plant Profile: Page 324

'Gumdrops' Begonia
(10 plants from 4.5" pots)
Plant Profile: Page 280

Supertunia (Petunia) 'Mini Rose Veined'
(10 plants from 4.5" pots)
Plant Profile: Page 317

Dragon Wing Beg
(10 plants from 4.5" po
Plant Profile: Page 2

The addition of these 'Gumdrops' double wax begonias (from Bodger Botanicals through Michell's) lit this arrangement up. It literally glowed when viewed from a distance. We only scattered a few sweet potato vines around the sides, so they wouldn't take over the begonias. We used brilliant red salvia as our top centerpiece plants; they held their own admirably in this arrangement full of bright-colored plants.

Light: Light shade to full sun.
Season: October through May. Protect them from frost.
Lifespan: About four to five months in this container.
Care: Fertilize with a slow-release mix on planting day. Water when the soil feels dry, about every other day (see page 354). Trim the sweet potato vine if it starts to overtake the other plants.
Pot: 20" basket mounted on a post.

See pages 346-354 to learn how to plant, mount, hang, and water your hanging baskets. And our companion DVD really makes it easy!

Golden Globe
(11 plants from 4.5" pots)
Plant Profile: Page 304

'Wizard Rose' Coleus
(11 plants from 4.5" pots)
Plant Profile: Page 287

'Supertunia Blushing Princess'
(11 plants from 4.5" pots)
Plant Profile: Page 317

The addition of 'Wizard Rose' Coleus to any basket gives you so much color that it's almost a three-for-one plant. The 'Golden Globes' looked good for only a short while. They peaked after about one month but were worth it for that time. We used 'Golden Globe', 'Wizard Rose' coleus, and pale petunias for this arrangement, planting top and sides with a total of about thirty-three plants.

Light: Light shade to full sun.
Season: October through May. Protect them from frost.
Lifespan: About three to four months in this container.
Care: Fertilize with a slow-release mix on planting day. Water when the soil feels dry, about every other day. We occasionally trimmed the 'Golden Globe' to keep it from overtaking the other plants. The petunias bloom more if you remove the dead flowers.

Baskets on Posts in Lime and Orange

Since baskets on posts are part of your garden, use plants in your baskets that complement the plants in the ground. The orange flowers planted in the baskets repeat the orange of the impatiens and crotons planted in the ground.

This was our first experience with the 'Little Lizzie' impatiens (from Bodger Botanicals through Michell's) , and we were quite impressed. They did beautifully when planted in the sides of the pots.

'Margarita' Sweet Potato
(3 plants from 4.5" pots)
Plant Profile: Page 324

Dragon Wing Begonia
(5 plants from 4.5" pots)
Plant Profile: Page 280

Red Salvia
(3 plants from 4.5" pots)
Plant Profile: Page 321

'Little Lizzie' Impatiens
(5 plants from 4.5" pots)
Plant Profile: Page 299

Orange Marigolds
(5 plants from 4.5" pots)
Plant Profile: Page 305

For container sources, go to www.easygardencolor.com

See pages 346-354 to learn how to plant, mount, hang, and water your hanging baskets. And our companion DVD really makes it easy!

The pansies ended up lost behind the more aggressive sweet potatoes after a few months, but their beauty for a short time was worth the cost. The 'Margarita' sweet potato vine did beautifully, as usual. They were planted along the top edge of the pot and filled in quickly.

Right & Left: We simply let the lime green sweet potato vine trail on both these baskets.

Light: Light shade to full sun.

Season: November through May. Protect them from frost.

Lifespan: About three to six months in this container.

Care: Fertilize with a slow-release mix on planting day. Water when the soil feels dry, about every other day. If the spring is unusually warm, you could end up watering these baskets every day because the sweet potato vines and impatiens are thirsty plants. Trim the sweet potato vine to keep it from overtaking the other plants.

Salvia
(3 plants from 4.5" pots)
Plant Profile: Page 321

Pansies
(5 plants from 4.5" pots)
Plant Profile: Page 315

Sweet Potato
(3 plants from 4.5" pots)
Plant Profile: Page 324

'Little Lizzie' Impatiens
(5 plants from 4.5" pots)
Plant Profile: Page 299

More Bright Baskets

| **Supertunia 'Mini Rose-Veined'** (5 plants from 4.5" pots) Plant Profile: Page 317 | **'Margarita' Sweet Potato** (5 plants from 4.5" pots) Plant Profile: Page 324 | **Double Impatiens** (5 plants from 4.5" pots) Plant Profile: Page 299 | **'Blackie' Sweet Potato** (5 plants from 4.5" pots) Plant Profile: Page 324 | **Yellow Snapdragon** (3 plants from one-gallon po...) Plant Profile: Page 32... |

This basket is an excellent example of leaves mixed with flowers. Since the centerpiece of yellow snapdragons doesn't bloom constantly, the other plants have to provide enough color to take up the slack. Double impatiens (from Bodger's through Michell's) and 'Supertunias' (from Proven Winners) are so dependable that they never missed a day of blooming. These flowers, coupled with the leaf color, provide lots of color even when the centerpiece is resting.

Light: Light shade to full sun.

Season: February through May. Protect them from frost.

Lifespan: About four to five months in this container.

Care: Fertilize with a slow-release mix on planting day, and repeat every two or three months. Water when the soil feels dry, about every other day. Trim the sweet potato to keep it from overtaking the other plants.

For container sources, go to www.easygardencolor.com

See pages 346-344 to learn how to plant, mount, hang, and water your hanging baskets. And our companion DVD really makes it easy!

Purple Pansy
(5 plants from 4.5" pots)
Plant Profile: Page 315

'Little Lizzie' Impatiens
(5 plants from 4.5" pots)
Plant Profile: Page 299

Persian Shield
(1 plant from a one-gallon pot)
Plant Profile: Page 316

Yellow Pansy
(5 plants from 4.5" pots)
Plant Profile: Page 315

Dragon Wing Begonia
(5 plants from 4.5" pots)
Plant Profile: Page 280

This basket started out as a blaze of color as you can see. Then, as the weather warmed up, the other plants overtook the pansies. After that, the arrangement became a huge glove of purple, red, and green. We used pansies, impatiens, begonias, and Persian shield for a seriously-colorful arrangement. We planted the top and sides with a total of about twenty-one plants.

Light: Light shade to full sun.

Season: November through May. Protect them from frost

Lifespan: About three to four months in this container.

Care: Fertilize with a slow-release mix on planting day and repeat every two or three months. Water when the soil feels dry, about every other day.

Chapter 5

Wall Pots & Window Boxes

After

Before

Ti Plant
(1 plant from a three-gallon pot)
Plant Profile: Page 325

Canna Lily
(2 plants from one-gallon pots)
Plant Profile: Page 285

Coleus 'Wizard Rose'
(12 plants from 4.5" pots)
Plant Profile: Page 287

Upright Torenia
(12 plants from 4.5" pots)
Plant Profile: Page 326

Dragon Wing Begonia
(12 plants from 4.5" pots)
Plant Profile: Page 280

Coleus 'Bellingrath'
(12 plants from 4.5" pots)
Plant Profile: Page 287

Wall pots are extremely useful in Florida gardens.

Most are flat on the back, designed to hang on flat surfaces. Or you can use pot clips to hang round pots on walls. When I was designing gardens, I used wall pots in at least half of the houses I did. They worked well next to front doors, on stucco columns, and on the walls and fences that surround so many Florida gardens. Basically, wall pots transform any boring space - whether it's next to a garage door or on a lattice for privacy - by providing a splash of color and interest.

Window boxes are also fun and decorative. I have them

on most of the windows in my house. Besides adding a welcoming note to the exterior of your home, window boxes allow flowers to be viewed up close from inside. The new fiberglass boxes are easy to install and a snap to maintain, so even novices can simply transform the look of their homes.

Left: This is the largest wall pot I have ever planted - it's a full thirty inches across, empty. By the time it was planted, the whole arrangement measured over forty inches across! The pot is made of the same material as the hanging baskets and works well with the same plants shown on pages 78-79 planted in the sides. (Look at the photo above to see what this type of pot looks like empty.) It provided a fabulous focal point above a bench on my pool pavilion. The only mistake I made was planting canna lilies in the top. The label said 'dwarf canna,' and I thought it would top out at about two feet tall. Not so. It rocketed up to over four feet tall, and we had to cut it down because it ruined the proportion of the arrangement. So much for 'dwarf' plants in Florida! Luckily, the pot had so many plants in it that the cannas were not even missed.

Light: Light shade to full sun.
Season: Spring through fall.
Lifespan: About three to four months in this container. The torenia only lasted about two months. By that time, the other plants were so large, it wasn't missed.
Care: Fertilize with a slow-release mix on planting day. Water when the soil feels dry, about every other day. Pinch back the coleus monthly to keep it from getting leggy. If you pinch the coleus this often, it will look good, even right after it's been pinched. If you wait longer, the plants will look bare for a while.

Wall Garden by a Pool

The owners of this pool garden asked me to land-scape a one-foot space wedged between the screen and the wall located behind their pool enclosure (see photo, right). Since the space was too small to plant, I suggested mounting a lattice in front of the screen and attaching a wall garden. The lattice formed a much more attractive background than the blank wall behind the screen.

Before, Right: The pool screening had a one-foot space between it and the wall. That space was too small to plant anything large enough to break up the large expanse of tall wall behind it.

After, Below: The wall behind the pool is softened with pots - both those mounted on the lattice and those on the floor. All the contain-ers are planted with low-maintenance plants - bromeliads, palms, and crotons - that don't shed much on the floor.

After, Below and Right: The small bed that is visible in the far left of the photo below is planted with material that coordinates with the container plantings.

Before

After

I tried to find the source of the pot clips I used below and on the next two pages. They were great because they were invisible once they were installed. I couldn't find the same ones, but many similar products are on the market. Put 'pot clips' in an internet search engine and push 'go.' Lots of interesting products pop up.

After

Wall Pots: Ideal for the concrete walls.

Many Florida bathrooms are surrounded by walled gardens. Wall pots are ideal for these areas.

Above: I was asked to perk up this bath atrium that was just outside a window. It featured only a triple Christmas palm and a crinum lily. I simply added containers of orchids and bromeliads. The bromelaids on the walls are attached with the same pot clips I found for the garden on the previous pages. The orchids were mounted on the window frame so the flowers would show from inside the window and the pots were hidden.

Left: I placed bromeliads in terra cotta pots on the ground inside the atrium. The homeowner put some shelves next to the the air conditioning unit (where not many people would see them) to store the bromeliads and orchids when they were not flowering.

For container sources, go to www.easygardencolor.com

that surround many Florida homes.

Courtyard homes are filled with windows that overlook walled gardens.

Above: This wall is the focal point of a courtyard home - all the windows of the main house and the guest house overlook it. In a planting area this narrow (two feet), it is difficult to achieve much interest by just planting in the ground. Containers do the trick, both for the palms in the ground pots and the bromeliads in the wall pots.

Right: The wall pots are made of terra cotta and painted with a concrete stain. The paint doesn't last forever, and it's more practical to look for pots with glazed finishes if you want color. But the pot clips are a great idea. Notice how the pots seem to be floating in the air because no support hooks are visible.

Wall pots come in many colors.

The inspiration for this grouping started with the wall pots. After they were hung, the 'outdoor room' craved more bright, Mexican pots - which were added as floor pots and animals.

Above: These colorful wall pots and hanging animals make an impact on their own, which makes designing with them very easy. Just hang them up and fill the Masart Mexican pots with colorful flowers. These are the first patterned wall pots I have found that are large enough to grow good-sized plants. The size also accomodates enough water you don't have to water them every five minutes.These pots looked so good that they inspired me to add three more coordinating groupings of Masart pots by the chairs, as shown opposite.

Opposite: More Masart pots form groupings around the furniture to complement the wall grouping. The different pot patterns mix together easily, complementing rather than overwhelming each other. The pots are also quite lightweight. I had no problem lifting any of them (empty) that you see on these pages. The animal pots are so decorative that they look good empty, especially if combined with pots of bright flowers and foliage.

For container sources, go to www.easygardencolor.com

Dracaena Reflexa
Profile: Page 292

Mammey Croton
Profile: Page 288

Hybrid Geranium
Profile: Page 296

Hybrid Diascia
Profile: Page 292

Coleus
Profile: Page 287

Dwarf White Striped Sweet Flag
Profile: Page 329

New Guinea Impatiens
Profile: Page 300

Lobelia
Profile: Page 331

Goldilocks
Profile: Page 303

Scaevola
Profile: Page 332

Coleus 'Defiance'
Profile: Page 287

Impatiens
Profile: Page 298

More Wall Pots

Wall pots are designed to fit against a wall, fence, or any flat surface. The wall pots on this page are wire (pictured, below), similar to the hanging baskets in the previous chapter, except they are flat on one side. They're planted in the sides and top. See pages 356-359 for planting details. They work well on walls, columns, or even swings, as shown.

Use plants in the sides that are recommended on pages 78-79 - the same ones that do well in the sides of hanging baskets.

For container sources, go to www.easygardencolor.com

See pages 356-359 to learn how to plant wire wall pots. And our companion DVD really makes the side-planting technique really easy!

Above: These wall pots are made of terra cotta and planted only in the top. They are flat on the back, with a rounded front. Their 18-inch length gives you enough space to plant at least three plants. This generous container size fits enough soil to allow the plants space to grow. Many wall pots are quite a bit smaller, making them harder to plant and water.

These terra cotta containers look best with a plant that trails slightly over the edge. The pot on the left features a bromeliad in the center and pothos trailing over the edge. The other one has yellow and purple lantana planted in it.

Above: These wall pots are made of wire, like the ones on the opposite page. They are flat on the back, with a rounded front, and measure 16 inches long. These pots are planted in the tops and through the sides, like the hanging baskets in the previous chapter. The side-planting technique gives you an instant look.

The pot on the left is planted with a wide variety of plants, including coleus, impatiens, and torenia. The pot on the right is simply planted with three different coleus and uses a ti plant as the centerpiece.

More Wall Pots

Golden Shrimp Plant
(2 plants from one-gallon pots)
Plant Profile: Page 322

'Dark Star' Coleus
(8 plants from 4.5" pots)
Plant Profile: Page 287

Dragon Wing Begonia
(8 plants from 4.5" pots)
Plant Profile: Page 280

'Gay's Delight' Coleus
(8 plants from 4.5" pots)
Plant Profile: Page 287

For container sources, go to www.easygardencolor.com

See pages 356-359 to learn how to plant wire wall pots. And our companion DVD really makes the side-planting technique really easy!

Wall pots in key locations should look dynamite and not mediocre. These two pots definitely fill the bill.

Left: This wall pot, measuring 22 inches across, is a great size and large enough to have a major design impact. The combination of two very different colors of coleus - lime green and dark (almost black) blue - contrasts dramatically with the pink dragon wing begonias and golden shrimp plants. The coleus are from Proven Winners.

Light: Full sun to light shade during the cool months. Light shade in summer. Although many of these plants take medium shade when planted in the tops of containers, they need more light when planted in the sides.
Season: Spring, summer, or fall.
Lifespan: The arrangement lasts about four to six months in this container. Plant the shrimp plant in your garden after it has outgrown the pot if you live in zones 9 through 11.
Care: Fertilize when planting, and repeat every three months with a slow-release mix. Water when soil feels dry, about twice a week in light shade, more often in sun. Pinch back the coleus monthly.
Pot: 22" half basket, shown empty below.

Above: This Kinsman wall arrangement is made of two parts - a flat, metal trellis that attaches to the wall and a hayrack (a long, thin planter made the same way as the wall pot shown below) hung in front of the trellis. It comes in a myriad of different sizes and is one of the most useful wall planters I have seen. This photo came from Kinsman Company. The hayrack includes variegated pandorea vine, red ivy geraniums, and trailing vinca vine. It was not grown in Florida, but I believe the plants would grow here. It is important to plant a vine that grows up the trellis as well as trailing plants that cascade over the edges.

Light: Full sun to light shade.
Season: November until April; protect from freezes.
Lifespan: The arrangement lasts about four to six months in this container.
Care: Fertilize when planting and repeat every three months with a slow-release mix. Water when soil feels dry.

Pots on Pedestals to Accent Walls

Sanchez and Maddux, landscape architects from Palm Beach, were presented with a special challenge with the wall in this garden, which has been designated as a Palm Beach landmark.

Above: They softened the wall itself with espalied vines. The antique urn and pedestal provide a wonderful focal point in the center of this formally planted garden. The urn plantings are incidental to the pot itself and are changed seasonally.

Left: Here another urn and unique pedestal break up a long expanse of wall that must be preserved. As Phil Maddux said when he's working with important antique pots that he leaves unplanted, "We let the pots speak for the sake of art itself."

As he does for many of the Palm Beach estates he landscapes, Phil Maddux searched the world for the classical urn and pedestal he used in this formal setting.

The arch of podocarpus above the urn is repeated in the entrance to this garden and enhances the urn as the focal point of the entire landscape.

Sanchez and Maddux are fond of purple and yellow color schemes. The round, purple flowers are ruellia 'Purple Showers' (see 'Easy Gardens for Florida') while the spiky ones are Mexican sage. The yellow flowers are seasonal annuals.

Window Boxes Made of Fiberglass.

I have had great luck with the fiberglass window boxes shown on these two pages. They are not only very attractive and durable, but well-sized. While many window boxes are only six inches square, these measure a full nine inches square, giving the plants enough room to fill out.

Because they come with all the necessary hardware, they are very easy to install. I have had them on three windows at my house for nine years. They come in white or dark green. The white can be painted to coordinate with your home.

These window boxes also work well hung from balconies, provided the balcony can handle the weight.

Top: Shrimp plants and impatiens liven up this window box, which is outside the kitchen sink. The cook enjoys the view while inside the kitchen. For more information about the purple bougainvillea, see "Best Garden Color for Florida," pages 194-195.

Bottom: Pothos and bromeliads pair up in this shade window box. In time, the pothos will cascade over the edge of this box.

For container sources, go to www.easygardencolor.com

are ideal for Florida's tough climate

'Perfecta' Bromeliad
Plant Profile: Page 284

Impatiens
Plant Profile: Page 298

Orchids
Plant Profile: Pages 160-169

Top: Where is the window box? It's hidden behind the caricature plants (bronze shrubs). The orchids are simply placed in the box in their plastic pots. When they are finished blooming (in about two months), they are either thrown away or attached to a tree.

Bottom: I have window boxes hung on most of the windows of my house because I like looking at them from inside as well as out-side. I enjoy not only flowers but also close views of butterfies and bumblebees. These boxes can be custom-sized to fit any area. They hang easily and securely with the enclosed hardware. This box is filled with impatiens and pothos.

Window Boxes Filled with...

Planted on August 13

Photographed on August 29, two weeks later.

Most window boxes look best with plants cascading over the edges. The sweet potato vines trailed faster than any other of the plants we tested. They almost completely covered the sides of the fiberglass window box (above) in just two weeks!

See how great the same sweet potato vines look in the Kinsman hayrack (opposite) hung from the second-story window. But remember, this fast success comes with a price. Snails love this plant, so use snail bait when planting them. And these vines are quite thirsty, requiring almost as much water as impatiens.

sweet potato vines, the fastest trailers.

Chapter 6

Containers as
Garden Accents

Once you choose your containers, where do you put them? Containers are garden accents, and their placement is important. You want as much visual impact as possible.

This chapter gives you ideas for accenting five different areas of your gardens with containers:

- Flower beds and other landscaped areas

- Gazebos

- Arbors

- Pool areas

- Entries

By familiarizing yourself with the design concepts used in these examples, you will find ideas for many areas of your own gardens. I was continually surprised and delighted with the impact the containers made in my trial gardens while I was working on this book. I would love to see your successes! Send me photos at info@easygardencolor.com

Left: The swing garden in our trial gardens. See the next two pages for more details about these containers. The green pedestals are also featured on page 189.

Accent a flower bed with containers.

For container sources, go to www.easygardencolor.com

Pots accent the swing and flower beds in my garden. The top of the swing is a terrific locale for flat-backed wall pots. These wall pots filled with annuals bring the eye to higher level than the ground plantings. The dark green pots on this page are the focal point of a garden accent area that is surrounded by white begonias and flat river rocks.

Wall pots, left: Red salvia, midnight blue petunias, and variegated ivy are planted in the top of the wall pot. The impatiens are planted through the sides.
Light: Light shade to full sun; blooms most in full sun.
Season: October through April. Protect from frost.
Lifespan: About eight to twelve weeks in this small container.
Care: Fertilize with a slow-release mix on planting day. Water when the soil feels dry or the impatiens wilt. I watered these about every other day when the plants were new. As they grew and the weather warmed up, I watered them daily.
Pot: Kinsman Company, round hayrack stuffed with lose coco-fiber, 16" W. See pages 356-357 for planting instructions.

Green pots, above: Geraniums, petunias, marigolds, and begonias are planted in these glazed pots.
Light: Full sun.
Season: October through April. Protect from frost.
Lifespan: About three to four months.
Care: Fertilize with a slow-release mix on planting day, and repeat every three months. Water when the soil feels dry, every two or three days (see pages 338-340 for more watering info). These pots are watered by the sprinkler system, which makes them really easy. The geraniums and marigolds flower more and look better if the old blooms are pinched off.
Pot: Anamese. These were one-of-a-kind pots that are no longer available. If you see pots you like, buy them fast!

Accent a gazebo with containers.

Use the design concepts shown in this gazebo with any seating area.

1. Place small containers next to chairs.
2. Use larger containers between chairs and loveseats so the flowers show over the furniture.
3. Use low pots on tabletops so you can see over them.
4. Use hanging baskets wherever you can!

Note: The plants in these containers will shed on the floor. For plants that don't shed, see pages 132-133. The mulch is pine straw, which is ideal for pathways because it is soft to walk on and it maintains its dark brown color for much longer than most other natural mulches.

For container sources, go to www.easygardencolor.com

Yellow pansies accent the table.

Red dragon wing begonias, blue lobelia, and yellow marigolds.

Red dragon wing begonias, blue lobelia, and lime green sweet potato.

Red dragon wing begonias, blue lobelia, and yellow marigolds.

Accent an arbor with containers.

I designed this arbor to accommodate a seating area as well as lots of containers. It works great, holding hundreds of colorful flowers just as I wanted. The mulch floor is ideal for flowers because they can shed their little hearts out without making a mess.

The arbor also forms a strong focal point for the entry garden to my home and office.

Measuring only eight by ten feet, this arbor is ideal for someone who wants a lot of flowers in a small space. It was constructed by my friend, Tim Hadsell, of Lake Worth.

For container sources, go to www.easygardencolor.com

Wall pot, right: The back of the arbor is covered with wall pots that are flat on the back. This example mixes cool-season annuals with both lime green and black sweet potato vines. These fast-growing vines cascade quickly.

Light: Light shade to full sun.

Season: October through April. Protect from frost.

Lifespan: About two to four months.

Care: Fertilize with a slow-release mix on planting day. Water when the soil feels dry or the impatiens wilt (see pages 338-340 for more watering info). Trim the vines so they don't take over the arrangement.

Pot: Kinsman round hayrack, 16"W.

Hanging basket, right: Hanging baskets are very attractive when hung from arbors. This one features a yellow elder (which is a large shrub or small tree at maturity) as an unlikely centerpiece. I found one in a three-gallon pot that was filled with blooms, and I couldn't resist it. Although it only bloomed for about a month, the other cool-season annuals in the arrangement took over when it was done. They include red double impatiens, yellow marigolds, red salvia, and both lime green and black sweet potato vines.

Light: Light shade to full sun. Blooms most in full sun.

Season: October through April. Protect from frost.

Lifespan: About four to six months.

Care: Fertilize with a slow-release mix on planting day. Water when the soil feels dry or the impatiens wilt (see pages 338-340). Trim the vines so they don't take over the arrangement. Marigolds and red salvia look better and bloom more if the dead flowers are pinched off.

Pot: Wire hanging basket, 20"W.

Accent a pool pavilion with containers

Like the arbor on the previous two pages, I designed this pool pavilion to provide a strong focal point for the pool garden that would incorporate seating and plenty of space for containers. It is larger than the previous arbor, measuring 12 by 17 feet, which keeps it in proportion to the over-sized pool.

The photo on the opposite page shows the south view, while the photo on this page shows the north view. This pavilion has provided a great training space for me to learn how to mix containers and accessorize a seating area. I hope it gives you some ideas you can use.

The pavilion was constructed by Gazebo Depot from Delray Beach, Florida.

For container sources, go to www.easygardencolor.com

Simple Entry Pots

Before

After

For container sources, go to www.easygardencolor.com

Use containers to mark entries to both homes and gardens. These pots don't have to be complex, as these four examples of simple entry plantings show. All of the gardens on this page were designed by Sanchez and Maddux, landscape architects, Palm Beach.

Opposite page: The 'before' photo shows a cold entry that features hard, white, stucco walls. Look at the difference in the 'after' photo, with only the addition of five simple containers and a flower border.
Above, left: The entry of this Palm Beach home shows the power of repetition. Six simple pots are filled with white impatiens to soften the safety rail and grace each side of the landing. The plantings are changed seasonally.
Above, right: Two formal urns on pedestals mark the entry to the garden of this landmark Palm Beach house. Notice how well the containers frame the gate. These important pieces are left unplanted for art's sake.
Right: Bright red begonias welcome guests from this attractive balcony.

Low-Shed Plants for Pools and Patios

Agave
Sculptural look with very little water or care required.

Alocasia or Elephant Ear
Tropical look with huge, green leaves. Great with palms.

Anthurium
Very easy plant for shady areas; lasts for years in the same pot.

Bromeliad
Tropical drama with little dropping; very low maintenance.

Caladium
Lots of leaf color with very little care during the warm months.

Calathea
Tropical glamour during the warm months.

Canna Lily
Showy, tropical color with very little dropping.

Coleus
One of the world's most popular container plants.

Colocasia or Elephant Ear
Similar to alocasia. Some have black leaves.

Copperleaf
Tropical foliage plant that is gaining favor throughout the world.

Croton
One of the easiest container plants. Leave it in the same pot for years on end.

Dieffenbachia
Great choice for deep shade. Very easy plant.

For container sources, go to www.easygardencolor.com

Grasses
Light texture that looks beautiful in tropical breezes.

Heliconia
One of our best summer container plants for exotic flowers; need little care.

Iris, Walking
One of the few plants that blooms in deep shade.

Ivy
The world's favorite trailing plant for containers.

Orchids
Ground orchids bloom for up to six months at a time with little care.

Palms
Naturals for containers around Florida pools and patios.

Peace Lily
Great flowering plant for shady areas, but watch out for snails!

Perilla 'Magilla'
A new plant superstar that resembles coleus.

Persian Shield
One of the world's most beautiful leaves.

Shrimp Plant
Blooms every day of the year in frost-free areas.

Ti Plant
Great centerpiece plant that provides constant color with very little mess.

White Bird of Paradise
Easy plant that gives a tropical look to pools and patios.

Pool Pots: Arrangements that Work Well

Phil Maddux, co-owner of the Palm Beach landscape architecture firm, Sanchez & Maddux, Inc., worked here with owners who have collected interesting pots for years. His design incorporated their garden art - from the classic stone eagle to the graceful bronze swans - as well as their Mexican pig pots. The historical designation of their pool wall called for minimal plant material.

Right: This wall is part of the original Phipps estate and is designated a Palm Beach historical landmark. Obviously, the owners wanted landscaping to enhance it rather than cover it. The espaliered vines are kept to a minimum. The row of Mexican pig pots collected by the owners are filled with wax begonias. The dish gardens are filled with geraniums.

Light: Light shade to full sun.
Season: Cool season.
Lifespan: About four to six months.
Care: Fertilize with a slow-release mix on planting day. Water when the soil feels dry or the impatiens wilt.
Pots: Handmade Mexican terra cotta, 10" to 14"H.

For container sources, go to www.easygardencolor.com

Pool Pots: Arrangements that Work Wel

This beachfront estate provides fabulous views of the Palm Beaches and the Atlantic Ocean. However, the sun, wind, and salt take a terrific toll on all but the hardest terra cotta containers. Italian pots that have been kiln-fired, like Ipruneta, will withstand the harshest elements for years, while the sun-dried and oven-baked terra cotta will disintegrate much faster.

As far as style, these Italian pots are in keeping with the classic Mediterranean architecture of the spa, pool, and house.

Background: The urns that serve as a backdrop for the spa are Balazara's large *Orcio Con Manici*. Left unplanted, they serve as architectural elements to help balance the tile-roofed fountain.

Foreground: Topiary citrus trees grow in Balazara's *Vaso Festonato* terra cotta pots, which are paired along the length of the pool.

   For container sources, go to www.easygardencolor.com

Pool Pots: Crotons and tis are ideal.

'Madame Chaoul' Ti Plant
(1 plant from a three-gallon pot)
Plant Profile: Page 325

Golden Shrimp Plant
(2 plants from one-gallon pots)
Plant Profile: Page 322

Mammey Croton
(2 plants from one-gallon pots)
Plant Profile: Page 288

'Margarita' Sweet Potato
(4 plants from 4.5" pots)
Plant Profile: Page 324

For container sources, go to www.easygardencolor.com

*Both ti plants and cro-
tons are ideal for pool
decks because they give
continuous color with
very little care. Many
different types of ti
plants and crotons are
on the market. Check
this book's index to
locate the different varieties in this book as well
as the other volumes of
this series.*

Left: A 'Madame Chaoul' ti plant forms the centerpiece of this arrangement, with a mammey croton planted directly in front of it. Shrimp plants are planted on either side of the croton, with a sweet potato vine in front, trailing over the edge.
Light: Medium shade to full sun.
Season: Year round. Protect from frost.
Lifespan: About six months in this container. All of the plants except the sweet potato vine last for years in frost-free locations. Move them into larger pots or into your frost-free garden when they outgrow this one.
Care: Fertilize with a slow-release mix on planting day. Water when the soil feels dry or the sweet potato vine wilts (see pages 338-340 for more watering info). Trim the vines so they don't take over the arrangement. Use snail bait as needed, if you see holes in the leaves of the vines.
Pot: International Pottery Alliance's *Rolled Rim Planter* from their Marco Polo Collection. Saddle red. 20" W.

'Margarita' Sweet Potato
(4 plants from 4.5" pots)
Plant Profile: Page 324

Piecrust Croton
(1 plant from a three- gal. pot)
Plant Profile: Page 288

Blackie Sweet Potato
(4 plants from 4.5" pots)
Plant Profile: Page 324

Above: A piecrust croton forms the centerpiece of this arrangement, with black and lime green sweet potato vines around the edges. This is a very easy arrangement to plant and maintain.
Light: Medium shade to full sun.
Season: Year round. Protect from frost.
Lifespan: About six months in this container. The croton lasts for years in frost-free locations. Move them into a larger pot or into your frost-free garden when they outgrow their container.
Care: Fertilize with a slow-release mix on planting day. Water when the soil feels dry or the sweet potato vine wilts (see pages 338-340). Trim the vines so they don't take over the arrangement. Use snail bait as needed, if you see holes in the leaves of the vines.
Pot: Terra cotta 20" W rolled rim. Source unknown.

Chapter 7
Containers for
Shade and Indoors

Shading our plants is one of the most valuable tools used for adapting to the south Florida environment. Trees cool the temperatures and provide cover for wildlife. Shade gardens use only one half to one third as much water as sun gardens. Moreover, trees protect the plants from wind and cold damage. All of our trial gardens are in light shade at least part of the day. People are often amazed at how good our plants look after wind storms or cold snaps.

Container gardens require much less maintenance in shade. Watering, which is the most time-consuming chore for container gardens, is cut by as much as two-thirds in shade gardens over sun gardens. Since plants don't grow as fast in shade, trimming is also lessened.

Assessing the degree of shade can be tricky. Different plants like different degrees of shade. Anthuriums, for example, like dense or medium shade but sometimes burn in light shade. This chapter covers the important task of assessing the amount of shade you have in your garden.

Above: Three glazed bowls filled with double impatiens. These high performers are excellent plants for shade color because they are easy to grow, dependable, and have a long bloom period.

Left: My favorite flower for shade containers is the dragon wing begonia. They offer spectacular color, especially when grown in large containers, like these from Sabu.

Assessing Shade

Above: While many orchids prefer light shade, phalaenopsis orchids (pictured) prefer medium shade.

As I design gardens, the most difficult challenge I face is assessing the degree of shade in any given spot. If the sun stayed in the same place all the time, it would be easy. But, it moves from east to west every day and from north to south every year.

I have developed a simple method, which works most of the time. Get a compass, and go to the spot you are considering. Pretend you are the container. Put your eye at the level of the plant and look around. Look up, down, and 360 degrees around. Since the sun moves throughout the day, do this mid-morning, noon, and mid-afternoon. This observation will give you a good understanding of the amount of light the container will receive at different times of the day.

Understand that the angle of the sun moves. At noon in June, the sun is almost straight overhead. At noon in December, it is further south. Imagine this change as you observe the sun. The seasonal difference can be significant for plants. Some locations are in full sun in summer and in medium shade during winter. I put sun plants in a container one summer, and they did well. The next winter, I planted sun plants again in the same location. They struggled, until I realized that the same spot was shady that time of year. Luckily, because the plants were in a container, I could move the whole thing to a sunny spot.

To make matters more complicated, the sun is less intense in winter than summer. Impatiens grow well in full sun during the winter but would burn up in the same location during summer. This change is due to cooler temperatures and shorter days. Many northern annuals that thrive during the summer in New Hampshire, when the summer temperatures are similar to Florida's winter, will not bloom in Florida's winter because the days are too short. Each plant in this book was tested in Florida to know, for sure, whether they would bloom in our winters.

Learn to understand your shade! To determine the degree of shade in your garden, try the following tests. Sit in the same location you are considering for a container and look around:

DENSE SHADE: Look up, and you will see the dense shade of trees - like ficus, bischofia, or black olive - or the roof of a building. Less than 30% of the sky is visible. Look down, and see almost nothing growing, except possibly a few weeds. Look all around, and you will still see very little sky but more thick-leafed trees or buildings.

MEDIUM SHADE: Look up, and you will see medium shade from trees, such as oaks, mahoganys, palms, or pines. Look for about 50% or more of sky. Look down, and see ferns or other shade plants growing. St. Augustine grass is thin at best, as it needs more sun to grow. Look around, and see more trees but not much open sky on the south or west sides. Sun from the south or west is strong and too much for most medium-shade plants.

LIGHT SHADE: Look up, and you will see about 20%-30% leaves and the rest sky. The trees are planted farther apart in light shade than in medium shade. Look down, and notice many types of plants growing, including St. Augustine grass. Look around, and see many patches of sky from any direction.

MIXED LIGHT: These areas get both direct sun and full shade and are normally found near buildings. The change in light is due to the movement of the sun, either from morning to evening or from winter to summer. If the movement is from winter to summer, it can be difficult to assess without a compass. Be sure to picture the seasonal sun movement when assessing the light. Plants in mixed light need the ability to adapt to extremes.

Top 12 Container Plants for **Outdoor Shade**

Anthuriums
Anthuriums bloom all the time and have the ability to stay in the same container for years. Although they are quite cold-sensitive, they are also tolerant of very low light. This means you can bring them inside for extended periods during cold spells, as long as you move them out again within a month or so.

Bromeliads
Although most bromeliads don't offer constant color, they produce spectacular flowers that bloom for months on end with very little care. Other varieties have very colorful leaves. They also have the ability to stay in the same container for years on end.

Crotons
Crotons produce constant color with very little care. They are not anywhere near as thirsty as many other colorful container plants. They also offer the benefit of being happy in the same container for years.

Dieffenbachia
Talk about low maintenance! I have four of these in containers that I haven't touched (other than watering) since they were planted eight months ago! They could go on for years that way! And they don't drop much, either.

Dragon Wing Begonias
This is my favorite shade plant. It actually produces fabulous color with very little care. I plant them in the fall and don't touch them until spring, other than watering. They don't even seem to mind if you forget their fertilizer occasionally!

Impatiens
Although you may be tired of seeing impatiens everywhere, there is a reason why they are the most popular bedding plant in the world. They quite simply bloom their little heads off for months on end without any dead-heading (removing dead blossoms) at all. If only they weren't so thirsty!

Ivy
Ivy is one of the most useful container plants from our trials. I buy the small containers that are almost always at the garden centers and pull small pieces of ivy off the main root ball. They come apart easily, making it possible to tuck them into many different container styles for an instant trailing effect.

Palms
Palms are easy in containers. They also do not require frequent transplanting, remaining happy in the same container for well over a year. Since many palms are inexpensive in Florida, they give you the opportunity for instant container height.

Shrimp Plants
Shrimp plants bloom for 365 days a year, which is unusual. Their flower is quite showy, and the yellow color is difficult to find for shade. They make great centerpiece plants. Be sure to plant something around them because they can get leggy.

Sweet Potato Vines
These are the fastest-growing trailers we have. They come in three colors - lime green, dark bluish black, and the mixed colors of the tricolor, shown above. They offer almost instant maturity but do like a lot of water, and the snails love them.

Ti Plants
Ti plants offer constant color for little care. They also are happy in the same container for more time than most colorful plants, although not as long as crotons. And tis make great instant centerpieces.

Trailing Torenia
Trailing torenia blooms all the time and lasts longer than any other blooming trailer we tried - up to a year with constant flowers. Do not confuse its performance with that of its close relative, upright torenia, which lasts only a few months in a container.

Top 12 Long-Lasting Container Plants for **Indoor Shade**

Bamboo Palm

This is a great plant for corners or wherever indoor height is required. It is one of the easiest palms for indoor use.

Chinese Evergreen

Also commonly known as aglaonema, this is one of the most popular house plants in the world. It grows indoors for years without problems and actually cleans the air inside your house. This plant is also used outdoors in south Florida but is very susceptible to cold damage there.

Corn Plant

Another old favorite, it has appeared in living room corners throughout the world for generations and is very easy to grow. It's another air cleaner recommended by NASA.

Dieffenbachia

Talk about low maintenance! I have four of these in containers that I haven't touched (other than watering) since they were planted eight months ago! They could go on for years that way! And they don't drop much, either.

Dracaena 'Lemon-lime'

Since it is difficult to get much color indoors, the variegated leaves of this draceana add textural interest indoors. All dracaenas absorb toxins from the air inside your home.

Kentia Palm

This palm has been one of the most popular indoor plants for over a hundred years. Its form is quite graceful.

Lady Palm

This palm does well inside provided it gets a lot of light - more than the kentia or the bamboo palm. It offers the additional benefit of a resistance to indoor pests, particularly spider mites. *(Photo from Lechuza.)*

Peace Lily

The peace lily is one of the few plants that blooms indoors and lasts for years inside a building. It needs more water than the others on this page and is quite susceptible to snails. *(Photo and container from Lechuza.)*

Pothos

Pothos is one of the easiest plants I have ever had. I kept the same one inside for fifteen years! But, be careful because this plant is invasive outside in south Florida.

Snake Plant

Another really easy plant, the snake plant grows indoors or out in south Florida. Be careful with it outdoors, however, as it has a tendency to take over an area. *(Photo and container from Lechuza.)*

White Bird of Paradise

This plant is especially appropriate for interiors with a tropical theme. Palms and bromeliads make excellent companions. See 'Easy Gardens for Florida' for more information about this plant in the landscape.

ZZ Plant

This plant is a relatively new introduction that is taking the interior plant market by storm. The ZZ plant offers an interesting texture and is very easy to grow indoors.

Shade Plants for Containers, Arranged by Size

TRAILING

BLUE DAZE
M, L, X

DIASCIA
L

DWARF CHENILLE
M, L, X

FUCHSIA
M, L

GERANIUM,
TRAILING L

'GOLDILOC
M, L

IVY
D, M, L

LAMIUM
L

LYSIMACHIA 'OUTBACK
SUNSET' L

MINT, VARIEGATED
L

PETUNIA
L

POTHOS
D, M, L

SWEET POTATO
M, L, X

TRAILING TORENIA
M, L, X

TRIFOLIUM, 'DARK
DANCER' L

VINCA
'ILLUMINATION' L

'WHITE LICORICE'
M, L, X

UNDER 1'

ANTHURIUM
D, M, L

AZALEA
L

BEGONIA, DRAGON
WING M, L

BEGONIA,
TUBEROUS M, L

BEGONIA, WAX
M, L

BUGLEWEE
(AJUGA) M

CALADIUM
M, L

CAST IRON PLANT,
D, M, L

CHINESE
EVERGREEN D, M

COLEUS
M, L, X

CROTONS
M, L, X

DIASCIA
L

DIEFFENBACHIA
D, M, L

DWARF SWEET
FLAG M, L, X

ELEPHANT EAR
D, M, L

FUCHSIA
M, L

GARDENIA
L

GERANIUM
L

GRASS, 'FIBER
OPTIC' L

HYDRANGEA
L

IMPATIENS
M, L

KALANCHOE
M, L, X

NEW ZEALAND
SEDGE M, L

PANSIES
L

PEACE LILY
D, M

PENTAS
L

PERILLA 'MAGILLA'
L

PETUNIA
L

POLKA DOT PLANT
D, M, L

PURPLE QU

Dense shade   M = Medium shade   L = Light shade   X= Mixed light

Shade tolerance is based on summer light. Many of these plants, like impatiens, will take mixed light in winter but not in summer.

NDER 1'

SNAKE PLANT D, M, L	SNAPDRAGON L	TORENIA L	TORENIA, TRAILING M, L	VIOLA L	FERN, WART D, M, L

1' - 3'

ANGEL'S TRUMPET M, L	ANTHURIUM D, M	ARBORICOLA D, M, L, X	AZALEA L	BEGONIA, ANGELWING M, L	BEGONIA, DRAGON WING L, M
BEGONIA, ORANGE ANGELWING L, M	BEGONIA, WHITE L, M	BROMELIAD L, M	CALADIUM L, M	CAST IRON PLANT M	CHENILLE L
CHINESE EVERGREEN D, M	COLEUS L	CROTONS L	DIEFFENBACHIA D, M, L	DRACAENA, CORN PLANT D, M, L	DRACAENA REFLEXA D, M, L, X
ELEPHANT EAR D, M, L	FICUS TREE D, M, L, X	FISHTAIL FERN D, M, L	FUCHSIA M, L	GARDENIA L	GERANIUM L
GROUND ORCHID L	HELICONIA L	HYDRANGEA L	IMPATIENS M, L	JATROPHA L	MELAMPODIUM M, L
MONA LAVENDER L	PALM, CARDBOARD D, M, L, X	PALM, THATCH D, M, L, X	PEACE LILY D, M, L	PENTAS L	PERLILLA 'MAGILLA' M, L, X
PERSIAN SHIELD M, L	PLUMBAGO L	REED-STEM ORCHID L	SALVIA L	SHRIMP PLANT L, M	SNAKE PLANT D, L, M

Shade Plants for Containers, Arranged by Size

1' - 3'

SNAPDRAGON
L

TI PLANT
L, M

TORENIA
L

WALKING IRIS
D, L, M

WART FERN
D, L, M

ZZ PLANT
D, L, M

2.5' - 4'

ANGEL'S TRUMPET
L, M

ARBORICOLA
D, L, M, X

AZALEA
L

BEGONIAS, ANGELWING
L, M

BROMELIADS
L, M

CARDBOARD PA
D, L, M, X

CHENILLE
L

CROTON
L, M, X

DIEFFENBACHIA
D, L, M

DRACAENA CORN PLANT
D, L, M

DRACEANA REFLEXA
D, L, M, X

ELEPHANT EA
D, L, M

FICUS TREE
D, L, M, X

FISHTAIL FERN
D, L, M

GARDENIA
L

HELICONIA
L

JATROPHA
L

PALM, AREC
D, L, M, X

PALM, BAMBOO
D, L, M

PALM, LADY
D, L, M

PALM, PYGMY DATE
D, L, M, X

PALM, THATCH
D, L, M, X

PEACE LILY
D, M

PLUMBAGO
L

SHRIMP PLANT
L, M

STARBURST
L, M, X

TI PLANT
L, M

WHITE BIRD OF
PARADISE D, L, M, X

ZZ PLANT
D, L, M

4' - 6'

ANGEL'S TRUMPET
L, M

ARBORICOLA
D, L, M, X

AZALEA
L

BEGONIA, ANGELWING
L, M

CARDBOARD PALM
D, L, M, X

CROTON
L, M

DRACAENA, CORN
PLANT D, L, M

DRACAENA REFLEXA
D, L, M

ELEPHANT EAR
D, L, M

FICUS TREE
D, L, M, X

FIDDLE LEAF FIG
D, L, M, X

GARDENIA
L

4' - 6'

HELICONIA
L

JATROPHA
L

PALM, ALEXANDER
D, L, M, X

PALM, ARECA
D, L, M, X

PALM, BAMBOO
D, L, M

PALM, CAT
D, M, L

PALM, FISHTAIL
D, L, M

PALM, KENTIA
D, L, M

PALM, LADY
D, L, M

PALM, PYGMY DATE
D, L, M, X

PALM, THATCH
D, L, M, X

PALM, TRAVELER'S
D, L, M, X

6' - 8'

ANGEL'S TRUMPET
L, M

DRACAENA, CORN
PLANT D, L, M

DRACAENA REFEXA
D, L, M

ELEPHANT EAR
D, L, M

FICUS TREE
D, L, M, X

FIDDLE LEAF FIG
D, L, M, X

PALM, ALEXANDER
D, L, M, X

PALM, ARECA
D, L, M, X

PALM, BAMBOO
D, L, M

PALM, CHRISTMAS
D, L. M. X

PALM, FISHTAIL
D, L, M

PALM, KENTIA
D, L, M, X

PALM, LADY
D, L, M

PALM, PYGMY DATE
D, L, M, X

PALM, TRAVELER'S
D, L, M, X

RUBBER PLANT
D ,L, M, X

STARBURST
D, M, L

WHITE BIRD OF
PARADISE D, L, M, X

8' - 15'

FICUS
D, L, M, X

PALM, ALEXANDER
D, L, M, X

PALM, BAMBOO
D, L, M

PALM, CHRISTMAS
D, L, M, X

PALM, FISHTAIL
D, L, M

PALM, KENTIA
D, L, M

PALM, TRAVELER'S
D, L, M, X

RUBBER PLANT
D, L, M, X

WHITE BIRD OF
PARADISE D, L, M, X

**LOWERING
TANDARDS**
(SMALL FLOWERING
TREES)

AZALEA
L

CAPE HONEYSUCKLE
L

CHENILLE PLANT
L

JATROPHA
L

TURK'S CAP
L

Creative Ideas for Interiors...

Interior shade is similar to the dense shade found in the darkest areas outside. As you can see on the plant charts on pages 146-149, most plants that grow in dense shade are green and somewhat boring if just placed in a blah container with no companions. These two containers designed by Karen O'Brien of Garden Tender (email address: wob111@hotmail.com) take dense shade arrangements to a new and exciting level. The arrangement on this page is indoors, and the arrangement opposite is outdoors. Indoors is always a more challenging environment for plants.

Below: Limelight Dracaenas and anthuriums are combined in this striking, contemporary, indoor arrangement. The space gets a lot of light from a huge skylight above it. I have had numerous problems with anthuriums indoors, but they really liked this space. Remember, never put anthuriums outdoors in sun.

Light: High light for an interior space; dense to medium shade outdoors.

Season: All year. Protect from temperatures under 45 degrees.

Lifespan: About six to eight months in this container.

Care: Fertilize with a slow-release mix on planting day. The anthuriums were watered routinely, once a week. The dracaena was watered when the soil felt dry, every week or two. Remove dead leaves and flowers.

Container: This wooden container was custom-made for the spot. It includes a metal liner but no drainage holes. To insure drainage, a layer of gravel is placed in the container prior to planting. Plants are placed on top of the gravel in their plastic nursery pots. The area around the nursery pots is filled in with more gravel.

Mix textures and colors.

'String Bean'
Peperomia
Plant Profile: Page 331

Variegated Cast
Iron Plant
Plant Profile: Page 328

'Neoregelia Carolinae'
Bromeliad
Plant Profile: Page 284

'Giant Black Heart'
Sweet Potato Vine
Plant Profile: Page 324

Above: This arrangement is placed at the front entry to a country clubhouse, just outside the room that is home to the opposite arrangement. It gets very little light, which makes choosing plants difficult because most shade plants don't thrive in shade this dense. The textural differences of these plants add a lot to the interest of the design.

Light: Dense to light shade outdoors.

Season: All year.

Lifespan: The whole arrangement lasted about six months. The peperomia and sweet potato vines died first. The cast iron plant lives for years, so transplant it into a larger pot or into the ground (in frost-free areas) when it outgrows this pot. The bromeliad lasts for years as well.

Care: Fertilize with a slow-release mix on planting day. Water when the soil feels dry, about once a week. Remove dead leaves and flowers.

Container: This container is custom-made of wood. It does have drainage holes. Wood is a great material for custom-made containers because it is easy to work with. But, remember to line it with something that will keep the moisture off the wood. I used black plastic garbage bags once, and they worked just fine.

Creative Ideas for Interiors...

Bright-colored walls make a great backdrop for indoor plants, particularly when quality plants in good containers are repeated.

Above: Three cacti *(Echinocactus grusonii)* in Lechuza choco design *Cubico 40* self-watering containers that measure 16"W x 16"D x 30"H.

Right: The lime green of the ferns *(Nephrolepis exaltata)* contrasts well with the purple wall. Ferns look great in containers but drop a lot! Lechuza charcoal *Quadro 35* self-watering containers that measures 14"W x 14"D x 13"H.

Opposite page: Dramatic yucca plants show well in these Lechuza choco design *Classico 50* self-watering containers that measure 20"W x 19"H.

For container sources, go to www.easygardencolor.com

Dramatic plants against bright walls

Self-Watering Containers...

Self-watering containers are ideal for indoor use for two reasons. First, you don't have to water as often. Second, you don't have the mess of leaving the pot to drain in the sink for hours - and then facing the dirty sink. These containers hold extra water in the base, which the plant takes up naturally as needed. We tested the containers shown on these two pages with great success - they were very easy to use, and we enjoyed the freedom of not having to water so often! The Lechuza Cubicos (shown on this page) can also be used outdoors. Simply pull a small, red plug out of the bottom to allow excess water to escape. This is a useful feature in times of heavy rains.

Left: The water is stored in the bottom of the column. The plant is planted in the liner and fits on top. A tube with a clear, plastic gauge is positioned between the water chamber and the top of the pot. You water the plant from the top, through the tube that is clearly visible. When the gauge next to the watering tube shows low water, simply pour water down through the tube.

Center: See the clear plastic water gauge on top of this container? That gauge shows you when you need to water. Simply pour the water down the tube that sits right next to it - the gauge shows you when you've filled it up. Talk about easy!

Right: Sanseveria (snake) plant is an easy plant for indoors or outdoors (in frost-free areas). It takes on a contemporary appearance in this choco design *Cubico 40* planter that measures 16"W x 16"D x 30"H.

For container sources, go to www.easygardencolor.com

make indoor gardening easier!

The Lechuza Mini-Cubi is one of my favorite containers. The water is stored in the bottom of the column, and the plant is planted in the separate, small cube. Simply remove the top with your hand to see when more water is needed. We watered ours only about once a month. Mini-Cubis are especially effective when used in groups. They also make a great gift. These Mini-Cubis are designed for indoor use only and measure 4"W x 4"D x 7"H.

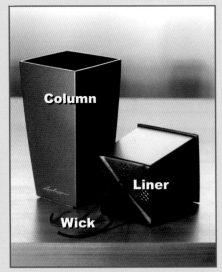

Water is stored in the bottom of the column. The plant is planted in the liner that fits inside the top half of the column. Water gets to the roots through the wick.

Dieffenbachia in *Mini-Cubi*. Look for the small plants in tiny pots in the house plant section of a garden center. They are ideal for these *Mini-Cubis*.

Peace lily in a *Mini-Cubi*. Many new and exciting plants are now sold in tiny pots in the house plant section of your garden center.

Repeating *Mini-Cubis* is a very effective design tool, as shown by these seven identical bromeliad arrangements.

Self-Watering Containers...

The containers shown on these two pages are from Lechuza's 'Quadro' and 'Classico' collection. They work slightly different than the columns on the previous two pages, but the concept is the same - the water is stored below and monitored by the handy gauge.

Left: This grouping repeats the same plant (*Dieffenbachia 'Camilla'*) in three containers that are the same size but vary in color. The containers are Lechuza *Quadro 21* and measure 8"W x 8"D x 8"H. The colors are charcoal, white, and silver. Notice the little, clear-plastic gauges at the top of the soil? These gauges monitor the water so you can easily see when the plants are thirsty.

Below: This office grouping would be much more difficult to maintain planted in regular containers with drainage holes than in these easy, self-watering containers. Every time you watered, you would have to be so careful that the water didn't spill through the drain holes onto that gorgeous wood floor! Since the water is stored in the sealed base of these Lechuza *Quadro* containers, you never face the danger of damage from overflows. The container on the desk is a *Quadro 21* (8"W x 8"D x 8"H) in choco design planted with a small ponytail. A *Quadro 50* (20"W x 20"D x 18"H) in the same choco design is planted with a peace lily (*Spathiphyllum wallisii 'Sensation'*) near the window.

For container sources, go to www.easygardencolor.com

make indoor gardening easier!

Simple plants and containers make an impact if they are quite large. Current architectural designs frequently feature high ceilings that are accentuated by tall plants. Plants in containers this large are also easy to care for because they can last for years in the same pot before they need root-pruning or transplanting.

Above, left: Lady palm in Lechuza *Classico 70* container in black that measures 28"W x 26"H. Lady palms are one of the easiest palms for indoor use.

Above, right: A dramatic yucca plant shows well in this Lechuza *Classico 60* container in black. The container measures 24"W x 22"H.

Right: Containers often do better if they are rotated for even light exposure. Order a rolling stand that fits under these pots for easy rotation. They are too heavy to move without wheels.

Orchids for Interiors...

Orchids are ideal for interiors because they bloom longer than most other plants inside a building. Prices are quite low now - an orchid plant often costs less than a cut-flower arrangement. The orchid may bloom for one to three months while the cut flowers ususally die within a week! After your orchid stops blooming, either put it in the trash as you would cut flowers, transplant it to a growing pot , or mount it on a tree if you live in a frost-free area. See pages 160-169 to learn about growing orchids outdoors after they have finished blooming indoors.

Right: A simple container filled with beautiful cattleya orchids provides a dramatic focal point in this white office. Cattleya orchid flowers - known for being featured in corsages - are more spectacular than phalaenopsis, but they don't bloom as long. The container is Lechuza self-watering *Cubico 40* in white that measures 16"W x 16"D x 30"H.

Left: Imagine seeing these orchids first thing every morning! I can't think of a better accent for a bedroom than with these white phalaenopsis orchids in Lechuza white *Quattro 35* self-watering containers that measure 14"W x 14"D x 13"H. Phalaenopsis orchids bloom longer indoors than most other orchids. These flowers can last up to three months inside. And with this container, you will seldom have to water them.

Right: This design shows the power of repetition. Spectacular yellow cymbidium orchids (difficult to grow outdoors in Florida) fill this *Cubico 40* self-watering container that measures 16"W x 16"D x 30"H. Behind the couch, dendrobium orchids fill three Lechuza *Classico 21* containers that measure 8"W x 8"D x 8"H. Dendrobiums are one of the easiest orchids to grow outside in Florida.

Opposite page: Phalaenopsis orchids planted in Lechuza *Mini Cubis* (4"W x 4"D x 7"H) provide a spectacular centerpiece for this dining room table.

For container sources, go to www.easygardencolor.com

Planted in self-watering containers

Orchids Outdoors...

Keep Them Indoors When Blooming and Then Move Them Out

The previous two pages show ideas for displaying orchids indoors, with the intent of moving them when they stop flowering. Since orchid plants are not particularly attractive when they are out of bloom, many people have a growing area outside for the orchids that is not a focal point of their homes or gardens (move the plants to a key area only when they are in bloom). Where they are moved when they are not blooming is up to you - to a growing area inside or outside your home. Orchids are commonly grown indoors or in greenhouses throughout the world, and there are hundreds, if not thousands, of books written on that subject, so I will not cover it here. Florida offers an excellent climate for growing orchids outdoors for that part of the year when the temperatures are warm enough. Volumes have been written about that as well. All I want to do here is give beginners a start - and encourage Floridians who have never grown an orchid to give it a try.

How I Started

I started growing ground orchids years ago (see page 162), confident enough to plant an orchid that grew in the ground like my other plants. But, for years, I never bought an epiphytic (tree) orchid (see page 163), which represents most of what you see for sale at our garden centers, because I thought it was hard to grow. I bought several books on these orchids and only became more intimidated because of the unbelievably complicated instructions. Then, I started buying them for indoors, planning to throw them away when they stopped blooming. When the time came, I didn't have the heart to toss them in the garbage, so I put a few of them under a tree, pots and all, and forgot about them. About six months later, I saw flowers on the ground under that tree and spotted some of my forgotten orchids blooming their heads off! They had been through two hurricanes and were completely blown out of their pots - just lying on the ground - roots, flowers, and all. This experience taught me a lesson - epiphytic orchids may be different, but some are unbelievably easy.

Survival of the Fittest

Above: Gene Joyner found that Cattleya (pictured) and Dendrobium orchids are easy to grow outside in Florida. This photo was taken at R.F. Orchids in Homestead.

Gene Joyner, the county extension agent in Palm Beach County, has been growing epiphytic orchids attached to his trees for thirty years. He follows the "survival of the fittest" growing method. He attaches all of them to trees and leaves them alone - completely - no fertilizer, no irrigation, no spraying, no cold protection. Palm Beach County seldom freezes, but it does get much colder than most of the books say that orchids prefer.

Gene mounts the new orchids to his trees at the beginning of the rainy season, so they can become established with natural water. His orchids grow like orchids do in nature - they get their water from rain and their nutrients from decaying tree leaves or any other organic substances that fall on them.

Gene loses half of the orchids in his garden. But half of them live! Imagine having an orchid garden with no maintenance! He says the phalaenopsis orchids proved hardest for him.

Orchids that receive no care from you will not look as good as the ones that receive a lot of care. You won't win any prizes for your orchids, but you will have gorgeous flowers.

What if you live in central or north Florida where most orchids would die from cold during their first winter attached to a tree? Grow them in pots. Hang them from your trees in the warm months and move them onto your porch or even inside your home if the temperatures are too cold for them. Buy several outdoor thermometers that record the low temperature from the night before, and find out how cold it actually gets on your porch in winter. It could be warmer than you think, and you could have potted orchids hung in your trees for most of the year, just moving them to your porch from Christmas through February.

For container sources, go to www.easygardencolor.com

Tips for Beginners *(See potting and mounting demo on page 355.)*

Orchid Prices

Orchid prices are lower than I have ever seen them. Years ago, one couldn't experiment much with orchids - each plant was quite expensive because it was very labor-intensive to propagate them. Tissue culture is now the norm - a propagation method that is done in test tubes, with thousands of baby orchids produced at once in one small tube. This method has resulted in orchids that cost less than a cut-flower arrangement and has led to much more use by people like you and me.

Great Places to Shop and Learn

Above: R.F. Orchids in Homestead is a wonderful place to spend the day.

I have extensive personal experience with most of the plants I write about. Not so for epiphytic orchids. I am a novice. But I know enough to be quite excited about their potential in other people's gardens (who know even less than me). They are ideal for today's typical, small-space gardens because the plants themselves are smaller than most flowering perennials, and they can be hung vertically, putting the flowers at eye-level, where they can be enjoyed the most.

I consulted with experts to learn more. Gene Joyner told me all about his low-maintenance orchids. Doris Happel, a master gardener, has grown quite a few orchids as a home gardener. She helped me shop for orchids and also showed me how to mount them to trees and pot them. The staff at **Turtle Pond Nursery** (9232 155TH Lane South, Delray, 561-498-2126) spent several hours with me. I also had a delightful phone interview with the legendary **Robert Fuchs of R.F. Orchids** (28100 SW 182 Avenue, Homestead, 877-482-6327, www.rforchids.com). Robert has been a key person in the orchid industry for years, as were his parents before him. I spent a day at his nursery and toured his private gardens with Julia Rosenberg, who works at R.F. Orchids. She has been growing and writing about orchids for 30 years and even served on the Board of Directors of the South Florida Orchid Society. Their Web site, **www.rforchids.com**, is a great place to shop. Madeline Michalowski of the **American Orchid Society** (16700 AOS Lane, Delray, 561-404-2000) showed me the easier orchids at that fabulous facility. You might want to follow my footsteps and visit these wonderful places.

Want to Learn More?

Above: Paphiopedilums are one of many orchids not covered in this book.

You will learn enough in this book to get you started. If you would like to learn more, I recommend a fabulous book called *Ortho's All About Orchids* published by Meredith Books, Des Moines, Iowa, with the help of the American Orchid Society. It is far and above the best book I have ever seen for orchid beginners. It is almost entirely oriented to growing orchids indoors, which is quite different from outdoors for most of the year in Florida. For example, dendrobiums are the easiest orchids to grow outdoors in Florida but are difficult indoors, so this book reports that they are difficult to grow. Conversely, phalaenopsis are one of the easiest to grow indoors and more difficult outdoors in Florida - and this book reports that they are easy to grow. However, the information on potting and general care is the best I have ever seen. Once you've learned the basics, buy the South Florida Orchid Society's *An Introduction to Orchids*, edited by Julia Rosenberg. Their Web site is www.SouthFloridaOrchidSociety.org. This book gives you lots of information about specific orchids that do well outdoors in Florida.

Some orchids naturally grow in the ground.

Six Important Points about Orchids that Grow in the Ground

1. They are called 'garden orchids' because they grow in the ground just like other landscape plants.

2. The flowers on garden orchids are not as showy as the flowers of the orchids that naturally grow in trees, but they bloom for much longer, often as long as six or eight months each year.

3. The two I have grown quite successfully in Florida are *Spathoglottis spp.* and *Epidendrum spp.*

4. They do better outside than inside.

5. Garden orchids thrive in containers.

6. Garden orchids are an excellent plant for orchid beginners because their care is easy and familiar, and they use regular potting soil, water, and fertilizer.

Spathoglottis Orchids: The Best One to Start With

Spathoglottis orchids are the easiest orchids to start with because they are simple to grow and bloom for a long time. They grow in the ground like other garden plants and require regular potting soil and containers. The plants themselves look better than the *Epidendrums*, but the leaves brown routinely in the winter outdoors when in zone 10. They need no support in containers - the flowers stand up naturally on their own stems. They bloom during the warm season, thriving in the worst heat that Florida has to offer. To learn about Spathoglottis in the landscape, see "Best Garden Color for Florida," pages 104 and 105.

Spathoglottis orchids come in a variety of sizes and colors. We have tested quite a few and find the light purple one in the photo to be quite dependable. It takes more cold than the 'Grapette,' which is darker purple. We've tried three different yellows with mixed results - one did poorly and two did quite well.

Epidendrum Orchids: Another Easy Garden Orchid

Epidendrum orchids (particularly *Epidendrum ibaguense,* shown at left*)* are beautiful, tried-and-true orchids, some of which grow in the ground in frost-free areas of Florida and flower for about six months each year. Like many orchids, the plant itself is not particularly attractive, a bit of a sprawler. It looks best if supported in a container with a small stake or trellis. These orchids are sold in landscape nurseries planted in regular potting soil. However, look for them as well in the orchid section of many nurseries, where it is displayed with the epiphytic (tree) orchids and planted in an orchid mix. See "Best Garden Color for Florida," pages 92 and 93 for information about growing this plant in your garden.

Many epidendrums are epiphytes, meaning they naturally grow in trees. However, they are quite adaptable, and the majority of the ones you see at your garden center can grow in the ground or in trees.

For container sources, go to www.easygardencolor.com

While others prefer trees. *(See potting and mounting demo on page 355.)*

11 Important Points about Orchids that Grow in Trees

1. Orchids that naturally grow in trees are called epiphytes.

2. Most of the orchids you see for sale are epiphytes.

3. Epiphytic orchids require a special potting mix when grown in containers because their roots must have air. Regular potting mixes are too heavy. Special orchid mixes are available at most garden centers in the orchid section.

4. Some of these orchids, like vandas, require no soil at all, even when grown in containers! They are sometimes easier to keep watered if they do have some orchid mix around their roots, but they are often sold with no soil at all and can live that way if they get enough water.

5. Epiphytic orchids require special containers because, once again, their roots must have air circulation. We used the Lechuza *Mini-Cubis* while we kept the blooming orchids indoors. The gravel that comes with these containers is ideal for orchids, allowing the proper air circulation. After we moved them outdoors, we transplanted them into wooden baskets with open areas between the slats.

6. You can also attach them to your trees if you live in a frost-free area, but they may require cold protection during cool spells. Most epiphytic orchids are more cold-sensitive than landscape plants commonly used in zone 10. Wrap them with cloth, like old towels or dish rags, if cold approaches. Be sure to shelter them from cold wind, which can damage them more than low temperatures.

7. These orchids have flowers that are showier than the garden orchids (that naturally grow in the ground), but they do not bloom as long.

8. Most epiphytic orchids grow inside or out, but they need more light inside to begin blooming than most other houseplants, like pothos or dieffenbachia. However, if they begin blooming outside or in a greenhouse, you can move them into a dense-shade interior, and they will keep blooming.

9. There are many different types of epiphytic orchids. Some, like dendrobiums, are quite easy to grow outdoors in Florida; others, like paphilopedilums, are more difficult. Each species has its own growing requirements.

10. Many of these gorgeous orchids are quite easy to grow, once you understand how they differ from most other garden plants. I frequently buy one for my kitchen window sill and put it outside, under a palm tree, in its original plastic nursery pot. It gets water from my sprinkler system. For two years, I have never fertilized, transplanted, or trimmed these orchids. They bloom anyway, despite the neglect!

11. Many epiphytic orchids require small stakes to support the flowers when they are in pots.

Top: Epiphytic orchids naturally grow on trees. Bottom: The flowers of epiphytic orchids - in this case, phalaenopsis, are generally more spectacular than ground orchids. But their bloom period is shorter.

Tree (epiphytic) Orchids for Beginners

Cattleyas (cat-LAY-yah)

Cattlyea orchids are most commonly associated with corsages. They, along with dendrobiums, are generally considered the easiest tree (epiphytic) orchids to grow outside in Florida because their native environment is similar to Florida. They are more difficult to grow indoors than phalaenopsis orchids because of higher light requirements. However, I buy cattleyas in bloom and start them off inside on my window sill. They live just fine there for the short, few week bloom period, after which I move them outside.

Cold Tolerance: Cattleyas take cold weather down to 35 to 40 degrees for short periods, provided they are protected from wind. This cold tolerance is less than most other landscape plants commonly grown in zone 10 but more than phalaenopsis or strapleaf vanda orchids. Many orchid hobbiests who live in zone 10 have cattleyas attached to their trees, which have never been moved indoors for cold spells. These orchids might not win any orchid shows but do provide beautiful flowers! Cattleyas grown in zone 8 or 9, of course, would have to be moved indoors during cold spells.

Water: Cattleyas have thick leaves and pseudo bulbs (thick, bulbous structures at the juncture of the stem and the root) that hold water, so they require less water than the thirsty, strap-leaf vandas or phalaenopsis. They are used to a climate that has wet and dry seasons, like Florida. In the summer, they require few waterings because of our frequent rains, and luckily, require drier conditions in our dry winters. I keep mine in trees that have sprinklers in them. They get water whenever I water the landscape. If you hand water, be sure to give them several passes with the hose so the roots are saturated. Then, let them dry out completely between waterings so the roots will grow to search for water and nutrients. I know many people who mount their cattleyas to a tree or slab at the beginning of the rainy season so they establish naturally, and they never give them any supplemental water. These cattleyas may live and produce flowers, but they won't win any orchid shows!

Bloom Period: Cattleyas flower in the cool season for a short time - a few weeks to a month. This short bloom time is the only drawback to cattleyas. There are some hybrids with multiple bloom periods.

Light: Cattleyas take a fair amount of light, more than phalaenopsis. Their leaves should be light green, not dark green. Light shade, as described on page 142, is ideal.

Pests: They are particularly susceptible to fungus and scale. Many orchid growers spray at the beginning of the rainy season with a fungicide to discourage fungus. Many other gardeners have never sprayed their cattleyas but are careful to place them in a location with good air circulation, which discourages fungus.

Soil: Cattleyas will not grow in regular potting mix. They require a special orchid mix that is commonly sold at garden centers.

Fertilization: Cattleyas are not as heavy feeders as many other orchids. Serious orchid growers spray them with liquid (like Peters or Miracle Grow) once every two weeks during the growing season (spring and summer) and cut it down to once a month in the fall and winter. Use a 20-20-20 unless the potting mix you use contains

Top: Cattleya orchid in a Lechuza Mini-Cubi that is appropriate for indoor use. Bottom: Cattleya in a terra cotta pot with open sides hanging from a tree.

For container sources, go to www.easygardencolor.com

The orchids shown in these containers are similar in size to the ones for sale at your local garden center. To make them easy to identify, take the book with you when you go plant shopping to help you make informed choices. See potting and mounting demo on page 355.

fir bark which would require a 30-10-10. Dilute one teaspoon of fertilizer in one gallon of water. I know other gardeners who have had cattleyas in their trees and never fertilized them for 20 years! These plants won't win any prizes, but you'll see some flowers at least half of the time.

Pot preferences: Any pot with open sides so the roots can get air. Or, mount them on a slab or tree.

Common mistakes: The two most common mistakes with cattleyas are overwatering and not giving them enough light. If the leaves are dark green, they are not getting enough light. Too much sunlight produces bleaching and burning of the leaves. If the leaves feel hot, then they are getting too much light.

Dendrobiums (den-DROE-bee-ums)

Dendrobiums (opposite) are great orchids for beginners. Along with cattleyas, they are generally considered the easiest tree (epiphytic) orchids to grow outside in Florida because they handle our temperature ranges and high outdoor light conditions better than some of the others. Some orchid growers say that dendrobiums can almost be ignored outdoors. And, they bloom much longer than the easy cattleyas. Their flowers are not as spectacular as cattleyas, but mature dendrobiums have so many flowers they can stop traffic.

The genus dendrobium contains over 1000 species. *Dendrobium phalaenopsis* is the one you are most likely to see at your garden center, and it is the only one described here. I treat them like cattleyas, buying them in bloom, enjoying them inside, and moving them outside when the blooms fade.

Cold Tolerance: Less cold-tolerant than cattleyas; they drop their leaves with too much cold.

Water: Same as cattleyas (see opposite page). Also, avoid watering the buds if possible.

Bloom Period: Dendrobiums bloom during the winter and spring, with flowering continuing for several weeks to a few months. Many flower more than once a year.

Light: Same as cattleyas (see opposite page). Be careful about moving them from the shade of a house to light shade outdoors because they might sunburn. Acclimate them slowly.

Pests: They are particularly susceptible to fungus and snails. Many orchid growers spray at the beginning of the rainy season with a fungicide to discourage fungus. Many other gardeners have never sprayed their dendrobiums but are careful to place them in a location with good air circulation, which also discourages fungus. Dendrobiums also occasionally drop their buds before they open, if they go through periods of change - like sudden temperature, humidity, or watering changes.

Soil: Dendrobiums will not grow in regular potting mix. They require a special orchid mix commonly sold at garden centers.

Fertilization: Same as cattleyas (opposite page).

Pot preferences: Any pot with open sides so the roots can get air. They do best in containers that are a little too small for them. Or, mount them on a slab or tree.

Common mistakes: Overwatering and not giving them enough light. Air circulation is important for all orchids.

Top: Dendrobium orchid in Lechuza indoor container.
Bottom: Dendrobium flower.

Tree (epiphytic) Orchids for Beginners

Phalaenopsis (fay-len-NOP-sis)

Top: Phalaenopsis orchid in a Lechuza Mini-Cubi that is appropriate for indoor use. Center: Phalaenopsis growing as it does in nature, on a tree with the leaves pointed down. Bottom: Mixed colors of phalaenopsis.

Phalaenopsis is the most commonly used indoor orchid because its flowers last longer than most other orchids' and it thrives in low-light situations. It doesn't do as well outdoors in Florida as the others in this book because it likes warmer weather than Florida in the winter - it suffers in temperatures under 50 degrees. And since it has no water-holding psuedobulb at the base - like cattleyas, dendrobiums, and oncidiums - it needs water more often.

I use quite a few phalaenopsis orchids, starting them out indoors in a self-watering container until the flowers die. I then pot them in a slatted basket with a standard orchid mix because they die in regular potting mix. The slatted pots allow air circulation around their roots, which they require.

It is easier to keep up with phalaenopsis water needs if it is potted rather than grown on trees. The potting mix retains water that is not available if the orchid is growing on a tree. They hang from an oak tree in my garden that has a sprinkler head in its branches.

Many serious orchid growers would never consider planting a phalaenopsis in a pot because the leaves can catch water and cause crown rot. Phalaenopsis in garden centers are planted with the leaves facing up - making it possible for water to accumulate in the middle of the leaves. In nature, they grow with the leaves growing down, as shown in the photo of the tree-mounted phalanopsis at left. If you plant them in pots, place the plant at an angle so the water will fall out naturally.

Cold Tolerance: This orchid suffers from cold when temperatures dip below 50 degrees. If you grow them outside, be prepared to bring them inside a good bit in the winter. Many Floridians grow this orchid outside in spring, winter, and fall and bring it inside, or at least onto a screened porch, for the winter. They require temperatures of about 55 degrees for a few weeks to initiate flowering.
Water: Unlike the easier cattleyas, dendrobiums, and oncidiums, these orchids have no natural storage area for water. So they need frequent watering. They are native to areas that receive the same amount of rainfall all year, which is quite different from Florida.
Bloom Period: Phalaenopsis orchids usually bloom in late winter and spring when grown outdoors. I have occasionally seen them bloom later as well. The blooms last for one to five months, which is one of its best advantages.
Light: Medium shade. The leaves burn in sun. These orchids require more shade than cattleyas, oncidiums, or vandas.
Pests: They are susceptible to mealy bugs, scale. and spider mites - more bugs than the other orchids in this book.
Soil: Phalaenopsis will not grow in regular potting mix. They require a special orchid mix commonly sold at garden centers.
Fertilization: Same as cattleyas (page 165).

For container sources, go to www.easygardencolor.com

The orchids shown in these containers are similar in size to the ones for sale at your local garden center. To make them easy to identify, take the book with you when you go plant shopping to help you make informed choices. See potting and mounting demo on page 355.

Pot preferences: Any pot with open sides so that the roots can get air. They do best in containers that are a little too small for them. Or, mount them on a slab or tree.

Common mistakes: Overwatering and not giving them enough light. Air circulation is also important for all orchids.

Oncidium (on-SID-ee-um)

Oncidium orchids are a good choice for a beginner because they are easy to grow and put on a great show when they bloom. Many oncidiums are large plants, quite happy growing on trees.

However, there are so many on the market now that it can be difficult to find the easy ones. Different oncidiums come from very different environments - some warm and some cool. For a listing of specific types that do well in Florida, see the South Florida Orchid Society's *An Introduction to Orchids* (pages 46-47) edited by Julia Rosenberg. Their Web site is www.SouthFloridaOrchidSociety.org. Or, buy your oncidiums from a nursery that knows which orchids do well outside in Florida.

Cold Tolerance: Different oncidiums require different temperatures - some warm and some cold. I have been lucky so far - the ones I have purchased locally do fine in my zone 10 garden without covering in winter. Rule of thumb for most of the oncidiums sold by local growers is to protect them from temperatures under 45 degrees. Many old oncidiums are growing in trees throughout south Florida without such protection, but they could be in a warm microclimate, naturally protected from cold, northwest winds.

Water: The water needs vary by type. Some are the same as cattleyas (see page 164), adapting well to Florida's wet season/dry season rainfall patterns. Others, particularly the oncidiums with small, thin leaves, need even moisture all the time.

Bloom Period: Oncidiums generally bloom in late spring for a period of two to three weeks.

Light: Light shade.

Pests: Flower thrips and mealy bugs.

Soil: Oncidiums will not grow in regular potting mix. They require a special orchid mix commonly sold at garden centers. **Fertilizer:** Most oncidiums are not as heavy feeders as many other orchids. Serious orchid growers spray them with liquid (like Peters or Miracle Grow) once every two weeks during the growing season (spring and summer) and cut it down to once a month in the fall and winter. Use a 20-20-20 unless the potting mix you use contains fir bark, which requires 30-10-10. Dilute one teaspoon of fertilizer in one gallon of water. I know other gardeners who have had oncidiums in their trees and never fertilized them for 20 years! These plants won't win any prizes, but you'll see some flowers at least half of the time.

Pot preferences: Any pot with open sides so the roots can get air. Larger oncidiums do particularly well mounted in the crook of a tree as long as they are protected from too much cold.

Common Mistakes: Under or over watering.

Top: Oncidium orchid in a Lechuza Mini-Cubi that is appropriate for indoor use. Bottom: Oncidium sphacelatum photographed at R.F. Orchids in Homestead. It is not only spectacular but also quite easy - it "grows like a weed" according to Julia Rosenberg, who works at that nursery. This is a large plant, so start it out in a pot with at least an 8 inch diameter or mount it onto something big.

Tree (epiphytic) Orchids for Beginners

Strapleaf Vandas

Strapleaf vanda orchids offer longer bloom periods than most other epiphytic orchids. Some bloom almost constantly outdoors in warm weather but need too much light to do well indoors. But their colors are fabulous - yellow, brown, pink, apricot, purple, blue, and violet.

Strapleaf vandas, as their name implies, have leaves that are shaped like straps. This leaf shape distinguishes them from other vandas.

Many vandaceous hybrids do very well outdoors in Florida. Julia Rosenberg from R.F. Orchids recommends the *Ascocenda Princess Mikasa 'Indigo'*, which is a vanda cross and behaves like a strapleaf vanda. It is the purple orchid in the center photo on this page, shown with yellow oncidium orchids and crotons. It flowers freely for most of the year. She also recommends the *Ascocenda Su-Fun Beauty 'Orange Belle'* shown in the bottom photo on this page. Its magnificent flowers appear on and off for most of the year. See R.F. Orchid's Web site at www.rforchids.com for more information.

Cold Tolerance: Bring inside if the temperature dips below 50.
Water: Since strapleaf vandas have no pseudo bulb in which to store water, they need frequent waterings. This need for water is accentuated by the fact that they prefer no soil around their roots, which also stores water. They will dehydrate in winter without supplemental irrigation.
Bloom Period: Many vandas bloom for most of the year.
Light: Light shade. They prefer more light than cattleyas.
Pests: They are particularly susceptible to fungus and flower thrips. Many orchid growers spray at the beginning of the rainy season with a fungicide, which discourages fungus. Many other gardeners have never sprayed their cattleyas but are careful to place them in a location with good air circulation, which also discourages fungus.
Soil: None at all! Yes, that's right. The vanda shown at the top (left) is just placed in that basket without any soil at all.
Fertilization: Same as cattleyas (page 164).
Pot preferences: Any pot with open sides so that the roots can get air.
Common mistakes: Over or under watering.

Semi-Terete Vandas

Semi-terete vandas are hybrids between terete and strapleaf vandas and are quite similar to the strapleafs in terms of their care. They bloom for much of the year and do better outside than indoors because of high light requirements. They take full sun, however, which is more light than the strapleafs can handle. Water them two or three times a week if there is no rain. They prefer no soil but require large containers - start them out in a pot that is 8 to 12 inches in diameter. These orchids have similar pest problems to the terete vandas. Their leaves are wider than teretes but more rounded and fleshy than the strapleafs.

Top: Vanda orchid in pot without soil. Upper middle: Ascocenda Princess Mikasa 'Indigo' with yellow oncidiums and crotons. Lower middle: Ascocenda Su-Fun Beauty 'Orange Belle'. Bottom: A semi-terete vanda.

For container sources, go to www.easygardencolor.com

Terete (ter-EETE) Vandas

Terete vandas are the orchids commonly used in leis in Hawaii and grown as hedges in Singapore. They prefer brighter light than is available indoors, so keep this one outside during warm weather. These orchids are semi-terrestrial - they like their roots in the ground yet climb up trees with aerial roots. They have been grown outside in the ground in south Florida for generations.

Terete vandas are easy to recognize because they have leaves that are round like pencils.

These vandas bloom for about two months a year, on the average, which is much less than the ground orchids discussed on page 162. But they are worth growing because the flowers are so pretty. They require support - remember that, in nature, they climb trees. Many Floridians grow them next to fences for this support.

Above: Both of these are the same terete orchid, Vanda 'Miss Joaquim,' The top photo shows it in a container and the bottom photo shows it planted in the ground.

Cold Tolerance: Terete vandas are commonly grown throughout south Florida outdoors with no cold protection. But be careful, and place them in a warm spot in your garden (see 'Microclimates' page 8). Protect from freezes and from temperatures in the low 40's if you can.

Water: About one inch of water a week, preferably in two waterings of one-half inch each time. This is the same watering requirement as any other landscape plant. Terete vandas are not too picky about water!

Bloom Period: They bloom for about a month once or twice a year. The season depends on the type of terete vanda.

Light: Light shade to full sun. These orchids like much more light than most of the others.

Pests: Flower thrips.

Soil: Use the same potting mix you use for regular container plants. Pro Mix, Lambert's, or Miracle Grow are all good brands. If you plant them in the ground, prepare the bed with this mix so they are not planted in our native soil.

Fertilization: Fertilize with the same product you use in the landscape. I use Nutricote 13-13-13, a slow-release granular product. Dynamite is another brand that is good. See "Easy Gardens for Florida" under "Fertilizer" for the contents of a good landscape product.

Pot preferences: Since this orchid grows in the ground, any regular container pot works as long as it drains well.

Common mistakes: Don't forget this orchid needs support!

Brassovola Nodosa: Lady of the Night

I learned about this orchid from Julia Rosenberg, who works at R.F Fuchs Orchids in Homestead (www.rforchids.com). She said it is one of the easiest orchids around - almost carefree - a great orchid for beginners. At night, it perfumes the whole garden. Grow lady of the night in light shade. It does best mounted on a tree or on a slab of tree fern, cork, or driftwood. Mounted this way, it requires no soil and will stay on the same slab for many years. Water it a few times a week. It flowers without fertilizer but blooms more with feedings (see cattleyas on page 164). It blooms in fall and winter - the larger the plant, the longer the bloom period - up to two months. Lady of the night tolerates temperatures into the mid-40's. It is relatively pest-free.

More Ideas for Orchids and Bromeliads

'Blue Tango' bromeliads are featured in both of these arrangements. It is one of my favorite bromeliads because it is quite tough and blooms for a full four months each year. Lipstick impatiens surround the 'Blue Tango' in the above arrangement, with white 'odorata' begonias planted in the ground around it. Dendrobium orchids accent the bromeliad to the right, which was photographed at RF Orchids in Homestead.

For container sources, go to www.easygardencolor.com

Wall Pot for Dense/Medium Shade

Empty Wall Pot

Dracaena Reflexa
(2 plants from 6" pots)
Plant Profile: Page 293

Ivy
(8 plants from 3.8" pots)
Plant Profile: Page 300

Variegated Peperomia
(3 plants from 5" pots)
Plant Profile: Page 332

Variegated Ivy
(5 plants from 3.8" pots)
Plant Profile: Page 300

Above: I found the plants for this wall pot in the house plant section of a garden center. I used small, individual pots of ivy. It would have been much cheaper to buy larger pots of ivy and separate them into small pieces, as shown on page 343. This arrangement is designed for deep shade, but it would be difficult to handle indoors because it drops a lot of coco-fiber when it is watered. See pages 356-357 to learn how to plant this type of container.

Light: Dense, medium, or light shade.

Season: All year. Protect from frost.

Lifespan: About six to eight months in this pot.

Care: This arrangement is really easy to care for. Fertilize with a slow-release mix on planting day, and repeat every two or three months. Water when the soil feels dry to the touch. We planted this pot in July and were pleasantly surprised at how little water it needed compared to many of our other containers. Trim as needed.

Pot: 16" wall pot (shown empty above).

For container sources, go to www.easygardencolor.com

Hanging Basket for Dense/Medium Shade

Dracaena 'Combo'
(6 plants from 3.8" pots)
Plant Profile: Page 317

Vreisia Bromeliad
(3 plants from 4" pots)
Plant Profile: Page 317

Vreisia Bromeliad
(1 plant from an 8" pot)
Plant Profile: Page 317

Croton
(3 plants from 3.8" pots)
Plant Profile: Page 317

Pothos
(18 plants from 3.8" pots)
Plant Profile: Page 317

Above: Like the plants on the opposite page, I found these plants in the house plant section of a garden center. Although the bromeliads form the focal point of this arrangement, they only bloom for about four months and won't re-bloom in dense shade. I planted the arrangement so it would be full on planting day and probably used way too many plants. A few pothos around the edge of the container would have covered the sides in no time at all!

Light: Dense, medium, or light shade.

Season: All year. Protect from frost.

Lifespan: About six to eight months in this pot.

Care: Fertilize with a slow-release mix on planting day, and repeat every two or three months. Water when the soil feels dry to the touch. We planted this pot in July and were pleasantly surprised at how little water it needed compared to many of our other containers. Trim as needed. Take care to keep the pothos from escaping into the ground because it is invasive.

Pot: 18" Imperial Basket.

My favorite plant for shade container color.

Dragon wing begonias are one of the best container plants available today for color. They offer as much color as impatiens without the high-water use. And talk about easy! They bloom continuously with very little care through our cool season (in sun or shade). Put them in cobalt blue pots, as shown above, for great contrast and color impact. We use two groups (of three each) to mark the entry to one of our trial gardens. They bloom heavily and continuously for at least five months. The sprinklers hit them well, so we never have to hand water them.

Pot source: Sabu's *Butterfly* pots in indigo; item number 320-028, sold in sets of three. From largest to smallest: 21"W x 23"H, 15"W x 17.5"H, and 12"H x 14"W.

Is the dragon wing begonia.

Dragon wing begonias work well with a variety of landscape styles. The blue pots (shown left and below) offer a casual look, while the cast stone pots (right) are much more formal.

They grow in sun (in winter only) or shade but do best in light shade. When grown in full sun, their leaves bleach out as the cool season warms up. The pot on the right is in medium shade, while the one on the left is in light shade. Note that the plant in light shade has more flowers than the one in medium shade.

Dragon wing begonias give a higher percentage of color than the similar angelwings. However, angelwings last as a perennial in the frost-free landscape, while the dragon wings are an annual.

More bromeliad ideas and...

Large, low bowls filled with bromeliads were placed on gravel. Notice that smaller gravel is used as mulch in the containers. The pots are quite large, a full 38 inches across, but lightweight because they are made of polyethylene. These large containers are *Magna Grecia Bowls* in a weathered stone finish from the Campania Polyethylene Collection.

This shell planter contains several bromeliads and one orchid. Bromeliads are easy to mix in a planter, and many keep blooming for up to four months after you plant them. They require almost no care other than occasional watering. I keep my collection that is not blooming in a utility area and move them into a container when they flower.

Bromeliads are taking the indoor plant industry by storm because they bloom longer than most other indoor plants. I found this lovely arrangement of assorted *Guzmanias* at the Breakers Hotel in Palm Beach. Some of these newer hybrids are bred in Japan or Holland and won't re-bloom after their initial flowering in Florida.

This *Neorogelia 'Fireball'* is a spreading bromeliad - one of the few that sends out runners like many groundcovers. It is ideal for containers because it will actually cascade down the sides of a pot. 'Fireball' works well in a strawberry jar, as shown, or in any container that gives it room to run. Be sure to use a light or bright-colored container to show off the dark burgundy leaf color.

Tall, red bromeliad in huge blue Campania pot featured on page 68. The fence is six-feet tall, which gives you an idea of the overall size of this dramatic arrangement!

Talk about easy! Just go to your garden center and find one tall and two short bromeliads that look good together! This arrangement features a tall (*Aechmea 'Fredericke'*) bromeliad accented with two *Neoregelia 'Tricolor Perfectas.'* The white container repeats the color of the white stripe in the leaves.

simple shade ideas with easy-to-find plants

I couldn't resist these African violets and bought five to plant in this strawberry jar. I accented the violets with impatiens and begonias in complementary colors. The violets only lasted about a month or two, but I enjoyed them anyway. Containers give you a convenient spot to try new things. This photo was taken in December.

Easy-to-find dieffenbachia (left) and two colors of coleus (right) coordinate well in this planting at the entry to my porch. The Masart pot (left) is described on pages 48 and 49. The solid green container is Sabu *Champa Glazed Series* #310-026. It measures 29 inches tall by 29 inches wide.

Elephant ears (*Alocasia spp.*) are an excellent choice for shade containers because their large leaves show up well with smaller-leafed plants. And, they have a sense of drama. Look for green ones, as shown, or the new, black ones, which are a great addition to contemporary gardens.

Double impatiens are available in many colors at most Florida garden centers in the cooler months. They are one of my favorite container plants because the flowers look like little roses. These pink double impatiens were planted in the sides and along the top edge of this basket. A white 'odorata' begonia forms the centerpiece.

Shade Containers In Other Chapters

Page 15

Page 16

Page 16

Page 17

Page 18

Page 20

Page 32

Page 32

Page 33

Page 37

Page 38

Page 39

Page 40

Page 43

Page 48

Page 54

For container sources, go to www.easygardencolor.com

Page 57

Page 61

Page 66

Page 70

Page 125

Page 138

Page 139

Page 205

Page 206

Page 206

Page 207

Page 212

Page 244

Page 245

Page 254

Page 260

Chapter 8
Containers for Sun

The containers on these two pages can be found throughout Universal Orlando Resort - (which consists of two theme parks, Universal Studios and Universal's Islands of Adventure, an entertainment complex called Universal CityWalk, and three luxurious onsite hotels - The Portofino Bay Hotel, Hard Rock Hotel, and Royal Pacific Resort).

These photos were taken in January, when the variety of cool-season flowers available is almost unlimited in south and central Florida. Let these container designs inspire you to experiment with new flowers that you see and love but have never tried before.

The Universal Orlando Horticulture staff underneath the roller coaster that towers over their offices, from left to right: Jon Schultz (supervisor), Alan Jordan (supervisor), Barry McKently (director), Barbara Busha (supervisor), David Turner (supervisor), and Pat McCarty (manager).

Top 12 Container Plants for **Sun**

Bougainvillea

Bougainvillea is good and bad for containers. Its major benefits are gorgeous winter color and the ability to stay in the same pot for years. Its disadvantage is that it drops a lot - more than almost any other plant. And it goes through bloom spurts, meaning it all blooms at once and then all stops at once, looking bare.

Coleus

Although many types of coleus are considered shade plants, we found lots of them that love the sun. They do especially well in the sides of hanging baskets in sunny spots. Coleus offers constant color during our warm months and hundreds of different leaf patterns and colors.

Crotons

Crotons produce constant color for very little care. They are not anywhere near as thirsty as many other colorful container plants. They also offer the benefit of being happy in the same container for years.

Goldilocks

This is a new plant for our container trials, and we just love it! It is attractive, versatile, easy, and dependable. The lime green color is great for many striking combinations, and the trailing growth habit is quite useful. The unique texture also adds to its value in container gardens.

Grasses

We tested both large and small grasses and were thrilled with both. They offer great textural interest as well as ease of care. See pages 192 and 193 for more info.

Mona Lavender

This plant is another new one - we tested it for just one year but were thrilled with its performance in containers (it did poorly planted in the ground). It thrives in the cool season but didn't like summer. It blooms constantly for at least six months with absolutely no trimming.

Palms

Palms are easy in containers. They also do not require frequent transplanting, remaining happy in the same container for well over a year. Since many palms are inexpensive in Florida, they give you the opportunity for instant container height.

Pentas

Most pentas bloom constantly, but some of the newer cultivars, like the butterfly pentas, bloom profusely for a few weeks and then go out of bloom for about two weeks before blooming again. But, again they are tough, dependable plants for containers

Petunias

We love petunias when we get the right ones. Some cultivars do quite well in Florida, blooming for months on end with very little care. Others die from fungus shortly after getting them home. We had great luck with the 'Supertunia' petunias from Proven Winners.

Sweet Potato Vines

These are the fastest-growing trailers we have. They come in three colors - lime green, dark bluish black, and the mixed colors of the tricolor, shown above. They offer almost instant maturity but do like a lot of water, and the snails love them.

Ti Plants

Ti plants offer constant color for little care. They also are happy in the same container for a longer period of time than most colorful plants, although not as long as crotons. And ti plants make great instant centerpieces.

Trailing Torenia

Trailing torenia blooms all the time and lasts longer than any other blooming trailer we tried - up to a year with constant flowers. Do not confuse its performance with that of its close relative, upright torenia, which lasts only a few months in a container

We tested diascia for the first time during the cool season preceding publication of this book and were thrilled with the results. It bloomed for five months straight with very little care. The container is Campania cast stone ('Rappallo Garland Urn' in CH finish, 17"W x 22.5"H). The diascia came from Bodger Botanicals (through Michell's), a seedling company that supplies wholesale nurseries.

Sun Plants for Containers, Arranged by Size

TRAILING

BLUE DAZE

BOUGAINVILLEA

CALIBRACHOA

DWARF CHENILLE

FUCHSIA

GERANIUM

GOLDEN GLOBE

GOLDILOCKS

LAMIUM, 'WHITE NANCY'

LANTANA, PURPLE

LANTANA, YELLOW

LICORICE PLANT, SILVER

LOBELIA

OUTBACK SUNSET

PETUNIAS

SCAEVOLA 'BLUE WONDER'

SWEET POTATO VINE

TORENIA, TRAIL

VERBENA

VINCA 'ILLUMINATION'

UNDER 1'

AGERATUM

AJUGA

ALYSSUM

BLUE DAZE

CACTUS

CALIBRACHOA

COLEUS

CROWN OF THORNS

DAISY, CALIFORNIA BUSH

DAISY, DAHLBERG

DAISY, MARGUERITE

DAISY, OSTEOSPERMU

DAISY, 'OUTBACK JUMBO'

DIASCIA

DUSTY MILLER

FUCHSIA

GRASS, DWARF SWEET FLAG

GRASS, FIBER OPTIC

GRASS, 'FROSTED CURLS'

HIBISCUS

IMPATIENS, NEW GUINEA

JUNIPER, SHORE

KALANCHOE

KALANCHOE THURSIFOLIA

LANTANA, PURPLE   LANTANA, YELLOW   LOBELIA   MARIGOLDS   MOSS ROSE   PANSIES

PERILLA 'MAGILLA'   PETUNIAS   PHLOX   PURPLE QUEEN   PURSLANE   ROSE

SALVIA   SALVIA, 'VICTORIA BLUE'   SEDUM   SNAPDRAGON   SUCCULENTS   TORENIA, UPRIGHT

VERBENA   VIOLA   ZINNIAS

1' - 3'

AGASTACHE   AGAVE   ANGEL'S TRUMPET   ARBORICOLA   BOUGAINVILLEA   BROMELIAD, IMPERIAL

CACTUS   CLEOME   COLEUS   COPPERLEAF   CROTONS   CROWN OF THORNS

DAISY, CALIFORNIA BUSH   DESERT ROSE   DRACAENA REFLEXA   ELEPHANT EAR   FRANGIPANI   FUCHSIA

GERANIUM   GRASS, FOUNTAIN   HIBISCUS   IMPATIENS, NEW GUINEA   JATROPHA   LANTANA, YELLOW

Sun Plants for Containers, Arranged by Size

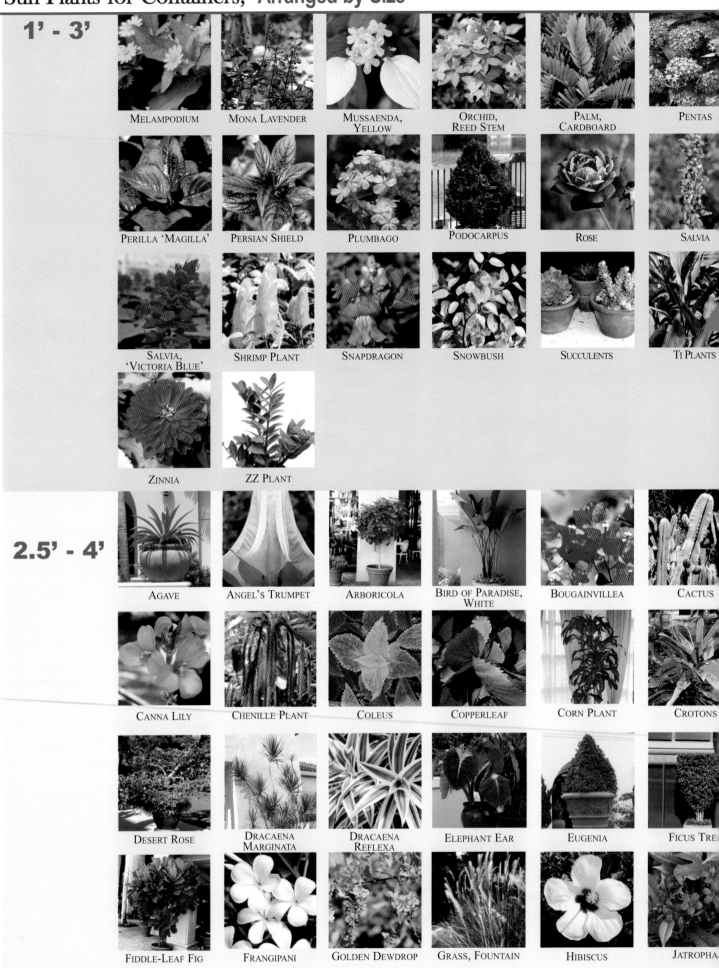

1' - 3'

MELAMPODIUM

MONA LAVENDER

MUSSAENDA, YELLOW

ORCHID, REED STEM

PALM, CARDBOARD

PENTAS

PERILLA 'MAGILLA'

PERSIAN SHIELD

PLUMBAGO

PODOCARPUS

ROSE

SALVIA

SALVIA, 'VICTORIA BLUE'

SHRIMP PLANT

SNAPDRAGON

SNOWBUSH

SUCCULENTS

TI PLANTS

ZINNIA

ZZ PLANT

2.5' - 4'

AGAVE

ANGEL'S TRUMPET

ARBORICOLA

BIRD OF PARADISE, WHITE

BOUGAINVILLEA

CACTUS

CANNA LILY

CHENILLE PLANT

COLEUS

COPPERLEAF

CORN PLANT

CROTONS

DESERT ROSE

DRACAENA MARGINATA

DRACAENA REFLEXA

ELEPHANT EAR

EUGENIA

FICUS TRE

FIDDLE-LEAF FIG

FRANGIPANI

GOLDEN DEWDROP

GRASS, FOUNTAIN

HIBISCUS

JATROPHA

.5' - 4'

MONA LAVENDER

MUSSAENDA, SALMON

MUSSAENDA, YELLOW

OLEANDER

PALM, ARECA

PALM, CARDBOARD

PALM, FISHTAIL

PALM, PYGMY DATE

PALM, THATCH

PERILLA 'MAGILLA'

PLUMBAGO

PODOCARPUS

ROSE

RUBBER PLANT

SILVER BUTTONWOOD

SNOWBUSH

TI PLANTS

ZZ PLANTS

4' - 6'

ANGEL'S TRUMPET

ARBORICOLA

BIRD OF PARADISE, WHITE

BOUGAINVILLEA

CACTUS

CANNA LILY

CHENILLE PLANT

CORN PLANT

CROTON

DRACAENA MARGINATA

DRACAENA REFLEXA

ELEPHANT EAR

EUGENIA

FICUS TREE

FIDDLE-LEAF FIG

FRANGIPANI

GOLDEN DEWDROP

JATROPHA

MUSSAENDA, SALMON

MUSSAENDA, YELLOW

OLEANDER

PALM, ALEXANDER

PALM, CARDBOARD

PALM, CHRISTMAS

PALM, FISHTAIL

PALM, PYGMY DATE

PALM, THATCH

PALM, TRAVELER'S

PLUMBAGO

PODOCARPUS

Sun Plants for Containers, Arranged by Size

4' - 6'

ROSE | RUBBER PLANT | SHRIMP PLANT | SILVER BUTTONWOOD | TI PLANTS

6' - 8'

ANGEL'S TRUMPET | ARBORICOLA | BIRD OF PARADISE, WHITE | BOUGAINVILLEA | CACTUS | DRACAENA MARGINAT

DRACAENA REFLEXA | EUGENIA | FICUS TREE | FIDDLE-LEAF FIG | FRANGIPANI | GOLDEN DEW

MUSSAENDA, SALMON | OLEANDER | PALM, ALEXANDER | PALM, ARECA | PALM, CHRISTMAS | PALM, FISHT

PALM, PYGMY DATE | PALM, THATCH | PALM, TRAVELER'S | PODOCARPUS | RUBBER PLANT | SILVER BUTTONWOO

8' - 15'

ANGEL'S TRUMPET | BIRD OF PARADISE, WHITE | FIDDLE-LEAF FIG | FRANGIPANI | JUNIPER | OLEANDER

PALM, ALEXANDER | PALM, CHRISTMAS | PALM, FISHTAIL | PALM, TRAVELER'S | PODOCARPUS | RUBBER PLA

FLOWERING STANDARDS

(SMALL FLOWERING TREES)

BOUGAINVILLEA | CHENILLE PLANT | GOLDEN DEWDROP | HIBISCUS | JATROPHA | TURK'S CA

Both of these pots feature petunias, which are one of our best performers for sun.

Above: Purple petunias and red dragon wing begonias fill this container from the Breakers in Palm Beach.
Light: Light shade to full sun. The dragon wing begonias take sun well during the cool months but not in the summer.
Season: October until April.
Lifespan: About six months in this container.
Care: Fertilize with a slow-release mix on planting day, and repeat every two to three months. Water when the soil feels dry to the touch.
Pot: Source unknown.

Right: Purple petunias, red salvia, and yellow marigolds fill this container from our trial gardens.
Light: Light shade to full sun.
Season: October until April.
Lifespan: About four months in this container.
Care: Fertilize with a slow-release mix on planting day, and repeat every two to three months. Water when the soil feels dry to the touch.
Pot: Source unknown.

Bright Ideas for Sun

Gaillardia 'Torch Yellow'
(1 plant from a one-gallon pot)
Plant Profile: Page 330

Mona Lavender
(1 plant from a three-gallon pot)
Plant Profile: Page 306

Petunia
(4 plants from 4.5" pots)
Plant Profile: Page 317

Since light absorbs color, bright colors do not show up as much in bright light as they do in shade. The reds, yellows, and purples that might look garish in New England are much more muted in the Florida sunshine.

Left: Mona lavender is the centerpiece of this bright arrangement. It did really well, blooming non-stop for over six months. This new introduction could become one of our superstar plants. Gaillardia 'Torch Yellow' (another new introduction) and petunias surround the Mona lavender. The gaillardia also did well, provided we removed the dead blooms. If not, ugly seed pods persisted for quite some time.
Light: Light shade to full sun.
Season: October until April.
Lifespan: About six months in this container.
Care: Fertilize with a slow-release mix on planting day, and repeat every two to three months. Water when the soil feels dry to the touch. Trim the dead flowers off the gaillardia.
Pot: Italian terra cotta, 22" wide, rolled rim.

Peach Crossandra
(2 plants from 4.5" pots)
Plant Profile: Page 329

Blue Salvia
(1 plant from a one-gallon pot)
Plant Profile: Page 321

Yellow Lantana
(2 plants from one-gallon pots)
Plant Profile: Page 302

Above: This attractive composition is the garden of my friend, Christopher James. Christopher has a florist shop called Christopher's Creative Designs in North Palm Beach (www.christopherscreativedesigns.com). He is the man you see in the DVD demonstrating potting and display techniques for orchids. This pot features blue salvia surrounded by peach crossandra and yellow lantana.
Light: Light shade to full sun.
Season: April to June or July.
Lifespan: About four months in this container.
Care: Fertilize with a slow-release mix on planting day, and repeat every two to three months. Water when the soil feels dry to the touch.
Pot: Source unknown.

Grasses for Sun

Grasses are exciting additions to container plantings. They are easy to grow and add an interesting texture to container arrangements. Grasses are available in both large and small sizes, as shown on these two pages.

Right: The red fountain grass flowers look like plumes and are clearly visible in this photo. Although it doesn't flower all the time, this grass still gives a very attractive texture, even when it's not blooming. Coleus surrounds the grass.

Light: Light shade to full sun.
Season: All year. Protect from frost.
Lifespan: About four to six months in this container.
Care: Fertilize with a slow-release mix on planting day, and repeat every two to three months. Water when the soil feels dry to the touch (see page 338-340 for more info).
Pot: International Pottery Alliance, Marco Polo Collection, *Octagon Planter,* 20" W, cream.

Below are small grasses that did well in our trials. Grasses are not only for centerpieces - like the one shown above. We were thrilled to find some small ones from Proven Winners that added interesting textures to our arrangements.

'Fiber Optic' Grass
Plant Profile: Page 296

Dwarf White Striped Sweet Flag
Plant Profile: Page 329

Carex 'Frosty Curls'
Plant Profile: Page 297

Right: I am thrilled with the appearance and performance of the grasses in these blue containers. All the containers on this page feature white-striped pampas grass (*Cortaderia selloana 'Silver Comet').* The texture shows up quite well against the background of larger-leafed plants.

Light: Light shade to full sun.
Season: All year for the grasses. Fall through spring for the verbena that surrounds them in the pots. Protect from frost.
Lifespan: About six months in this container.
Care: Fertilize with a slow-release mix on planting day, and repeat every two to three months. Water when the soil feels dry to the touch.
Pot: Anamese *Grande Jar,* set of two. (Large: 20"H x 23"W; Medium: 13"H x 15"W).

Left: This is the same grass as the pot shown above. It is surrounded by coleus, and it did beautifully through the spring and summer. Eventually, the grass got so heavy it fell over, and I changed the pot to other plantings. Planting a tall grass gives a pot instant height. This white-striped pampas grass was planted from a three-gallon pot and surrounded with 10 coleus from 4.5" pots.

Light: Light shade to full sun.
Season: All year. Protect from frost.
Lifespan: About four to six months in this container.
Care: Fertilize with a slow-release mix on planting day, and repeat every two to three months. Water when the soil feels dry to the touch.
Pot: Sabu *Champa Glazed Series* #310-026. It measures 29 inches tall by 29 inches wide.

Chapter 9

Cool-Season Containers

The cool season (October through April) is the most pleasant time of year in Florida because of the wonderful, cool-but-seldom-cold temperatures. This is the time we want to be outside enjoying our gardens.

This chapter features charts that organize the plants by size. These plant charts make designing easier by putting all the plants that work in a specific environment in one spot, so you can see all the possibilities at once. For example, if you are looking for a plant about four to six feet tall that peaks in the cool season, simply look at that size range on the plant charts.

Most annuals do better in the cool season than summer because of the cooler temperatures. We are the envy of many gardeners from other places because of our ability to grow such a wide variety of annuals in our ideal cool season.

The pot collection at left is based on the brilliantly-colored pots made at Addison Mizner's Los Manos potteries in the 1920s. The pots mirror the same cobalt blue that's seen in the pool tiles. Other antique elements, like the fountain and statuary, anchor the stunning backdrop created at the far end of the pool. Shade-tolerant varieties, like alocasia, bromeliads, and ferns, mix well with brilliant impatiens. Dracaenas and ti plants fill in the background. The plantings are all changed seasonally.

Above: The long, white container includes some of our best winter annuals: dragon wing begonias, and petunias. Confederate jasmine vines trail down the sides. The terra cotta companion pot includes different colored petunias. These pots are from The Breakers in Palm Beach.

Top 12 Container Plants for **the Cool Season**

Bougainvillea

Bougainvillea is good and bad for containers. Its major benefits are gorgeous winter color and the ability to stay in the same pot for years. Its disadvantage is that it drops a lot - more than almost any other plant. And it goes through bloom spurts, meaning it all blooms at once and then all stops at once, looking bare.

Bromeliads

Although most bromeliads don't offer constant color, they produce spectacular flowers that bloom for months with very little care. They also have the ability to stay in the same container for years on end.

Dragon Wing Begonias

This is my favorite shade plant. It actually produces fabulous color with very little care. I plant it in the fall and don't touch them until spring, other than watering. They don't even seem to mind if you forget their fertilizer occasionally!

Geraniums

Beautiful, traditional flowers th love Florida's cool season. Loc best if dead-headed (dead flowe pinched off). Great container plants that often do better in co tainers than in the ground in Florida.

Impatiens, Double

Double impatiens are one of the best choices for cool season color. The flowers are lovely, resembling miniature roses. These plants are not only easy, but very dependable, blooming constantly with very little care. They thrive in sun or shade during our cool season. They're well worth the extra water they demand.

Mint, Variegated or Swedish Ivy

This is a great variegated plant for Florida. The ones we planted in winter lived for about a year as long as we kept them out of the sun in summer. It will cascade quite a distance if you let it, or you can keep it trimmed as a mounding plant.

Mona Lavender

This plant is another new one - we tested it for just one year but were thrilled with its performance. It thrives in the cool season but didn't like summer. It blooms constantly for at least six months with absolutely no trimming.

Pansies

One of the few plants that blooms in the coldest parts of Florida in January without havi to bring them inside if it freezes Available in many colors and pa terns. Underused in the souther end of the state.

Perilla 'Magilla'

This is a new plant in Florida and a real super-achiever. We planted ours in January, and they are still going strong the following September! We first thought that this was a small plant until it grew to three feet tall!

Persian Shield

The most beautiful, iridescent leaves I have ever seen. Since it doesn't live long in the Florida landscape, containers are a great way to enjoy this gorgeous plant.

Petunias

We love petunias when we get the right ones. Some cultivars do quite well in Florida, blooming for months on end with very little care. Others die from fungus shortly after getting them home. We had great luck with the 'Supertunia' petunias from Proven Winners.

Salvia

Very dependable bloomer that comes in many colors and types Requires little care or water. On of the favorite foods of hummingbirds.

Our gazebo garden in winter. The hanging basket is shown on page 71. Planted in the ground, the white 'odorata' begonias contrast well with the bright New Guinea impatiens.

Cool Season Plants for Containers, Arranged by Size

TRAILING

BLUE DAZE · BOUGAINVILLEA · CALIBRACHOA · CHENILLE, DWARF · FUCHSIA · GERANIUM

GOLDILOCKS · IVY · LAMIUM, 'WHITE NANCY' · LANTANA, PURPLE · LICORICE PLANT, SILVER · LOBELIA

MINT, VARIEGATED · PETUNIAS · POTHOS · SWEET POTATO VINE · TORENIA, TRAILING · VERBENA

VINCA, 'ILLUMINATION'

UNDER 1'

ANTHURIUM · AJUGA · ALYSSUM · BEGONIA, DRAGON WING · BEGONIA, TUBEROUS · BEGONIA, WA

BLUE DAZE · BROMELIAD · CACTUS · CALIBRACHOA · CROWN OF THORNS · DAISY, CALIFORNIA BU

DAISY, DAHLBERG · DAISY, MARGUERITE · DAISY, OSTEOSPERMUM · DAISY, 'OUTBACK JUMBO' · DIASCIA · DUSTY MILLE

FERN, WART · FUCHSIA · GRASS, DWARF SWEET FIG · GRASS, 'FIBER OPTIC' · GRASS, 'FROSTED CURLS' · HIBISCUS

IMPATIENS

IMPATIENS, NEW GUINEA

JUNIPER, SHORE

KALANCHOE

KALANCHOE, THURSIFOLIA

LANTANA, PURPLE

LOBELIA

MARIGOLDS

MINT, VARIEGATED

PANSIES

PERILLA 'MAGILLA'

PETUNIAS

PHLOX

POLKA DOT PLANT

PURPLE QUEEN

ROSE

SALVIA

SALVIA, 'VICTORIA BLUE'

SEDUM

SNAKE PLANT

SNAPDRAGON

SUCCULENTS

TRIFOLIUM, 'DARK DANCER'

VERBENA

VIOLA

AGASTACHE

AGAVE

ANGEL'S TRUMPET

ANTHURIUM

ARBORICOLA

AZALEA

BEGONIA, DRAGON WING

BEGONIA, ORANGE ANGELWING

BEGONIA, PINK ANGELWING

BEGONIA, WHITE 'ODORATA'

BOUGAINVILLEA

BROMELIAD

BROMELIAD, IMPERIAL

CACTUS

CAST IRON PLANT

CHINESE EVERGREEN

CLEOME

CROTONS

1' - 3'

CROWN OF THORNS

DAISY, CALIFORNIA BUSH

DESERT ROSE

DIEFFENBACHIA

DRACAENA REFLEXA

ELEPHANT E

FERN, FISHTAIL

FERN, WART

FUCHSIA

GERANIUM

GRASS, FOUNTAIN

HIBISCUS

IMPATIENS

IMPATIENS, NEW GUINEA

IRIS, WALKING

JATROPHA

MONA LAVENDER

PALM, CARDBC

PALM, BAMBOO

PEACE LILY

PENTAS

PERILLA 'MAGILLA'

PERSIAN SHIELD

PODOCARP

ROSE

SALVIA

SALVIA, 'VICTORIA BLUE'

SHRIMP PLANT

SNAKE PLANT

SNAPDRAGO

SNOWBUSH

SUCCULENTS

TI PLANT

ZZ PLANT

2.5' - 4'

AGAVE

ANGEL'S TRUMPET

ARBORICOLA

AZALEA

BEGONIA, PINK ANGELWING

BEGONIA, WHITE 'ODOR

BIRD OF PARADISE, WHITE

BOUGAINVILLEA

BROMELIAD

CACTUS

CORN PLANT

CROTONS

2.5' - 4'

DESERT ROSE	DIEFFENBACHIA	DRACAENA MARGINATA	DRACAENA REFLEXA	ELEPHANT EAR	EUGENIA
FICUS TREE	FIDDLE-LEAF FIG	GRASS, FOUNTAIN	HIBISCUS	JATROPHA	MONA LAVENDER
OLEANDER	PALM, ARECA	PALM, BAMBOO	PALM, CARDBOARD	PALM, CAT	PALM, FISHTAIL
PALM, LADY	PALM, PYGMY DATE	PALM, THATCH	PEACE LILY	PERILLA 'MAGILLA'	PODOCARPUS
ROSE	RUBBER PLANT	SHRIMP PLANT	SILVER BUTTONWOOD	SNAKE PLANT	SNOWBUSH
TI PLANT	ZZ PLANT				

4' - 6'

ANGEL'S TRUMPET	ARBORICOLA	AZALEA	BEGONIA, PINK ANGELWING	BIRD OF PARADISE, WHITE	BOUGAINVILLEA
CACTUS	CORN PLANT	CROTONS	DRACAENA MARGINATA	DRACAENA REFLEXA	ELEPHANT EAR

Cool Season Plants for Containers, Arranged by Size

4' - 6'

EUGENIA

FICUS TREE

FIDDLE-LEAF FIG

JATROPHA

OLEANDER

PALM, ALEXAND

PALM, ARECA

PALM, CARDBOARD

PALM, CAT

PALM, CHRISTMAS

PALM, FISHTAIL

PALM, KENTIA

PALM, LADY

PALM, PYGMY DATE

PALM, THATCH

PALM, TRAVELER'S

PODOCARPUS

ROSE

RUBBER PLANT

SHRIMP PLANT

SILVER BUTTONWOOD

TI PLANT

6' - 8'

ANGEL'S TRUMPET

ARBORICOLA

BIRD OF PARADISE, WHITE

BOUGAINVILLEA

CACTUS

CORN PLANT

DRACAENA MARGINATA

DRACAENA REFLEXA

EUGENIA

FICUS TREE

FIDDLE-LEAF FIG

JUNIPER

OLEANDER

PALM, ALEXANDER

PALM, ARECA

PALM, BAMBOO

PALM, CHRISTMAS

PALM, FISHTA

PALM, KENTIA

PALM, LADY

PALM, PYGMY DATE

PALM, THATCH

PALM, TRAVELER'S

PODOCARPU

6' - 8'

RUBBER PLANT

SILVER BUTTONWOOD

FLOWERING STANDARDS 4' - 8'
(SMALL FLOWERING TREES)

BOUGAINVILLEA

CAPE HONEYSUCKLE

CHENILLE PLANT

GOLDEN DEWDROP

HIBISCUS

JATROPHA

SNOWBUSH

TURK'S CAP

8' - 15'

ANGEL'S TRUMPET

BIRD OF PARADISE, WHITE

FIDDLE-LEAF FIG

OLEANDER

PALM, ALEXANDER

PALM, CHRISTMAS

PALM, FISHTAIL

PALM, KENTIA

PALM, TRAVELER'S

Although bougainvillea peaks during the cool season in Florida, it is commonly used in summer and fall farther north. I found this gorgeous specimen at Landcraft Environments on Long Island. Owned by Dennis Schrader and Bill Smith, this unique nursery specializes in tropicals. Dennis, along with Susan Roth, wrote a great book called "Hot Plants for Cool Climates: Gardening with Tropical Plants in Temperate Zones." It really makes you appreciate living and gardening in Florida!

Cool-Season High Performer...

Double Impatiens
(3 plants from one-gallon pots)
Plant Profile: Page 299

'Little Lizzie' Impatiens
(6 plants from 4.5" pots)
Plant Profile: Page 299

Dragon Wing Begonia
(8 plants from 4.5" pots)
Plant Profile: Page 280

Above: A hanging basket that features double impatiens planted in the top of the basket. Purple 'Little Lizzie' impatiens and red dragon wing begonias are planted in the side. This basket did extremely well, with all the plants blooming constantly for six months through the entire cool season.

Light: Medium shade to full sun in the cool season. None of these plants take full sun in the summer.

Season: Cool season. Protect from frost. These plants also grow during the summer in Florida but do not do as well and require a lot more shade.

Lifespan: About six months in this basket.

Care: Fertilize with a slow-release mix on planting day, and repeat every two to three months. Water when the soil feels dry or the impatiens wilt (see pages 338-340 for more watering info). This is a very easy combination to grow, but it requires a lot of water.

Pot: 20" hanging basket.

For container sources, go to www.easygardencolor.com

Double Impatiens

Double Impatiens
(3 plants from 6" pots)
Plant Profile: Page 299

Yellow Calibrachoa
(8 plants from 4.5" pots)
Plant Profile: Page 285

Above: What a great idea for cobalt blue pots! This simple arrangement of red double impatiens surrounded by yellow calibrachoa is all this pot needs to become a striking combination. The impatiens filled in quickly, but the calibrachoa were planted small and took a few months to trail over the edge of the pot.

Light: Light shade to full sun in the cool season.

Season: Cool season. Protect from frost.

Lifespan: About six months in this container.

Care: Fertilize with a slow-release mix on planting day, and repeat every two to three months. Water when the soil feels dry or the impatiens wilt (see pages 338-340 for more watering info). This is a very easy combination to grow, but it requires a lot of water.

Pot: Source unknown.

Cool-Season High Performer...

Impatiens are one of the best choices for cool-season container color. The plants are easy, providing constant blooms with very little care. Many of the other annuals we tested went in and out of bloom, particularly in December and January; but the impatiens kept on blooming. And, they grow well in sun or shade during our cool season. Mix impatiens with pothos as shown above or use a single color, as shown to the left.

Above: This six-foot fiberglass window box is filled with impatiens and pothos. The pothos will trail over the edges of the box with time.

Left: A cast stone pot on a pedestal that sits in front of a column. This arrangement is just outside the front door of a residence, welcoming visitors. The container and pedestal are attractive enough to look great with simple plantings. Elaborate arrangements would detract from the beauty of the container.

For container sources, go to www.easygardencolor.com

Regular Impatiens

Below: This three-tiered planter contains lipstick impatiens and tricolored sweet potato. Two layers of flowers are planted in the ground around the planter. The inner layer is lipstick New Guinea impatiens, and the outer border is white wax begonias. **Light:** Medium shade to full sun in the cool season. **Season:** Cool season. **Lifespan:** The whole arrangement lasted about six months. **Care:** Fertilize with a slow-release mix on planting day. Water when the soil feels dry. Trim the sweet potato as needed. **Container:** This container is constructed like a three-level hanging basket connected with iron supports. See it planted with herbs on page 243.

Lipstick Impatiens
Plant Profile: Page 299

Sweet Potato
Plant Profile: Page 324

New Guinea Impatiens
Plant Profile: Page 300

White Wax Begonia
Plant Profile: Page 282

Cool-Season High Performer...

Bromeliad
(1 plant from a 6" pot)
Plant Profile: Page 284

Verbena
(1 plant from a 6" pot pulled apart to surround the bromeliad)
Plant Profile: Page 327

Begonia
(40 plants from 4.5" pots planted at the base of the pots)
Plant Profile: Page 282

While most bromeliads prefer shade in summer, almost all of them take sun well in winter. As long as you don't put them in an area of intense heat, like against a south-facing concrete wall, they thrive in our light winter sun. As a general rule, the thicker the leaves, the more sun it will take.

Above: The pot on the opposite page pairs unlikely companions of bromeliads and verbena. The height of the pot requires a tall center focal point, but the opening of the pot is quite small. Bromeliads don't require a lot of root space, so this one fits quite easily in the middle of the pot, giving much more height than plants with similarly small root systems. The next challenge is to choose a cascading plant that also requires a small root space. This verbena had to be pulled apart at the roots so small pieces could be slipped in along the edge. It took this abuse beautifully, never showing any shock. Although the verbena didn't flower as much as it would in a warmer season, its trailing effect was lovely. The pot is underplanted with white wax begonias to accent it further. White 'odorata' begonias and New Guinea impatiens are planted in the ground behind the pot.

Light: Medium shade to full sun in the cool season. This bromeliad doesn't take full sun in the summer.

Season: Bromeliads grow all year in Florida. Verbena does well most of the time, except during the worst summer heat. Begonias do best during the cool season.

Lifespan: About four to five months in this container.

Care: Fertilize with a slow-release mix on planting day, and repeat every two to three months. Water when the soil feels dry, about every three days (see pages 338-340 for more watering info).

Pot: Source unknown.

For container sources, go to www.easygardencolor.com

Bromeliads

Cool-Season High Performer...

Bougainvillea perform exceptionally well in pots. In fact, they bloom more when their roots are crowded, lasting for years in the same container. Masses of bougainvillea flowering during our cool weather can be quite stunning, but they also go through periods of bareness between bloom bursts. Over-pruning will decrease the blooms, and their thorns can be quite nasty; so, prune with long loppers and handle with thick gloves. And remember, bougainvillea drop quite a few flowers. See "Best Garden Color for Florida" on pages 192-193 and 208-209 for lots more information about bougainvillea.

Above: Purple bougainvillea is a better bet than red for surrounding entries because, when frequently trimmed, it blooms more than the red. The pots are from Balazara'a *Vaso Pestonato*, 22"H x 31"D with an 11" base. Krent Weiland, Landscape Architect, Lake Worth, Florida, designed this garden.

Right: A cast stone bowl with a gorgeous bougainvillea at the Portofino Bay Hotel and Resort, part of Universal Orlando Resort. Even small bowls like this one bloom well with bougainvillea because bougainvillea does not require much root space.

Bougainvillea

Cool-Season Performer...

These azaleas - found throughout Universal Orlando Resort - are evergreen shrubs for most of the year and flower for about a month in spring. Azaleas do better for long-term use the further north you go in Florida. However, they are ideal for quick container color, even in the southern parts of the state.

For container sources, go to www.easygardencolor.com

Azaleas

Chapter 10

Hot-Season Containers

Coleus 'Wizard Red Velvet'
(12 plants from 4.5" pots)
Plant Profile: Page 287

Coleus 'Wizard Golden'
(12 plants from 4.5" pots)
Plant Profile: Page 287

Coleus 'Painted Lady'
(12 plants from 4.5" pots)
Plant Profile: Page 287

The hot season runs from April until October. April through June are fine months for container gardening in Florida, some of the best. July is passable. August and September are unbearably hot. I have few containers out in the hottest part of summer other than year-round plantings, like palms and succulents.

This chapter features ideas for hot-season color as well as charts that organize the plants by size that do well in our hot season. These plant charts make designing easier by putting all the plants that work in a specific environment in one spot, so that you can see all the possibilities at once. For example, if you are looking for a plant about four to six feet tall that thrives during the hot season, simply look at that size range on the plant charts.

Although annuals are more difficult during the hot season, perennials are easier. More perennials bloom in summer than winter. Some, like mussaenda and heliconia, bloom profusely all summer long with very little care. These tropical perennials are gaining popularity throughout the world for summer container plantings.

Left: Three different coleus and a centerpiece of red fountain grass make an interesting combination in this basket on a post.
Light: Light shade to full sun. Coleus needs more sun when planted in the sides of a basket than when planted in the top of a container.
Season: Coleus and fountain grass grow all year in Florida if they are protected from frost.
Lifespan: Six months.
Care: Fertilize with a slow-release mix on planting day. Water when the soil feels dry, up to daily when the basket is mature and the temperature is very hot. Pinch back the coleus every month or two.
Container: 20" hanging basket mounted on a post. See page 352 for mounting instructions.

Above: Mixed coleus paired with pilea will take the worst of our summer heat.

Top 12 Container Plants for **the Hot Season**

Caladiums

Caladiums add color in summer, when most other annuals wilt from heat or rot from too much rain. They are native to tropical areas and are well adapted naturally to Florida's summer heat. Caladiums are available in a variety of sizes, from large ones to small dwarfs. Be sure you know what size you're buying!

Cannas

Cannas love our summer heat, blooming with showy, bright flowers almost continuously. However, they are quite susceptible to caterpillar damage, although not as much in containers as in the ground. And even the dwarfs grow large enough to fall over before summer ends.

Coleus

Interest in coleus is exploding all over the world, and the plant loves Florida's summer. They do especially well in the sides of hanging baskets in sunny spots. Coleus offers constant color during our warm months and hundreds of different leaf patterns and colors.

Ground Orchids

Orchids are the world's favorite flowers and are traditionally thought of as difficult to grow. Garden orchids are the exception, blooming in regular potting soil with the same care as other landscape plants. They bloom throughout our warm months.

Heliconia

Heliconia is one of the best choices for summer color. It blooms continuously all summer with very little care. There are many different kinds of heliconia, from dwarfs to large shrubs. The smaller varieties are the best for containers.

Mandevillea

This beautiful vine is used throughout the world as a summer container plant for sunny spots. In the warmest parts of Florida, it sometimes lives for a few years. In cooler spots, it lasts for just one summer.

Melampodium

This little-known plant is a good choice for yellow color in summer. Some years it is not as dependable as others, but its overall performance is good. Its daisy-like flower and mounding growth habit are appropriate for formal or informal gardens.

Mussaenda

Mussaenda is the most spectacular plant in our summer garden, with huge flowers that bloom for at least six months each year. It very easy to grow but most types are completely bare all winter.

Pentas

Most pentas bloom constantly, but some of the newer cultivars, like the butterfly pentas, bloom profusely for a few weeks and go out of bloom for about two weeks before blooming again. But they are tough, dependable plants for containers and love our summer heat.

Sweet Potato Vines

These are the fastest-growing trailers we have. They come in three colors - lime green, variegated with pink, and the blackish blue shown above. They offer almost instant maturity but do like a lot of water, and the snails love them.

Torenia, Trailing

Trailing torenia blooms all the time and lasts longer than any other blooming trailer we tried - up to a year with constant flowers. Do not confuse its performance with that of its close relative, upright torenia, which lasts a few months in a container.

Torenia, Upright

Although upright torenia doesn't last as long as trailing torenia, it is very useful in summer containers. The colors are great, particularly the blue. They did very well in the sides of hanging baskets.

White Mussaenda
(1 plant from a three-gallon pot)
Plant Profile: Page 308

Butterfly Pentas
(3 plants from 4.5" pots)
Plant Profile: Page 315

Torenia, Upright
(4 plants from 4.5" pots)
Plant Profile: Page 326

bove: White mussaenda, one of our most spectacular summer plants, forms the centerpiece of this arrangement. Pink but-rfly pentas and blue torenia surround it. We soaked the roots of the plants in water prior to planting them - so we could queeze the root balls into a little smaller size - in order to fit them all in a pot this small.

ight: Full sun.

eason: Summer.

ifespan: About six months in this container. The mussaenda flowers lasted for about six months. The pentas and torenia sted two to three months. Once the pentas and torenia have died, the mussaenda should be large enough to make a strong atement alone in this attractive container. Plant it in the ground when it outgrows the container if you live in zones 10 or 11.

are: Fertilize with a slow-release mix on planting day, and repeat every two to three months. Water when the soil feels dry the touch (see pages 338-340 for more watering info). The butterfly pentas look better if you remove the dead blooms. And, ey don't flower every day, like the other two plants. Expect them to take some bloom breaks.

ot: Global Pottery's *Elegante* in French yellow from their Classico Collection. 16"H x 14"W.

Hot Season Plants for Containers, Arranged by Size

TRAILING

CHENILLE, DWARF

GOLDILOCKS

IVY

LICORICE PLANT, SILVER

MINT, VARIEGATED

POTHOS

SWEET POTATO VINE

TORENIA, TRAILING

VINCA 'ILLUMINATION'

UNDER 1'

BROMELIAD

CACTUS

CROWN OF THORN

FERN, WART

GRASS, DWARF SWEET FLAG

GRASS, FIBER OPTIC

GRASS, 'FROSTED CURLS'

JUNIPER, SHORE

KALANCHOE THURSIFOLIA

MINT, VARIEGATED

PERILLA 'MAGILLA'

PORTULACA

PURPLE QUEEN

PURSLANE

SEDUM

SNAKE PLANT

SUCCULENTS

TORENIA, UPRIGHT

1' - 3'

AGAVE

ANGEL'S TRUMPET

ANTHURIUM

ARBORICOLA

BEGONIA, ORANGE ANGELWING

BEGONIA, PINK ANGELWING

CACTUS

CALADIUM

CAST IRON PLANT

CHINESE EVERGREEN

COLEUS

COPPERLEAF

CROTON

CROWN OF THORNS

DESERT ROSE

DIEFFENBACHIA

DRACAENA REFLEXA

ELEPHANT EAR

FERN, FISHTAIL	FERN, WART	FRANGIPANI	GRASS, FOUNTAIN	HELICONIA	HIBISCUS
IRIS, WALKING	JATROPHA	LANTANA, YELLOW	MELAMPODIUM	MUSSAENDA, YELLOW	ORCHID, GROUND
ORCHID, REED-STEM	PALM, CARDBOARD	PALM, CAT	PEACE LILY	PENTAS	PERILLA 'MAGILLA'
PERSIAN SHIELD	PLUMBAGO	PODOCARPUS	ROSE	SHRIMP PLANT	SNAKE PLANT
SNOWBUSH	SUCCULENTS	TI PLANT	ZZ PLANT		

AGAVE	ANGEL'S TRUMPET	ARBORICOLA	BEGONIA, PINK ANGELWING	BIRD OF PARADISE, WHITE	BROMELIAD
CACTUS	CANNA LILY	CHENILLE PLANT	COLEUS	COPPERLEAF	CORN PLANT
CROTON	DESERT ROSE	DIEFFENBACHIA	DRACAENA MARGINATA	DRACAENA REFLEXA	ELEPHANT EAR

2.5' - 4'

EUGENIA

FICUS TREE

FIDDLE-LEAF FIG

FRANGIPANI

GOLDEN DEWDROP

GRASS, FOUNT

HELICONIA

HIBISCUS

JATROPHA

MUSSAENDA, SALMON

MUSSAENDA, YELLOW

OLEANDER

PALM, ARECA

PALM, BAMBOO

PALM, CARDBOARD

PALM, CAT

PALM, FISHTAIL

PALM, LAD

PALM, PYGMY DATE

PALM, THATCH

PEACE LILY

PERILLA 'MAGILLA'

PLUMBAGO

PODOCARPU

ROSE

RUBBER PLANT

SHRIMP PLANT

SILVER BUTTONWOOD

SNAKE PLANT

SNOWBUSH

TI PLANT

ZZ PLANT

4' - 6'

ANGEL'S TRUMPET

ARBORICOLA

BEGONIA, PINK ANGELWING

BIRD OF PARADISE, WHITE

CACTUS

CANNA LIL'

CHENILLE PLANT

CORN PLANT

CROTON

DRACAENA MARGINATA

DRACAENA REFLEXA

ELEPHANT EA

4' - 6'

EUGENIA • FICUS TREE • FIDDLE-LEAF FIG • FRANGIPANI • GOLDEN DEWDROP • HELICONIA

JATROPHA • JUNIPER • MUSSAENDA, SALMON • MUSSAENDA, YELLOW • OLEANDER • PALM, ALEXANDER

PALM, ARECA • PALM, BAMBOO • PALM, CARDBOARD • PALM, CAT • PALM, CHRISTMAS • PALM, FISHTAIL

PALM, KENTIA • PALM, LADY • PALM, PYGMY DATE • PALM, THATCH • PALM, TRAVELER'S • PLUMBAGO

PODOCARPUS • ROSE • RUBBER PLANT • SHRIMP PLANT • SILVER BUTTONWOOD • TI PLANT

6' - 8'

ANGEL'S TRUMPET • ARBORICOLA • BIRD OF PARADISE, WHITE • CACTUS • CORN PLANT • DRACAENA MARGINATA

DRACAENA REFLEXA • EUGENIA • FICUS TREE • FIDDLE-LEAF FIG • FRANGIPANI • GOLDEN DEWDROP

JUNIPER • MUSSAENDA, SALMON • OLEANDER • PALM, ALEXANDER • PALM, ARECA • PALM, BAMBOO

Hot Season Plants for Containers, Arranged by Size

6' - 8'

PALM, CHRISTMAS
PALM, FISHTAIL
PALM, KENTIA
PALM, LADY
PALM, PYGMY DATE
PALM, THATC

PALM, TRAVELER'S
PODOCARPUS
RUBBER PLANT
SILVER BUTTONWOOD

FLOWERING STANDARDS 4' - 8'
(SMALL FLOWERING TREES)

CHENILLE PLANT
GOLDEN DEWDROP
HIBISCUS
JATROPHA
SNOWBUSH

8' - 15'

ANGEL'S TRUMPET
BIRD OF PARADISE, WHITE
FIDDLE-LEAF FIG
FRANGIPANI
OLEANDER
PALM, ALEXAN

PALM, CHRISTMAS
PALM, FISHTAIL
PALM, KENTIA
PALM, TRAVELER'S
PODOCARPUS
RUBBER PLAN

Dipladenia (left) and purslane (right) thrive in the summer heat at the Breakers, Palm Beach. The bright colors show well in the bright sun.

Above: The heliconia, croton, and shrimp plants are ideal for summer heat. They are also very easy to care for in containers. But where are the containers? The torenia has completely covered the green pots, which are also shown planted with other plants on pages 53 and 123. These plants get water from the garden sprinklers, which makes growing them much easier than if they were hand-watered.

Light: Light shade.

Season: Summer.

Lifespan: About six months in these containers. Transplant them to larger containers or into the garden when they outgrow these pots. Protect from frost.

Care: Fertilize with a slow-release mix on planting day, and repeat every two to three months. Water when the soil feels dry to the touch.

Pot: Dark green, glazed pots from Anamese.

Curcuma 'Purple Prince' (3 plants from 6" pots) Plant Profile: Page 329

Peacock Spike Moss (3 plants from 6" pots) Plant Profile: Page 331

Above: Curcuma 'Purple Prince' with blue peacock fern.
Light: Light shade.
Season: Summer.
Lifespan: About two to three months.
Care: Fertilize with a slow-release mix on planting day, and repeat every two to three months. Water when the soil feels dry to the touch (see pages 338-340 for more watering info).
Pot: Global *Flared Rectangle* from their Brass Collection in Ancient Red (16.5"L x 11"W x 7"H). See page 27 for more information about this metal pot.

Right: Gorgeous yellow ground orchids in an iron container make a great summer combination.
Light: Light shade to full sun.
Season: Summer and fall.
Lifespan: These orchids bloom for about six months during the warm months. They can be transplanted into the ground in frost-free areas.
Care: Fertilize with a slow-release mix on planting day, and repeat every two to three months. Water when the soil feels dry to the touch.
Pot: Campania *Browning Swag Urn* with wax rust patina (20"W x 19.5" H). See page 27 for more information.

For container sources, go to www.easygardencolor.com

I found all of these plants at Excelsa Gardens in Loxahatchee, Florida. Remember to explore your local garden centers!

Spathoglottis Ground Orchid
(1 plant from a three-gallon pot)
Plant Profile: Page 162

Tropicals that Like It Hot

Canna Lily
(1 plant from a three-gallon pot)
Plant Profile: Page 285

Persian Shield
(2 plants from one-gallon pots)
Plant Profile: Page 316

'Painted Pink' Coleus
(1 plant from a 4.5" pot)
Plant Profile: Page 287

Purslane
(2 plants from one-gallon pots)
Plant Profile: Page 320

Left: Orange canna lilies surrounded with Persian shield, coleus, and purslane. Prior to planting, we soaked the root balls in water - so we could easily squeeze them smaller - to fit into this pot. The only problem we had with this arrangement was that the canna eventually grew a bit too tall for the container.

Light: Light shade to full sun.
Season: Summer.
Lifespan: About four months in this container. The cannas can be transplanted to the garden (see 'Best Garden Color for Florida,' pages 28-29).
Care: Fertilize with a slow-release mix on planting day, and repeat every two to three months. Water when the soil feels dry to the touch. Pinch back the Persian shield and coleus as needed.
Pot: Rolled-rim terra cotta, 20" diameter.

Right: Orange heliconia surrounded by shrimp plants, mammey crotons, coleus, and sweet potato vine. I was very pleased with this combination because it lasted a full six months, looking great the entire time.

Light: Light shade to full sun, but not reflected sun (like in front of a white concrete wall).
Season: Summer.
Lifespan: About six months in this container. The heliconia, shrimps, and crotons can be transplanted into the garden in zone 10 or 11. The heliconia is not an ideal landscape plant (see 'Best Garden Color for Florida,' pages 152-153).
Care: Fertilize with a slow-release mix on planting day, and repeat every two to three months. Water when the soil feels dry to the touch. Trim the sweet potato vine when needed, about once a month.
Pot: International Pottery Alliance *Scallop Rim Planter* in Oxblood (20" D).

For container sources, go to www.easygardencolor.com

Heliconia
(1 plant from a three-gallon pot)
Plant Profile: Page 298

Mammey Croton
(2 plants from one-gallon pots)
Plant Profile: Page 288

Golden Shrimp Plant
(1 plant from a one-gallon pot)
Plant Profile: Page 322

Coleus 'Defiance'
(2 plants from 4.5" pots)
Plant Profile: Page 287

'Margarita' Sweet Potato
(2 plants from 4.5" pots)
Plant Profile: Page 324

Color that Likes It Hot

Snowbush
(1 plant from a three-gallon pot)
Plant Profile: Page 332

Periwinkle
(4 plants from 4.5" pots)
Plant Profile: Page 331

**'Florida Sweetheart'
Caladium**
(2 plants from 4.5" pots)
Plant Profile: Page 284

Left: Snowbush is the centerpiece of this arrangement surrounded by periwinkles and caladiums.
Light: Sun.
Season: Snowbush grows all year in the warmer parts of Florida but looks best during the warmer months. Caladiums and periwinkles are summer annuals. To learn more about them in the landscape, see "Best Garden Color for Florida," pages 26-27 and 66.
Lifespan: This arrangement is happy in this size pot for about four months. Be sure the caladiums are dwarfs, or they will quickly outgrow the snowbush. The snowbush can be planted in the garden in the warmer parts of Florida after it outgrows the pot. (Be careful if you plant it in the landscape because caterpillars feast on snowbush in the spring).
Pot: Global Pottery *Ribbed Planter* in Lead from the Fiberglass Collection (20"W x 13.5"H). See page 27 for more information about trial results on fiberglass containers.

Right: Diplademia is surrounded by dwarf caladiums and a silver licorice plant. We were quite surprised that the licorice plant breezed through our hot summer.
Light: Sun.
Season: Summer.
Lifespan: This arrangement is happy in this size pot for about three to four months. Be sure that the caladiums are dwarfs, or they will quickly outgrow the diplademia. Although diplademia is classed as a perennial, I have never had much luck with it living more than one season in the ground.
Pot: Global Pottery *Venice Urn* in Lead from their Fiberglass Collection (21"W x 18.5"H). See page 27 for more information about trial results on fiberglass containers.

Both of these pots are light-weight fiberglass, so I was able to carry them around a nursery in search of summer plants that looked good with them. Fiberglass is an excellent container material for Florida gardens. It is durable (think about it - boats are made of fiberglass!), easy to clean, and available in attractive finishes, like these two from Global Pottery. Pink is my favorite color to coordinate with these grey tones.

Diplademia
(1 plant from a three-gallon pot)
Plant Profile: Page 329

Silver Licorice Plant
(2 plants from one-gallon pots)
Plant Profile: Page 303

'Florida Sweetheart' Caladium
(4 plants from 4.5" pots)
Plant Profile: Page 284

Chapter 11

Year-Round Containers

Year-round containers are the ideal. We would love to plant a container once and have it stay like that for the rest of our lives. The only way to do that is with silk or plastic plants! Since plants grow, the roots need more space when they reach the edge of the pot. So, year-round containers don't mean you plant them and leave them forever. Rather, this chapter deals with plants that look good all year and do not go through any seasonal changes.

This chapter does not include plants that flower seasonally - only those that flower all year. Unfortunately, most plants have a shorter blooming season, like summer or winter. Blooming all the time is similar to being pregnant all the time - a not-too-frequent occurrence.

Many evergreen plants, like palms and podocarpus, do quite well in containers. This chapter features the best of them.

Left: Pots of ruellia provide color mainly during the warm months, while impatiens bloom during cooler weather. However, the pinwheel jasmine, the strong vertical shapes, and the undulating hedge in this landscape design provide interest all year in this garden designed by Sanchez and Maddux of Palm Beach.
Light: Full sun.
Season: Year round.
Lifespan: Ruellia lasts for years in the ground. They need transplanting annually.
Care: Plant with time-release fertilizer that includes minor elements. Repeat every three months. Water two to three times a week or when soil feels dry.
Pot: Balazara 'Italian Conca Toscana', 17"H x 24"W.

Above: A container this lovely looks great empty. This is another striking landscape by Sanchez and Maddux of Palm Beach.

Top 12 Container Plants that Grow **Year Round**

Anthuriums

Anthuriums bloom all the time and have the ability to stay in the same container for years. Although they are quite cold-sensitive, they are also tolerant of very low light. This means you can bring them inside for extended periods during cold spells, as long as you move them out again within a month or so.

Bromeliads

Although most bromeliads don't offer constant color, they produce spectacular flowers that bloom for months with very little care. They also have the ability to stay in the same container for years on end.

Crotons

Crotons produce constant color with very little care. They are not anywhere near as thirsty as many other colorful container plants. They also offer the benefit of being happy in the same container for years.

Dracaenas

Talk about low maintenance! An dracaenas love containers, lastin in the same pot for years. The one pictured is 'Lemon Lime', which features unique, two-tone green and lime striped leaves.

Elephant Ears

I tested the *Colocasia illustris* (above) and am very impressed with the length of time it lasted in the same container - it's going on eight months now, and it still looks great. This plant has required very little care - only occasional fertilization and removal of dead leaves.

Goldilocks

This is a new plant for our container trials, and we just love it! It is attractive, versatile, easy, and dependable. The lime green color is great for many striking combinations, and the trailing growth habit is quite useful. The unique texture also adds to its value in container gardens.

Ivy

Ivy is one of the most useful container plants from our trials. I buy the small containers that are almost always at the garden centers and pull small pieces of ivy off the main root ball. They come apart easily, making it possible to tuck them into many different container styles for an instant trailing effect.

Palms

Palms are easy in containers. They also do not require freque transplanting, remaining happy the same container for well over a year. Since many palms are inexpensive in Florida, they giv you the opportunity of instant container height.

Sweet Potato Vines

These are the fastest-growing trailers we have. They come in three colors - lime green, dark bluish black, and the mixed colors of the tricolor, shown above. Although they offer almost instant maturity, they require a lot of water and snail bait to combat frequent snail attacks.

Ti Plants

Ti plants offer constant color with little care. They are also happy in the same container for more time than most colorful plants, although not as long as crotons. And ti plants make great instant centerpieces.

Trailing Torenia

Trailing torenia blooms all the time and lasts longer than any other blooming trailer we tried - up to a year with constant flowers. Do not confuse its performance with that of its close relative, upright torenia, which lasts only a few months in a container.

White Bird of Paradise

I once kept a white bird in a 30' diameter container on my porch for five years without transplanting. The pot received rainwater and was so large it held enough water, I seldom had to add any water.

Bismarckia Palm
Plant Profile: Page 331

Yellow Firecracker
Plant Profile: Page 295

Variegated Ivy
Plant Profile: Page 300

Bismarckia palms are not uncommon in Florida, but in New York? Yes, I found this gorgeous specimen underplanted with yellow firecracker and ivy at Landcraft Environments on Long Island, New York. Owned by Dennis Schrader and Bill Smith, this unique nursery specializes in tropicals. Dennis, along with Susan Roth, wrote a great book called "Hot Plants for Cool Climates: Gardening with Tropical Plants in Temperate Zones."

Light: Light shade to full sun.
Season: All year.
Lifespan: This plant mix lasts about a year in the same container. Transplant the palm and firecracker to your garden (zones 10-11) when they outgrow the pot.
Care: Fertilize with a slow-release mix on planting day, and repeat every two to three months. Water when the soil feels dry to the touch (see pages 338-340). Trim the firecracker and ivy as needed.
Pot: Source unknown.

Year-Round Plants for Containers, Arranged by Size

TRAILING

DWARF CHENILLE · GOLDILOCKS · IVY · LICORICE PLANT · MINT, VARIEGATED · POTHOS

SWEET POTATO · TRAILING TORENIA · VINCA 'ILLUMINATION'

UNDER 1'

BROMELIAD · CACTUS · CROWN OF THORNS · FERN, WART · GRASS, DWARF SWEET FLAG · GRASS, FIBER OPTIC

JUNIPER, SHORE · KALANCHOE THURSIFOLIA · MINT, VARIEGATED · PERILLA 'MAGILLA' · PURPLE QUEEN · SEDUM

SNAKE PLANT · SUCCULENTS

1' - 3'

AGAVE · ANTHURIUM · ARBORICOLA · BEGONIA, ORANGE ANGELWING · BEGONIA, PINK ANGELWING · BROMELIAD

CACTUS · CAST IRON PLANT · CHINESE EVERGREEN · COPPERLEAF · CROTON · CROWN OF THO

DESERT ROSE · DIEFFENBACHIA · DRACAENA REFLEXA · ELEPHANT EAR · FERN, FISHTAIL · FERN, WART

1' - 3'

GRASS, FOUNTAIN

IRIS, WALKING

JATROPHA

PALM, CARDBOARD

PALM, CAT

PEACE LILY

PENTAS

PERILLA 'MAGILLA'

PERSIAN SHIELD

PODOCARPUS

SHRIMP PLANT

SNAKE PLANT

SNOWBUSH

SUCCULENTS

TI PLANT

ZZ PLANT

2.5' - 4'

AGAVE

ARBORICOLA

BEGONIA, PINK ANGELWING

BIRD OF PARADISE, WHITE

BROMELIAD

CACTUS

COPPERLEAF

CORN PLANT

CROTON

DESERT ROSE

DIEFFENBACHIA

DRACAENA MARGINATA

DRACAENA REFLEXA

ELEPHANT EAR

EUGENIA

FICUS TREE

FIDDLE-LEAF FIG

GRASS, FOUNTAIN

JATROPHA

PALM, ARECA

PALM, BAMBOO

PALM, CARDBOARD

PALM, CAT

PALM, FISHTAIL

PALM, LADY

PALM, PYGMY DATE

PALM, THATCH

PEACE LILY

PERILLA 'MAGILLA'

PODOCARPUS

Year Round Plants for Containers, Arranged by Size

2.5' - 4'

RUBBER PLANT

SHRIMP PLANT

SILVER BUTTONWOOD

SNAKE PLANT

SNOWBUSH

TI PLANT

ZZ PLANT

4' - 6'

ARBORICOLA

BEGONIA, PINK ANGELWING

BIRD OF PARADISE, WHITE

CACTUS

CORN PLANT

CROTON

DRACAENA MARGINATA

DRACAENA REFLEXA

ELEPHANT EAR

EUGENIA

FICUS TREE

FIDDLE-LEAF

JATROPHA

PALM, ALEXANDER

PALM, ARECA

PALM, BAMBOO

PALM, CARDBOARD

PALM, CAT

PALM, FISHTAIL

PALM, KENTIA

PALM, LADY

PALM, PYGMY DATE

PALM, THATCH

PALM, TRAVEL

PALM, CHRISTMAS

PODOCARPUS

RUBBER PLANT

SHRIMP PLANT

SILVER BUTTONWOOD

TI PLANT

6' - 8'

ARBORICOLA

BIRD OF PARADISE, WHITE

CACTUS

CORN PLANT

DRACAENA MARGINATA

DRACAENA REFLEXA

6' - 8'

EUGENIA

FICUS TREE

FIDDLE-LEAF FIG

PALM, ALEXANDER

PALM, ARECA

PALM, BAMBOO

PALM, FISHTAIL

PALM, KENTIA

PALM, LADY

PALM, PYGMY DATE

PALM, THATCH

PALM, TRAVELER'S

PALM, XMAS

PODOCARPUS

RUBBER PLANT

SILVER
BUTTONWOOD

**FLOWERING
STANDARDS
4' - 8'**
(ALL FLOWERING OR
COLORED-LEAF TREES)

JATROPHA

SNOWBUSH

8' - 15'

BIRD OF PARADISE,
WHITE

FIDDLE-LEAF FIG

PALM, ALEXANDER

PALM, FISHTAIL

PALM, KENTIA

PALM, TRAVELER'S

PALM, XMAS

PODOCARPUS

RUBBER PLANT

Year-Round Containers

Balazara's classic Italian pots are filled with year-round plants to accent these gardens.

Above: The centerpiece container of the courtyard (above) is planted with a lemon tree.

Left: Another fruit tree, a kumquat, grows happily in the handsome container shown left.

Right: This Eugenia topiary looks smashing in the *Vaso Festonato* container.

For container sources, go to www.easygardencolor.com

Left: Balazara containers planted with low-water agaves grace the entry to this home. Columns are a natural place for containers. The proportion and shape of these low, round containers complement the shape of the column.

Agaves are very easy to grow but the ones with sharp spines should not be placed in areas like this that are near walkways.

Right: In this North Palm Beach model home, an empty corner of the fountained courtyard comes alive with an eclectic mixture of pots and sun-hardy plants. The tall Greek oil jar (called a *stamna*) complements Balazara's *Vaso Festonato* (planted with areca palms) as well as the colorful Majolica ceramic pots. The variety of pots adds interest to what would have otherwise been dead space.

Left: No effort was spared to lend authenticity to this French style home in Wellington's equestrian district. However, substitutes have to be found for the Italian cypress, typical of formal French gardens, since it does not fare well in south Florida's climate. Here, Sanchez & Maddux, landscape architects from Palm Beach, have used podocarpus to achieve the same effect. Pots: Balazara's *Vaso Orlando*, 30"H x 46" W.

Containers as Architectural Accents.

With only four inches of depth in this roof-top garden, Palm Beach Landscape Architects Sanchez & Maddux chose to lay sod in a checkerboard pattern, interspersed with stepping stones to cover this surface. The container plantings add height in this formal Italian design. Jorge Sanchez often uses containers strictly as accent pieces because they add a more structural element to the garden. "Sometimes, I leave the containers for last because they help tie the garden together," Sanchez says. "I especially appreciate their adaptability because containers change with the architecture of the house." The podocarpus planted in the Italian pots eventually grew big enough to be shaped into tall, topiary pyramids.

Light: Full sun.
Season: Year round.
Lifespan: Remains in a pot this size about two years. After that, either trim the roots of the plant and place it back in the same pot or transplant it into the garden, where it will live another 20 years or so.
Care: Plant with time-release fertilizer that includes minor elements. Repeat every three months. Water two to three times a week or when soil feels dry.
Pot: Balazara, *Italian Vaso Festonato*, 27"H x 34"W.

in a roof-top garden

Tips for Growing Herbs...

Cooks know that fresh herbs have a much better quality than dried herbs. And, herbs are ideal for container planting. Even if you have very little space, you can grow an herb garden with a lot of variety. Remember, most herbs are annuals or short-lived perennials in Florida, so they don't last forever. If you want some variety in little space, use strawberry pots or tiered planters, like the ones shown.

An excellent reference for local herb growing is "Herbs and Spices for Florida Gardens" by Monica B. Brandeis.

I buy herbs in small pots at the grocery store or garden center and simply replace them once they die.

Left: This strawberry pot from Anamese is an ideal container for herbs. The side pockets fit 4.5" pots easily. And, it is quite easy to water. I do the top and the side pockets separately, which negates the need for a pipe down the middle of the pot, typical of many strawberry jars.

I bought all these herbs at the same time at Fresh Market in Boca Raton. They were in 6" pots, so I soaked the roots in water and sqeezed them a little to fit them in the side pockets.

I like to use herbs for cooking but don't know too much about growing them. I have a simple system that works. Keep a pot that can fit lots of herbs near the kitchen. Be sure the space gets at least a half a day of sun. Buy herbs when you are at the grocery store or nursery in 4.5" or 6" inch pots. Plant them, and replace the ones that die as needed.

Above: This three-tier planter from Kinsman Company is ideal for growing a variety of herbs. You can grow a complete herb garden right outside your kitchen in a space that's only three foot square! This planter includes pineapple mint, silver and golden thymes, basils, parsley, lavender, rosemary, sage, oregano, trailing tarragon, chives, and more! My thanks to Kinsman Company for this photo. The same planter is shown on page 207 but is planted with flowers and sweet potato vines; that one is found in my trial gardens. I have had that container in the same spot for six years, and it shows no signs of rust! The planter measures 23" wide by 36" tall.

Year-Round Color...

Both perennial begonias and dracaenas are easy to grow all year long in Florida. Begonias are a large plant family - many of which are annuals. The pink angelwing is one of the strongest perennials. The tricolor dracaena is similar to the more common dracaena marginata but offers more leaf color.

Above: Pink angelwing begonias are one of the few perennials that bloom every day of the year.
Light: Medium to light shade. Takes full sun in the cool season, but needs shade in the summer.
Season: All year. Blooms more during the cool season.
Lifespan: About five months in this container. Transplant it into your garden if you live in zones 9b-11.
Care: Fertilize on planting day, and repeat in three months. Water thoroughly when the soil feels dry to the touch, every few days (see pages 338-340).
Pot: Global Pottery *Ribbed Planter* in bronze from their Fiberglass Collection (20"W x 13.5"H).

Right: Dracaenas are one of the easiest container plants except for the fact that they drop a lot. Here, tricolor dracaena is combined with *Syngonium 'Bold Allusion'* and blue peacock fern.
Light: Medium to light shade.
Season: All year.
Lifespan: About five to seven months in this container. Transplant the dracaena into your garden if you live in zones 9b-11.
Care: Fertilize on planting day, and repeat in three months. Water thoroughly when the soil feels dry to the touch, every few days (see pages 338-340).
Pot: Lotus International, #GRS-1524 (15" W x 12" H). Color is dark red-orange but it looks brown.

Dracaenas and Perennial Begonias

Tricolor Dracaena
(1 plant from a three-gallon pot)
Plant Profile: Page 293

Syngonium 'Bold Allusion'
(2 plants from one-gallon pots)
Plant Profile: Page 325

Blue Peacock Fern
(1 plant from a 6" pot)
Plant Profile: Page 329

Year-Round Topiaries...

Topiaries are plants that are trimmed into various shapes. Look for slow-growing plants for topiaries because they don't need constant trimming. Podocarpus (above) and Eugenia compacta (below) are ideal because they grow both densely and slowly. Dress your topiary up by underplanting it with annuals, as shown in five of these examples from Universal Orlando Resort.

and palms

Palms are ideal for containers, lasting quite awhile in the same one. They look good when under-planted with smaller plants. The multi-trunked Christmas palm (right) is underplanted with coleus, alyssum, and New Guinea impatiens. These annuals are replaced seasonally. The areca palm, below, is underplanted with pothos and bromeliads. The pothos will last for years in the same pot. The bromeliads are changed when they stop flowering. Both of these palms were photographed at The Breakers in Palm Beach, Florida.

Year-Round Color

'Zebra Sunset' Canna Flower
(2 plants from three-gallon pots)
Plant Profile: Page 285

Ti 'Madame Chaoul'
(1 plant from a three gallon pot)
Plant Profile: Page 325

'Zebra Sunset' Canna Leaf
(2 plants from three-gallon pots)
Plant Profile: Page 285

Above: I planted this arrangement to last through the summer and was delighted to see it grow all year! The winter was warm, and the cannas, which normally die back in winter, breezed right through it.
Light: Light shade to full sun.
Season: All year. Protect from freezes.
Lifespan: The arrangement lasts for about 2 years in this container.
Care: Fertilize when planting, and repeat every three months with a slow-release mix. Water when soil feels dry. Groom when necessary - trim off brown leaves and flowers.
Container: Sabu *Four Lion* pot that measures19.5"H x 30" W.

Right: A Jatropha standard underplanted with Mammey Crotons. We soaked the root balls so we could fit them in this pot.
Light: Light shade to full sun.
Season: All year. Protect from freezes.
Lifespan: The arrangement lasts for about six months in this container. Transplant the plants into a frost-free garden, or move them into a larger pot at that time.
Care: Fertilize when planting, and repeat every three months with a slow-release mix. Water when soil feels dry. Trim the plants hard once a year in the summer, which leaves them bare for a time.
Container: Global Pottery's *Fiberglass Lattice Box*, 20"H x 20"D x 20"W. This pot is not only lightweight, it also looks just like metal but doesn't rust.

Jatropha
(1 plant from a seven-gallon pot)
Plant Profile: Page 301

Mammey Crotons
(5 plants from one-gallon pots)
Plant Profile: Page 288

Chapter 12
Low-Water Containers

Watering is the highest maintenance activity with container gardening. Many containers need daily watering, especially if they are in the sun. This chapter covers ways to cut down on the work involved in this monotonous task.

Plants need more water in containers than they do in the ground. A plant's roots can spread quite a distance when the plant is in the ground. This large root system gives the plant more area in which to absorb and store water.

Automatic sprinkler systems make watering much easier. See pages 338-340 to learn about them and other important watering basics. These pages also discuss water-saving polymers.

Here are some important factors that affect water use:

1. Sun or shade. Plants use half as much water in shade than in full sun.
2. Temperature. Plants use more water when the temperatures are high. I do not have many containers out in bright sun in July and August because I can't keep up with the watering.
3. Wind. Plants in windy areas require more water than plants in calm areas.
4. Reflections from walls. If you have a light-colored wall facing south with no shade, you may have to plant succulents to take the reflected heat.
5. Soil. Good-quality potting soil usually includes peat moss, which holds water better than cheaper, sandy soils.
6. Plant type. Plant species vary in their need for water. Impatiens, for example, need much more water than cactus.
7. Container size. Large containers with small plants require much less water than small containers filled to the brim with large plants.
8. Container type. We didn't notice a significant difference between the material used to make a container and water use.
9. How long the plant has been in the container. As plants age in containers, their roots fill the pot, leaving less space for water, so they need watering more often.

Left: A fabulous desert rose. Above: Small plants in large pots don't require watering as often as large plants in small pots. The coleus are planted in a very large pot that is 30" tall. They only need water about once a week.

Low-Water Container Plants, Arranged by Size

TRAILING

IVY

POTHOS

UNDER 1'

BROMELIAD

CACTUS

CROWN OF THORNS

JUNIPER

KALANCHOE

KALANCHO
THURSIFOLI

MOSS ROSE

PEPEROMIA

PURPLE QUEEN

PURSLANE

SEDUM

SNAKE PLAN

SUCCULENTS

1' - 3'

AGAVE

ANTHURIUM

ARBORICOLA

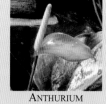
BROMELIAD

CACTUS

CAST IRON PL

CROTON

CROWN OF THORNS

DESERT ROSE

DRACAENA

PALM, CARDBOARD

SNAKE PLAN

SUCCULENTS

2.5' - 4'

AGAVE

ARBORICOLA

BROMELIAD

CACTUS

CROTONS

DESERT ROS

se plants need water at the most about once a week, if they are growing in shade and away from a lot of wind. This doesn't mean you have to r them once a week if they are outside because we normally get rain at least once a week for about 80 per cent of the year.

2.5' - 4'

DRACAENA PALM, CARDBOARD PALM, PYGMY DATE SNAKE PLANT

4' - 6'

ARBORICOLA CACTUS CROTONS PALM, PYGMY DATE

6' - 8'

ARBORICOLA CACTUS DRACAENA PALM, PYGMY DATE

Bromeliads do not require a lot of water, particularly if they are kept in shade. These pots are from Balazara.

Think Shade to Save Water

Container plants use much less water in shade. Many of our shade containers receive only rainwater for most of the year. We supplement them with a hose during the rare weeks when we go a full seven days without water - that is, if we remember! The pots on these two pages use low-water, shade plants that look attractive with very little water other than rainwater.

Above: This metal container, lined in moss, is planted with four, low-water plants: a snake plant, *Dracaena reflexa,* variegated peperomia, and ivy. I found this at Giverney Gardens in Jupiter, Florida.
Light: Medium shade.
Season: All year. Protect from freezes.
Lifespan: The arrangement lasts about four to six months in this container.
Care: Fertilize when planting and repeat every three months with a slow-release mix. Water when soil feels dry. This low-water arrangement should only need water about once a week in the shade.
Container: Giverney Gardens in Jupiter.

Left: This arrangement, designed by Sanchez and Maddux, landscape architects, Palm Beach, features bromeliads and ivy. These plants need little supplemental water when kept in shade.
Light: Light to medium shade.
Season: All year. Protect from freezes.
Lifespan: The arrangement lasts about six to nine months in this container.
Care: Fertilize when planting, and repeat every three months with a slow-release mix. Water when soil feels dry. This low-water arrangement should only need water about once a week in the shade.
Container: Source unknown.

Don't Forget Self-Watering Pots

The Planter Technology system for self-watering containers consists of a liner (shown, above left) and an outer, decorative pot (shown, above right). The liner has thick, double walls in which water is stored. The water is put in through the capped hole shown below. It flows into the potting soil as the plant needs it through an interior tube.

Plant the plant in the liner and then put the whole thing inside the decorative pot. This system is ideal for this variegated costus plant, which requires quite a bit of water when it is planted in a container.

Use Low-Water Plants...

like these succulents.

My first experiences with cacti and succulents in south Florida were not good. They thrived in the dry season and died from too much water in the wet season. I thought they were not adapted to south Florida, only the desert. I have since learned otherwise. Many cacti and succulents are native to areas that are similar to Florida, with a rainy season. And they are tough plants, well-adapted not only to drought situations but also areas of high salt and wind.

These two containers were designed and planted by Alan Stopek of Efflorescence, a nursery in Loxahatchee, Florida (www.efflor.com). He has containers with succulents on his patio that have been planted for years, and he rarely waters them. If we have no rain, he waters them every two to three weeks. They grow slowly and have few problems with disease or insects. Many of these plants can be maintained in the same pot for a very long time.

Left: Strawberry jars are excellent containers for mixed succulent gardens.
Light: Light shade to full sun.
Season: All year. Protect from freezes.
Lifespan: The arrangement lasts for a few years in this container.
Care: Fertilize when planting, and repeat every three months with a slow-release mix. Water when soil feels VERY dry (see left sidebar). Groom when necessary - pull off the pups (new plants) to maintain strong plants.
Container: Anamese blue strawberry jar (24"H x 20"W).

Above: This low, square bowl in blue shows off this succulent garden well.
Light: Light shade to full sun.
Season: All year. Protect from freezes.
Lifespan: The arrangement lasts for a few years in this container.
Care: Fertilize when planting, and repeat every three months with a slow-release mix. Water when soil feels VERY dry (see left sidebar). Groom when necessary - pull off the pups (new plants) to maintain strong plants.
Container: Sunlight low bowl, square, 17" diameter.

Agave univitata | Echeveria spp. | Aloe 'Black Doran' | Senecio radicans 'String of Bananas' | Aloe spinossissima
Echeveria spp. | Aloe vera | Portulacara afra variegated | Kalanchoe thursifolia | Aloe 'White Tooth'

More Ideas with Low-Water Plants

The staff at Giverney Gardens, a garden center in Jupiter, tell me that many of their customers want low-water container arrangements. So much so that they have a whole section of low-water plants in the garden center. Judy Traver, the manager of Giverney, created these arrangements to show that low-water doesn't have to be blah and boring! The mixture of colors and textures works quite well. Spiky plants work particularly well as centerpieces.

Right: Terra cotta container filled with low-water plants.
Light: Full sun.
Season: Warm months because the mandeville and portulaca are only available then.
Lifespan: About four to six months in this container.
Care: Fertilize when planting, and repeat every three months with a slow-release mix. Water when soil feels dry. Groom when necessary - remove dead leaves and overgrowth.
Container: 20" W, rolled-rim terra cotta container from Giverney Gardens, Jupiter

| **Purslane** (2 plants from one-gallon pots) Profile: Page320 | **Jewel of Opar** (2 plants from one-gallon pots) Profile: Page 331 | **Walking Iris** (1 plant from a one-gallon pot) Profile: Page 331 | **Diplademia** (1 plant from a one-gallon pot) Profile: Page 329 | **Rosemary** (1 plant from a one-gallon pot) Info: Page 242 |

Puerto Rican Purslane
(3 plants from one-gallon pots)
Plant Profile: Page 320

Yellow African Iris
(2 plants from one-gallon pots)
Plant Profile: Page 331

Devil's Backbone
(1 plant from a one-gallon pot)
Plant Profile: Page 329

Above: Low bowl filled to the brim with low-water plants.
Light: Full sun.
Season: Warm months because of the purslane. The other plants grow throughout the year if you protect them from freezes.
Lifespan: About four to six months in this container.
Care: Fertilize when planting, and repeat every three months with a slow-release mix. Water when soil feels dry. Groom when necessary - remove dead leaves and overgrowth.
Container: From Giverney Gardens, Jupiter.

Chapter 13

Containers for Salt and Wind

Salt and wind are hard on plants. Even the strongest plants native to beach areas show leaf burn fairly routinely in Florida. However, there is a lot you can do with container gardens in these difficult areas if you learn some basics:

1. It is important to know the amount of salt and wind your area gets. See the next page for information.

2. Ideas using dynamite containers planted with simple plants are shown throughout this chapter. If the tough environment kills the plants, at least you'll have the containers! And don't forget annuals. They are so inexpensive that you won't lose much if they get damaged.

3. The plant charts on pages 264-267 are great reference tools for choosing plants for this tough environment.

Left and above: Bromeliads with thick leaves take salt and wind well. Look how nice these simple plantings look in these beautiful, glazed containers from Sunlight, a wholesaler in Ft. Lauderdale. I took the empty containers to Tropical World Nursery in Boynton Beach to see what creative ideas they could come up with for this difficult environment. This nursery has a wonderful assortment of bromeliads, and the staff are experts in their use and care.

Assessing Your Location

Oceanfront Sites

Direct oceanfront sites (for example, on top of a dune) are easy to assess. They are very difficult for plants and need ones that can withstand high wind and salt. Areas very near the shoreline are traditionally landscaped with plants that are native to these areas. These plants are not within the focus of this book but are covered very well in "Seashore Plants of South Florida and the Caribbean" by David W. Nellis. Areas slightly back from the shore, but still within sight of the water, are ideal for the plants in this book that are classified as high-salt-and-wind-tolerant. And don't forget the impact of containers - simple plantings in fabulous containers have a strong impact.

Sites along Inland Waterways or Near the Ocean but not Directly on It

Plants with medium salt and wind tolerance do well in the majority of these sites. Exceptions include areas that are open to very wide expanses of water, where high winds are frequently a problem, or areas that get direct salt spray from a waterway. Use plants for high wind and salt in these locations. Other tricky locations are wind tunnels created by buildings. These frequently occur on the sides of buildings and definitely call for plants that are tolerant of high winds. Residents of these properties are the best sources of information about winds.

Expect Wind Damage on even the Most Tolerant Plants

Every few years, much of Florida experiences a winter storm that brings 30 to 40 mile per hour winds to our beach areas for a few days in a row. About a month later, my phone starts to ring. Many people ask questions about why their landscape has so many brown tips on its leaves. Wind damage often shows up about a month after the wind event (unless, of course, it is a hurricane). It is mainly characterized by brown tips on the leaves. Even the most wind-tolerant plants, like coconut palms (which are naturalized to beach areas all over the world), have brown tips on their leaves after a wind storm. The brown tips do not heal, but the leaves are eventually replaced with new growth. Occasionally tolerating brown leaf tips is a small price to pay for living near the ocean.

Simple, Creative Ideas

Left: This container garden on an inland waterway is fairly protected from both wind and salt spray. Many beautiful flowers are at home here.

Right: How about a container with no plants at all? I found this creative arrangement at Giverney Gardens in Jupiter.

Below: This simple blue bowl (from Sunlight, a wholesaler in Fort Lauderdale) is planted with just one 'Fiber Optic' grass. I found the shiny, black stones at Giverney Gardens. They added just the finishing touch this arrangement needed. The investment is in the pot and stones. If the plant dies, it is easy and inexpensive to replace.

Salt-and-Wind-Tolerant Plants for Containers, Arranged by Size

TRAILING

BLUE DAZE
M, H

BOUGAINVILLEA
M

GERANIUM
M, H

'GOLDILOCKS'
M

IVY
M

**LAMIUM, 'W
NANCY'** M

LANTANA, PURPLE
M, H

LANTANA, YELLOW
M, H

LOBELIA
M

PETUNIAS
M, H

POTHOS
M

SCAEVOLA
M, H

SWEET POTATO
M

TRAILING TORENA
M

VERBENA
M

VINCA
'ILLUMINATION' M

UNDER 1'

AGERATUM
M

ALYSSUM
M

**BEGONIA, DRAGON
WING** M

**BEGONIA,
TUBEROUS** M

BEGONIA, WAX
M

BLUE DAZE
M, H

BROMELIAD
M, H

CALADIUM
M

CROWN OF THORNS
M, H

**DAISY, CALIFORNIA
BUSH** M

**DAISY,
MARGUERITE** M

DIASCIA
M

DUSTY MILLER
M

**GRASS, 'DWARF
SWEET FLAG'** M

**GRASS, 'FIBER
OPTIC'** M

**GRASS, 'FROSTED
CURLS'** M

HIBISCUS
M

**IMPATIENS, NE
GUINEA** M

JUNIPER, SHORE
M, H

KALANCHOE
M

LANTANA, PURPLE
M, H

LANTANA, YELLOW
M, H

LOBELIA
M

MARIGOLDS
M

MOSS ROSE
M, H

PETUNIAS
M, H

PURPLE QUEEN
M, H

PURSLANE
M, H

ROSE
M

**SALVIA, 'VICTO
BLUE'** M, H

UNDER 1'

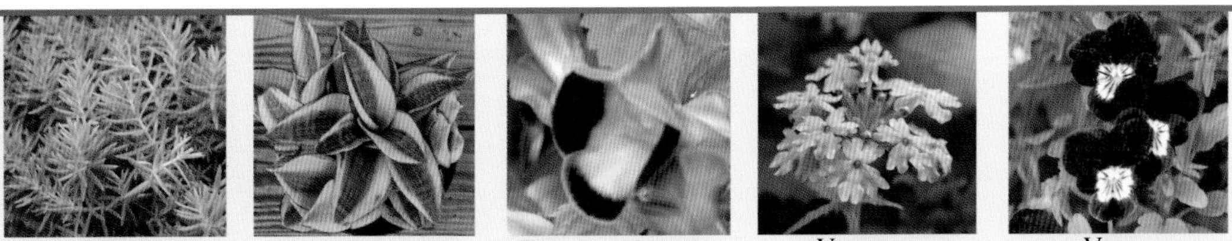

SEDUM M	SNAKE PLANT M, H	TORENIA, UPRIGHT M	VERBENA M	VIOLA M

1' - 3'

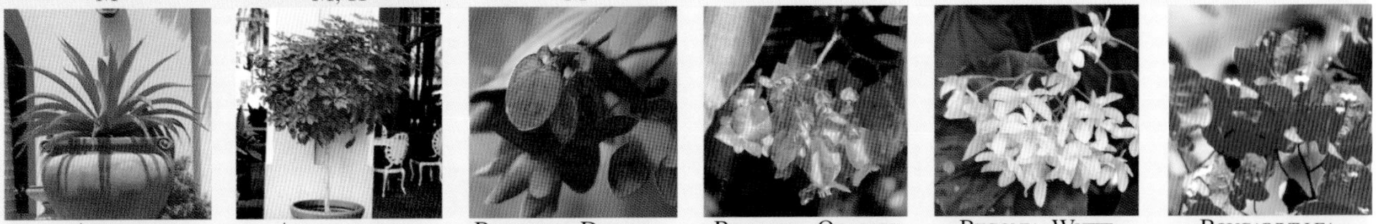

AGAVE M	ARBORICOLA M, H	BEGONIA, DRAGON WING M	BEGONIA, ORANGE ANGELWING M	BEGONIA, WHITE 'ODORATA M	BOUGAINVILLEA M
BROMELIAD M, H	CALADIUM M	CAST IRON PLANT M	COPPERLEAF M	CROTON M	CROWN OF THORNS M, H
DAISY, CALIFORNIA BUSH M	DESERT ROSE M	DRACAENA REFLEXA M	FRANGIPANI M, H	GERANIUM M, H	GRASS, FOUNTAIN M
HIBISCUS M	IMPATIENS, NEW GUINEA M	JATROPHA M	LANTANA, YELLOW M, H	MELAMPODIUM M	PALM CARDBOARD M
PENTAS M	PLUMBAGO M	PODOCARPUS M	ROSE M	SALVIA, 'VICTORIA BLUE' M, H	SNAKE PLANTS M, H
SNOWBUSH M					

2.5' - 4'

AGAVE M	ARBORICOLA M, H	BEGONIA, WHITE 'ODORATA' M	BOUGAINVILLEA M	BROMELIAD M, H	COPPERLEAF M

2.5' - 4'

CORN PLANT
M

CROTON
M

DESERT ROSE
M

DRACAENA
MARGINATA M

DRACAENA
REFLEXA M

EUGENIA
M

FICUS TREE
M

FIDDLE-LEAF FIG
M

FRANGIPANI
M, H

GRASS, FOUNTAIN
M

HIBISCUS
M

JATROPHA
M

OLEANDER
M, H

PALM, CARDBOARD
M

PALM, PYGMY
DATE M, H

PALM, THATCH
M, H

PLUMBAGO
M

ROSE
M

RUBBER PLANT
M

SILVER BUTTONWOOD
M, H

SNAKE PLANT
M, H

SNOWBUSH
M

4' - 6'

ARBORICOLA
M, H

BOUGAINVILLEA
M

CORN PLANT
M

CROTON
M

DRACAENA
MARGINATA M

DRACAENA
REFLEXA M

EUGENIA
M

FICUS TREE
M

FIDDLE-LEAF FIG
M

FRANGIPANI
M, H

JATROPHA
M,

OLEANDER
M, H

PALM, ALEXANDER
M

PALM, CARDBOARD
M

PALM, CHRISTMAS
M

PALM, KENTIA
M

PALM, PYGMY DATE
M, H

PALM, THATCH
M, H

PLUMBAGO
M

PODOCARPUS
M

RUBBER PLANT
M

SILVER BUTTONWOOD
M, H

6' - 8'

ARBORICOLA
M, H

BOUGAINVILLEA
M

CORN PLANT
M

DRACAENA
MARGINATA M

DRACAENA
REFLEXA M

EUGENIA
M

FICUS TREE
M

FIDDLE-LEAF FIG
M

FRANGIPANI
M, H

OLEANDER
M

PALM, ALEXANDER
M

PALM, CHRISTMAS
M

PALM, KENTIA
M

PALM, PYGMY DATE
M, H

PALM, THATCH
M, H

PODOCARPUS
M

RUBBER PLANT
M

SILVER
BUTTONWOOD M, H

**FLOWERING
STANDARDS
4' - 8'**
(SMALL FLOWERING OR
COLORED-LEAF TREES)

BOUGAINVILLEA
M

CAPE HONEYSUCKLE
M

HIBISCUS
M

JATROPHA
M

SNOWBUSH
M

8' - 15'

FIDDLE-LEAF FIG
M

FRANGIPANI
M, H

OLEANDER
M, H

PALM, ALEXANDER
M

PALM, CHRISTMAS
M

PALM, KENTIA
M

PODOCARPUS
M

RUBBER PLANT
M

Salt-and-Wind-Tolerant Pots...

Left: Madagascar olive underplanted with kalanchoe. The kalanchoe is a winter bloomer but doesn't bloom continuously all season. However, it tolerates salt and wind quite well and adds a dazzling spot of color at the base of this tough tree.

Below: Rubber tree underplanted with kalanchoe.

Right: Cardboard palm underplanted with baby sun rose. With the beauty of the ocean behind it, this container looks great, even though it is quite simple. Cardboard palms are incredibly tough plants and quite useful in difficult environments.

from the Breakers of Palm Beach

Colorful Containers...

The quality of light near the sea is intense - so bright that pale colors have a tendency to bleach out in the daytime. Bright colors not only show up well but also have a sense of fit with the bright blue water. Both of the containers on these two pages are from Masart.

These two arrangements were designed and planted by Alan Stopek of Efflorescence, a nursery in Loxahatchee, Florida (www.efflor.com). He has containers with succulents on his patio that have been planted for years, and he rarely waters them. If we have no rain, he waters them every two to three weeks. They grow slowly and have few problems with disease or insects. Many of these plants can be maintained in the same pot for a very long time.

Most cacti and succulents do well in many difficult environments - both low-water and high-salt-and-wind situations.

work well near the sea

Yes, You Can Have Flowers...

Frangipani 'Pudica'
(1 plant from a 15-gallon pot)
Plant Profile: Page 330

Star Grass
(7 plants from one-gallon pots)
Plant Profile: Page 333

Left: This frangipani 'Pudica' is ideal for high-salt-and-wind situations. It is one of the few evergreen frangipanis. The white flowers are gorgeous. The challenge with this planting in a high-wind situation is keeping the tree from blowing out of the pot. Keep it near walls or in a similar situation that gives it some protection.

Light: Full sun.

Season: Although the frangipani is evergreen, it blooms more in the warm months. Protect from frost.

Lifespan: About one to two years in this container.

Care: Fertilize when planting, and repeat every three months with a slow-release mix. Water when soil feels dry. Groom when necessary - remove dead leaves and overgrowth.

Container: From Giverney Gardens, Jupiter. They also did the planting.

in even the most challenging areas.

Right: Hybrid crown of thorns (which did very well in our trials) and variegated confederate jasmine.
Light: Full sun.
Season: Year round. Protect from frost.
Lifespan: About one years in this container.
Care: Fertilize when planting, and repeat every three months with a slow-release mix. Water when soil feels very dry. Groom when necessary - remove dead leaves and overgrowth.
Container: From Giverney Gardens, Jupiter. They also did the planting.

Below: Geraniums and variegated ivy photographed at the Breakers in Palm Beach. It's amazing that such a beautiful arrangement is so tough!
Light: Full sun to light shade in the cool months.
Season: Year round. Protect from frost.
Lifespan: About four to six monthsin this container.
Care: Fertilize when planting, and repeat every three months with a slow-release mix. Water when soil feels dry. Groom when necessary - remove dead leaves and flowers.
Container: Source unknown.

Chapter 14

The Top 100 Plants

Lilac Impatiens
Plant Profile: Page 298

Coleus 'Wizard Golden'
Plant Profile: Page 285

Mammey Croton
Plant Profile: Page 288

'Odorata' Begonia
Plant Profile: Page 328

Salvia (annual)
Plant Profile: Page 321

In Florida, choosing plants for containers is a lot easier than choosing landscape plants. While our success rate for testing landscape plants is about ten percent, most of the container plants we tested worked fairly well. You don't have to contend with Florida soils in containers nor do you expect the plants to live for as long as landscape plants.

We planted about 10,000 plants during our two years of intense container trials. Some were superior, like coleus, while others were mediocre or inconsistent, like angelonia.

This chapter gives you plant profiles of the top 100 we tested, along with shorter descriptions of another sixty-four plants that deserve mention. But don't limit yourself to only these plants because container gardening gives you the opportunity to really have fun experimenting with new varieties. Let us know how you do at info@easygardencolor.com!

Above: A "leftover" basket mounted on a post. Read more about "leftover" baskets on page 89.

Left: We test plants grown in the ground as well as in containers. The success rate for plants in containers is much higher. Also, notice how well the baskets on posts coordinate with the garden underneath.

The Top 12 Container Plants...

Begonias of all types are ideally suited for containers. Many of them give constant bloom for an extended period of time with very little care.

Bromeliads are one of the top container plants because they need very little care, are quite dependable, and need little water to thrive.

Coleus is my favorite container plant because of its dependability, variety, and ease of care.

Crotons are one of the easiest container plants. They last for at least a year in the same pot, offering constant color in sun or shade. Crotons don't require much water or care of any kind.

Goldilocks (the lime green plant) is one of the easiest cascading plants. Although it grows slower than the sweet potato vine, it requires less water and trimming. This attractive plant is also relatively pest resistant.

Grasses make ideal centerpiece plants for a myriad of container styles. They give an interesting texture to the arrangement and are very easy to grow. Grasses last longer than most container plants.

A Great Place to Start!

Ivy is one of the most useful container plants. Remove it from the nursery pot, and pull the individual pieces apart at the roots. Tuck them along the edges of a pot.

Palms are great for containers because they last for several years in the same pot without requiring transplanting, and they are quite easy to grow.

Salvia (annual) thrives in Florida and is a fool-proof container plant as long as you use it at the right time of year (see page 321).

Succulents performed beautifully in our trials, requiring less water and maintenance than any other plants we tried (design by Alan Stopek).

Ti plants are easy and attractive, offering constant color with very little care. Their vertical shape is ideal for the centerpiece in many container styles.

Trailing torenia is the highest-performing flowering plant (with a cascading habit) from our trials. It produces lots of flowers any time of the year—provided it is protected from frost.

Plant Profiles: The Top 100

Agastache *(Agastache spp.)*

Characteristics and Care

Use: Centerpiece plant.
Growth rate: Fast.
Size: About 12 to 18 inches tall by 8 inches wide.
Colors: Pink and peach tones.
Average life: Although it is grown as a perennial farther north, use as an annual in Florida.
Cautions: None known.
Care: Very easy. Plant with slow-release fertilizer, and leave them alone! Fertilize again in 2 or 3 months. Trim off the tips if the plants become too large.
Scent: Smells like anise and attracts pollinators.

Agastache performed wonderfully in our trial gardens once we figured out that it didn't bloom in winter. It needs longer days to bloom and came into its glory in April, lasting until June. The Salmon-Pink Bicolor from Bodger Botanical's Acapulco series (above) was our favorite and got more comments than any other plant at one of our garden tours. We had good luck with it in pots and in the ground as well.

Companions: We particularly liked it in the green pots shown on page 51. In that arrangement, we mixed it with pinks and purples. Agastache's spiky texture contrasts well with round flowers like petunias.

Growing Conditions

Season: Spring. Ours thrived from April until June.
Light: We tested them only in full sun.
Water: Medium.
Salt tolerance: Unknown.
Wind tolerance: Unknown.
Zone: Use as an annual in Florida.
Pest problems: Fungus.

See page 51 for some great companions for agastache.

Agave *(Agave spp.)*

Characteristics and Care

Use: Primarily used as a centerpiece plant or a single specimen.
Growth rate: Slow.
Size: Many different sizes available, up to 6 feet tall by 6 feet wide.
Colors: Green, silvery green, or variegated.
Average life: 10 to 30 years in the landscape.
Cautions: Many (but not all) agaves have very sharp tips that can inflict significant injury. And, the sap is a serious skin toxin, so be sure to wear long sleeves and gloves when trimming. Do not touch your eyes with the sap, or you could get a nasty infection.

Agaves not only offer bold, tropical texture but are also very easy to grow. If they receive rainwater, they seldom if ever need supplemental watering. And, they are quite tolerant of neglect - if you forget to fertilize them, they might not even notice! But look out for the varieties with sharp spines along the leaves because they can cause serious injuries. Some people trim the spines off the leaves. There are over 300 different kinds of agaves, many with no spines at all.

Companions: Agaves look particularly good when mixed with succulents.

Growing Conditions

Season: Year round.
Light: Full sun for best performance, although it takes some shade.
Water: Low. Grows in containers outside with only rainwater.
Salt tolerance: High.
Wind tolerance: High.
Zone: Grows in all of Florida.
Pest problems: Occasional scales.
Care: Very easy. Plant with slow-release fertilizer, and leave them alone! Fertilize again in 2 or 3 months. Carefully remove the old leaves when they die (see "Cautions" in opposite blue column).

Alyssum *(Lobularia maritima)*

Characteristics and Care

Use: Mounding plant that cascades slightly along the edges of any pot. Doesn't work in the sides of hanging baskets.
Growth rate: Medium.
Size: 3 to 6 inches tall by 8 inches wide.
Colors: White and different shades of rose, and purple.
Average life: A few months.
Cautions: None known.
Care: Very easy. Plant with slow-release fertilizer, and repeat every two to three months. **Also see pages 40-41 in "Best Garden Color for Florida" to learn about this plant in the landscape.**

Alyssum is a beautiful, sweet-smelling annual that grows fairly well in Florida provided it doesn't freeze or get too much heat. Although alyssum is not quite as dependable as impatiens or begonias, it is well worth the small cost because it gives a unique and lovely look to a container arrangement, particularly if planted at the edge of the pot. It is easier to grow in containers than in the ground. The white did better than the purple or rose in my trials.
Companions: Use alyssum with plants that have larger flowers and leaves. A classic, can't miss combination combines alyssum with geraniums and petunias.

Growing Conditions

Season: Cool-season annual. Plant in December or January in south Florida and around February 15 in central Florida. In north Florida, plant as soon as danger of frost has ended. Do not plant in summer!
Light: Full sun.
Water: Medium. Do not overwater or the plant will get fungus. But if you let the plant dry out completely, parts of it will turn brown.
Salt tolerance: Medium.
Wind tolerance: Medium.
Zone: 3 to 11.
Pest problems: None known.

Anthurium *(Anthurium spp.)*

Characteristics and Care

Use: Centerpiece.
Growth rate: Medium.
Size: The different types average 12 to 18 inches tall by 6 to 12 inches wide.
Colors: Pink, peach, orange, red, and white.
Average life: 2 to 10 years.
Cautions: Irritant.
Care: Very easy. Plant with slow-release fertilizer, and leave them alone! Fertilize again in 2 or 3 months. Trim off yellow leaves as they appear. One advantage to using anthuriums in containers is that they can stay in the same pot for at least a year.

Anthuriums are one of the easiest and longest-lasting container plants. They bloom all the time, need very little care or water, and can stay in the same pot for at least a year. They also bloom in less light than any other plant in this book. Plant your anthuriums in pots small enough to move inside during cold spells because they don't like temperatures below 45 degrees. Some people say they grow well for extended periods indoors, but mine didn't thrive inside for long.
Companions: Use anthuriums with tropical plants, like bromeliads, palms, crotons, or shrimp plants. **See pages 40 and 150 for more companion ideas.**

Growing Conditions

Season: Anthuriums bloom all year. Protect them from temperatures under 45 degrees.
Light: Deep to medium shade. The leaves burn with even a little sun.
Water: Low. We watered ours once a week.
Salt tolerance: Low.
Wind tolerance: Unknown.
Zone: 11 for outside use during the coldest days of winter.
Pest Problems: Holes in the leaves usually come from snails; leaf spot diseases.
Also see pages 78-79 in "Best Garden Color for Florida" to learn about this plant in the landscape.

Plant Profiles: The High Performers

Begonia, Dragon Wing *(Begonia 'Dragon Wing')*

Characteristics and Care

Use: Mounding or centerpiece plant. One of the best for the sides of a hanging basket.
Growth rate: Medium.
Size: In the top of a large container, grows 2 feet tall by 1 foot wide. Smaller if planted in the side of a basket, about 8 inches tall.
Colors: Red or pink.
Average life: 6 months.
Cautions: None known.
Care: Very easy. Plant with slow-release fertilizer, and leave them alone! Fertilize again in 2 or 3 months. Trim off the tips if the plants become too large.

Dragon wing begonias are one of the highest performers in our trials, blooming continually with an impressive percentage of color for at least six months. They provide more color than the more common wax or angelwing begonias. This is a great choice for someone who wants easy, profuse color during our cool months.
Companions: Use the reds with bright colors. They show beautifully in blue pots. Or, combine them with golden shrimp plants and Persian shield for shade drama. Mix the pink with more subdued yellows and blues.

Growing Conditions

Season: Does best from October to June.
Light: Medium shade to full sun in the cool season, but shade only in summer.
Water: Medium.
Salt tolerance: Medium.
Wind tolerance: Low.
Zone: Use as an annual. Tolerant of light frost but not a freeze.
Pest problems: Occasional fungus, caterpillars, or snails.

Also see pages 33, 37, 38, 71-72, 84-85, 101-102, 112, 174-175, and 140 in this book. See pages 22-23 in "Best Garden Color for Florida" to learn more about this plant in the landscape.

Begonia, Gumdrops *(Begonia x semper. Cultorum 'Gumdrops')*

Characteristics and Care

Use: Mounding plant that works well in the center, along the edges of any pot and in the sides of hanging baskets.
Growth rate: Medium.
Size: In the top of a container, grows about 6 to 8 inches tall. Smaller if planted in the side of a basket, about 4 inches tall.
Colors: Red or pink
Average life: 6 months.
Cautions: None known.
Care: Very easy. Plant with slow-release fertilizer, and repeat in two or three months. Trim if the plant become too large.

Gumdrop begonias are super performers - blooming non stop for up to six months with very little care. I was particularly impressed by the pink ones that glowed with color, showing up very well from quite a distance. The flowers look like little roses and are particularly useful in the sides of hanging baskets. Although the 'Gumdrops' resemble the old wax begonias, I like them much better because they show up better, both from a distance as well as close up. We tested the two colors. The red didn't show up anywhere near as well as the pink.
Companions: Most winter annuals are good companions, particularly petunias, geraniums, and salvia. See page 96 for an example.

Growing Conditions

Season: Cool season. Avoid planting from July through September.
Light: Medium shade to full sun in the cool season, but burns in the sun in early summer.
Water: Medium.
Salt tolerance: Medium.
Wind tolerance: Medium.
Zone: Use as an annual. Tolerant of light frost but not a freeze.
Pest problems: Uncommon in the landscape. Powdery mildew in humid, cool spring. Rare whitefly and snails in summer.
My thanks to Bodger Botanicals (through Michell's) for introducing me to this plant.

Begonia, Orange Angelwing *(Begonia 'Orange Rubra')*

Characteristics and Care

Use: Mounding plant that works well in the center or along the edges of any pot.
Growth rate: Medium.
Size: 12 to 18 inches tall by the same wide.
Colors: Orange.
Average life: About 2 to 3 years in the ground. Will stay in the same size container about 1 year.
Cautions: None known.
Care: Very easy. Plant with slow-release fertilizer, and leave them alone! Fertilize again in 2 or 3 months. Trim back hard, to about 6 inches tall, in summer if it looks leggy.

Orange rubra begonias are another superstar begonia for containers. They bloom all the time, require very little care, and last for years. These bright begonias also offer the advantage of being happy in the same container for up to a year, if they are trimmed hard in the summer. They also do very well planted in the ground in frost-free areas.

Companions: This begonia looks great with large, yellow flowers or bright-colored leaves that grow in shade. Try golden shrimp plants for yellow and red spot or mammey crotons for the bright-colored leaves.

Growing Conditions

Season: All year.
Light: Medium to light shade. Takes more sun in the winter.
Water: Medium.
Salt tolerance: Medium.
Wind tolerance: Medium
Zone: 9b to 11. Protect from freezes.
Pest problems: Spots on the leaves mean fungus. Spray only if it is really bad.

Also see pages 82 and 83 in "Best Garden Color for Florida" to learn about this plant in the landscape.

Begonia, Pink Angelwing *(Begonia coccinea 'Pink' aka Begonia flamingo)*

Characteristics and Care

Use: Centerpiece plant.
Growth rate: Medium.
Size: The size of this plant depends on the container size. In a medium container (10"W), it grows to about 2 feet tall by 2 feet wide. In a large container (17"W), it grows to about 4 feet tall by 3 feet wide.
Colors: Pink.
Average life: 10 years.
Cautions: None known.
Care: Very easy. Plant with slow-release fertilizer, and leave them alone! Fertilize again in 2 or 3 months. Trim the tall canes to 6 inches tall if they are falling over.

Pink angelwing begonias are one of the highest performers in our trials, blooming continually with an impressive percentage of color for years. They are quite easy, and are happy in the same pot for up to a year. This begonia is larger than any other begonia in this book. I have seen it grow five feet tall in huge containers. It is a great landscape plant for zones 10 to 11 as well.

Companions: Pink angelwings make a strong statement planted alone, especially in large, dark green, glazed pots. See an example on page 244.

Growing Conditions

Season: All year. Blooms more in winter.
Light: Medium to light shade. Takes full sun in the cool season, but burns in the summer sun.
Water: Medium. We water ours every third day.
Salt tolerance: Medium.
Wind tolerance: Low.
Zone: 10 to 11, although I keep hearing from people in Tampa who say they do well in warm spots there.
Pest problems: Occasional fungus, snails.
Also see "Easy Gardens for Florida."

Plant Profiles: The High Performers

Begonia, Tuberous *(Begonia spp.)*

Characteristics and Care

Use: Mounding plant or centerpiece. Some types trail over pot edges well.

Growth rate: Medium.

Size: Sizes vary by species, from 6 to 12 inches tall and wide.

Colors: Red, pink, peach, yellow, orange.

Average life: 2 to 4 months in Florida.

Cautions: None known.

Care: Very easy. Plant with slow-release fertilizer, and leave them alone! Fertilize again in 2 or 3 months. Trim off any dead leaves.

Growing Conditions

Season: Cool season, particularly January through March.

Light: Medium to light shade.

Water: Medium. We watered ours about every third day.

Salt tolerance: Medium.

Wind tolerance: Low.

Zone: Use as an annual in most of the world.

Pest problems: Fungus, leaf spot diseases.

Tuberous begonias are one of the most beautiful begonias but sometimes tricky to grow in Florida. I had inconsistent results from them in my trials. One year, none of them thrived. The next year, they did great, blooming like crazy for three full months and looking absolutely beautiful. So be careful with this one!

Companions: These flowers are so gorgeous that mixing them might dilute their impact. Mix different colored tuberous begonias in the same pot, but don't put different kinds of plants with them.

Begonia, Wax *(Begonia x semper. Cultorum)*

Characteristics and Care

Use: Mounding plant.

Growth rate: Medium.

Size: In the top of a container, grows about 8 inches tall by 5 inches wide. Smaller if planted in the side of a basket, about 4 to 6 inches tall.

Colors: Red, pink, or white flowers on green or bronze leaves.

Average life: 4 to 6 months.

Cautions: None known.

Care: Very easy. Plant with slow-release fertilizer, and leave them alone! Fertilize again in 2 or 3 months.

Growing Conditions

Season: Cool season. Avoid planting from July through September.

Light: Medium shade to full sun in the cool season, but burns in the summer sun. Bronze-leafed varieties are more sun-tolerant.

Water: Medium.

Salt tolerance: Medium.

Wind tolerance: Medium.

Zone: Use as an annual. Tolerant of light frost but not a freeze.

Pest problems: Occasional fungus, shown by leaf spots.

Also see pages 54, 78, 80, 88, 123, 134-135, 207, and 209 in this book; see "Best Garden Color for Florida," pages 24-25, to learn about using these begonias in the ground.

Wax begonias are one of the most commonly used annuals in the world because of their toughness and dependability. They are not as dramatic as dragon wing or gumdrop begonias but work well in the sides of hanging baskets. I find the white-flowered wax begonia with green leaves particularly useful.

Companions: Contrast these small flowers with larger ones, like geraniums and petunias. For a beautiful hanging basket, plant hot pink geraniums in the top. Then alternate white begonias and midnight blue petunias along the rim of the basket, as well as on the sides.

Bird of Paradise, White *(Strelitzia nicolai)*

Characteristics and Care

Use: Centerpiece.
Growth rate: Medium.
Size: In the landscape, grows to 15 feet tall. In containers, it depends on the size of the container, about 2 feet tall in a 10"W pot to 7 feet tall in a 24"W container.
Colors: Green leaves are more distinctive than the occasional white flowers.
Average life: 20 years plus.
Cautions: None known.
Care: Very easy. Apply a slow-release fertilizer every 3 months. Remove old leaves when they turn brown.

White birds of paradise are one of the most useful green specimen plants for containers, particularly in dense shade situations. It grows indoors as well as in the landscape but lasts much longer outside. I put one on my screened porch in a huge, 36 inch pot, and it lasted for seven years without transplanting. It was positioned to receive rainwater and seldom needed more than that because the pot was so large.
Companions: The white birds look best with other tropical plants, like the anthuriums shown above. Bromeliads are another great companion.

Growing Conditions

Season: All year.
Light: Very tolerant of different light conditions, from dense shade to full sun.
Water: Low.
Salt tolerance: Medium.
Wind tolerance: Low.
Zone: 9 to 11. Tolerates temperatures down to 25 degrees.
Pest problems: Scale is frequent under screening or indoors. Outside, the plant has few pests.

See "Easy Gardens for Florida" for info about this plant in the landscape.

Bougainvillea *(Bougainvillea spp.)*

Characteristics and Care

Use: Centerpiece plant.
Growth rate: Fast.
Size: Hundreds of cultivars are currently available that range in size from small hanging baskets to large trees.
Colors: Peach, orange, yellow, white, red, magenta, purple.
Average life: 20 years plus.
Cautions: Sharp thorns; the flowers drop a lot.
Care: Fertilize with a slow-release mix every 3 months. Trim hard every summer. See "Best Garden Color for Florida," pages 193, 195, 207, and 209 for more trimming info.

Bougainvillea is one of the best container plants for bursts of bright color. It has the added benefit of being comfortable in the same pot for years on end. But, it's a pain in the neck to maintain because it drops a lot and grows quickly enough to require frequent pruning, which can be painful because of its thorns. It also blooms in spurts, with bright spurts followed by dormant periods, when it is almost bare of leaves or flowers.
Companions: Plant single colors of bougainvillea alone in pots, and display pots of different-colored bougainvilleas together.

Growing Conditions

Season: Cool, dry season. Blooms best from late December until June.
Light: Full sun.
Water: Medium.
Salt tolerance: High.
Wind tolerance: Medium.
Zone: 9 to 11. Dies back in a severe freeze, especially in zone 9. Usually recovers.
Pest problems: Caterpillars.

Also see pages 203 and 210-211 in this book. See pages 192-195 and 206-209 in "Best Garden Color for Florida" to learn about growing this plant in the ground.

Plant Profiles: The High Performers

Bromeliad *(many different genuses and species)*

Characteristics and Care

Use: Centerpiece or accent.
Growth rate: Slow.
Size: Varies greatly by species, from tiny to over 5 feet tall.
Colors: All!
Average life: Single plant lives about 2 years but sends up babies to replace itself.
Cautions: Serrated leaves on some varieties can be quite hazardous.
Care: Fertilize every 3 months with a slow-release mix. Avoid getting fertilizer in the center of the plants.

Bromeliads are one of the highest performers in our trials. Over 2500 different types of bromeliads have been identified, varying greatly in size and color. Some have gorgeous flowers that bloom for two to four months at a time. They are quite happy in the same pot for years on end.
Trimming: The mother plant dies after flowering and producing pups (babies). Trim off the dead plant after it becomes brown. Leave the remaining pups to grow where they are or separate them to plant in other pots. Since this only has to be done every few years, this is truly an easy plant.

Growing Conditions

Season: All year. Protect from freezes.
Light: Medium to light shade. Takes more light in winter. If used inside, will continue to bloom in deep shade until that flower dies.
Water: Low, but tolerates daily watering if planted with impatiens.
Salt tolerance: High for thick-leafed varieties.
Wind tolerance: High for thick-leafed varieties.
Zone: 9b to 11. Protect from freezes.
Pest problems: None serious.
See the index of this book for page numbers of bromeliads in containers.

Caladium *(Caladium x hortulanum)*

Characteristics and Care

Use: Mounding plant or centerpiece.
Growth rate: Medium
Size: 6 to 30 inches tall, depending on variety.
Colors: Shades of white, green, red, and pink.
Average life: Normally used for just one summer.
Cautions: Poisonous.
Care: For instant effects, plant full-size plants rather than tubers. Fertilize every 3 months with a slow-release mix. If you feel really energetic, removing the nondescript flowers increases leaf production.

Caladiums are one of the highest performers for summer color. I used them extensively, both as centerpieces and mounding plants. Be sure you know the mature size of any caladiums you buy. I have made the mistake of thinking that one was a dwarf and watching it grow to 30 inches tall, completely overwhelming the other plants in the container!
Companions: Use caladiums at the base of tropical plants like the white bird of paradise or palms. Or mix them with flowering plants in colors that coordinate with the leaves. I frequently use them with begonias, torenia, and coleus.

Growing Conditions

Season: Summer.
Light: Medium shade to full sun, depending on type.
Water: Medium.
Salt tolerance: Medium.
Wind tolerance: Low.
Zone: Grown throughout the world as a summer annual.
Pest Problems: Slugs or snails.

Also see pages 38, 39, 54, 70-71, 132, 216, and 228-229 in this book. See pages 26-27 in "Best Garden Color for Florida" for info about propagation and using caladiums in the ground.

For container sources, go to www.easygardencolor.com

Calibrachoa, Trailing Petunia or Million Bells (*Calibrachoa x hybridus*)

Characteristics and Care

Use: Many different cultivars are currently available. Some are mounding and some trailing.

Growth rate: Medium.

Size: About 3 to 5 inches tall by 6 inches wide.

Colors: Many shades of red, pink, peach, yellow, and purple.

Average life: 4 to 6 months.

Cautions: None known.

Care: Very easy. Plant with slow-release fertilizer, and leave them alone! Fertilize again in 2 or 3 months. These plants seldom require trimming.

Calibrachoas are new for me - I've only used them for a year and still have a lot to learn. We tested plants from Proven Winners and Bodger Botanicals (through Michell's); all of these did well. They look like tiny petunias, with some varieties trailing and others upright. They are slow-growing, however, and it takes a long time for the trailing to be significant. The colors are lovely, and this is a very useful container plant.

Companions: Use with larger flowers that have different shapes, like geraniums, phlox, double impatiens, and daisies. Mixed colors of calibrachoas - like yellow, purple, and red - work well without any other plants added to the container.

Growing Conditions

Season: Cool season, from November until June. Avoid planting from July through September.

Light: Blooms best in full sun, but I had acceptable results in light shade.

Water: Medium.

Salt tolerance: Unknown.

Wind tolerance: Unknown.

Zone: Use as an annual.

Pest problems: Nematodes in landscape so keep pot off the ground. These plants do better in containers than in the ground in Florida.

Also see pages 51, 205, and 318 in this book.

Canna Lily (*Canna x generalis*)

Characteristics and Care

Use: Centerpiece.

Growth rate: Medium.

Size: 3 to 5 feet tall by 2 to 3 feet wide.

Colors: Pink, yellow, peach, coral, red, and orange flowers. Leaves come in bronze, green, purple, or burgundy, solid or striped.

Average life: They average about one summer in the same container, but I had some that lasted for up to 2 years.

Cautions: None known.

Care: Fertilize on planting day, and repeat every 3 months. Trim off the brown leaves and flowers.

Cannas are one of our showiest sources of summer color. Although they don't bloom constantly, the breaks in blooming are brief, and the beauty of the flowers overshadows this shortcoming. I didn't have as many caterpillar problems with cannas in containers as I had with them in the ground. Be careful with size - they are often sold when they are about eight inches tall, and it is hard to believe that they will quickly reach at least three feet tall, even the dwarf varieties.

Companions: I often use cannas alone in containers, sometimes single colors and sometimes mixed. The cannas with yellow and green striped leaves look great with red ti plants or Persian shield.

Growing Conditions

Season: Cannas are perennials that are most often used as summer annuals in Florida. Some last all year for several years in a row in the southern part of the state. The leaves die back in the cold of central and north Florida and reappear the next spring.

Light: Full sun.

Water: Medium.

Salt tolerance: Low.

Wind tolerance: Low.

Zone: 7 to 10.

Pest problems: Fungus and caterpillars. Also see pages 102, 103, 132, 216, and 226 in this book and pages 22-23 in "Best Garden Color for Florida."

Plant Profiles: The High Performers

Chenille, Dwarf *(Acalypha pendula)*

Characteristics and Care

Use: Trailing plant.
Growth rate: Medium.
Size: About 3 to 4 inches tall by 6 to 10 inches wide. This plant is a short trailer, growing about 6 to 8 inches down the sides of the pot.
Colors: Red.
Average life: 3 to 5 years in the ground. Lasts about a year in the same container.
Cautions: None known
Care: Very easy. Plant with slow-release fertilizer, and leave them alone! Fertilize again in 2 or 3 months. Trim off the tips if the plants become too large.

Dwarf chenille is an easy and attractive plant for the edges of pots and baskets. Since it grows in sun or shade, it works well in most Florida environments. It is a relatively short trailer, growing about six inches down the sides of a pot after a few months. Use it for its interesting texture, and move it into the ground in your garden after it has outgrown its pot.
Companions: Dwarf chenille is a very versatile plant, blending well with many container styles. It looks great with leaf color, like caladiums and coleus. It also blends well with cottage garden flowers, like pentas and torenia.

Growing Conditions

Season: Blooms most of the year.
Light: Medium shade to full sun.
Water: Medium.
Salt tolerance: Unknown.
Wind tolerance: Medium.
Zone: 7 to 11. Dies back in a freeze but grows back when the weather warms up.
Pest problems: None serious.

Also see page 39 in this book. This is an excellent landscape plant for all of Florida. For more information about this use, see "Easy Gardens for Florida."

Chinese Evergreen or Aglaonema *(Aglaomena spp.)*

Characteristics and Care

Use: Centerpiece.
Growth rate: Medium.
Size: Variable but averages 2 feet tall by 2 feet wide.
Colors: Green leaves with varying patterns of white to silver.
Average life: Unknown, but I have seen them last for 3 to 5 years indoors if transplanted or root-pruned annually.
Cautions: The sap is an irritant. Do not eat this plant, and handle it with gloves!
Care: Very easy. Plant with slow-release fertilizer, repeat every 3 months. Root prune or transplant annually to a larger container.

Aglaonema is one of the most common and dependable house plants in the world. There are hundreds of different varieties. It thrives in deep shade and adapts well to indoor or outdoor conditions. This is the plant for people who have killed every plant they have ever tried! It is quite cold-sensitive, however, and best moved inside if the temperatures dip to the mid-40's.
Companions: Use with other plants that like deep shade, like corn plants, pothos, dieffenbachia, and bamboo palms.

Growing Conditions

Season: All year. Protect from temperatures below 45 degrees.
Light: Dense, medium, or light shade.
Water: Medium.
Salt tolerance: Medium.
Wind tolerance: Medium.
Zone: 10a to 11 in the ground. Protect from temperatures under 45 degrees.
Pest problems: Occasional scale, mealybugs, and spider mites.

Coleus *(Solenostemon scutellarioides)*

Characteristics and Care

Use: Smaller types for mounding plants and larger ones for centerpieces.
Growth rate: Medium.
Size: Varies greatly by variety, 6 to 36 inches tall and equally as wide.
Colors: Shades of red, white, yellow, and green.
Average life: 6 months.
Cautions: None known
Care: Plant with slow release fertilizer and repeat again in 2 or 3 months. Pinch the tips monthly if plant becomes too large. If you delay this trimming, it may take them a while to look good again.

'Gay's Delight'   'Dark Star'
'Defiance'   'Crime Scene'

Coleus are one of the highest performers in our trials, thriving in every pot we used, even in the sides of hanging baskets. New ones are constantly appearing, which makes identifying their mature size sometimes difficult at the garden center. But their leaves are so varied that we put up with this inconvenience. They produce some of the most beautiful leaf patterns in the world.
Companions: Coordinate coleus leaves with other leaf or flower colors. Try lime green with dark burgundy for a dramatic theme. Many combinations are shown throughout this book.

Growing Conditions

Season: All year, if protected from frost.
Light: Prefers some shade, but many of the newer varieties take full sun.
Water: High.
Salt tolerance: Medium.
Wind tolerance: Medium.
Zone: Use as an annual.
Pest problems: Occasional aphids, mites, mealybugs, slugs, and snails.
Also see pages 23, 41-43, 46, 48-49, 57, 61, 65, 70-71, 72-75, 78, 80, 82-89, 94, 97, 102-103, 109-112, 132, 177, 182, 192-193, 214-216, and 226-227 in this book. See pages 58 and 59 "Best Garden Color for Florida" to learn about growing this plant in the ground.

Copperleaf and Chenille Plant *(Acalypha spp.)*

Characteristics and Care

Use: Centerpiece.
Growth rate: Medium.
Size: Varies greatly by variety, from 3 foot dwarfs to large, 8 foot shrubs.
Colors: Leaves are either green, variegated, or shades of peach. Flowers are white or red.
Average life: 15 to 20 years. Plant in your garden (in frost-free areas) when it outgrows your container. Lives in the same container for about 6 months.
Cautions: None known.

Mardi-Gras Copperleaf
Fire Dragon Copperleaf   Chenille Plant

Copperleafs and chenille plants are good centerpiece plants for containers, especially in the summer. They take heat very well. I don't use them in the cool season in containers because the leaves burn at temperatures that routinely occur into zone 10b.
Companions: The copper-colored leaves look great with lime green coleus or goldilocks. The red flowers look good with yellow or blue flowers.
Care: Very easy. Plant with slow-release fertilizer, and repeat every three months. Trim in the summer if it gets leggy, although the goal of using these shrubs in containers is to plant nice, full specimens in your decorative containers and transplant them to the garden before they get leggy.

Growing Conditions

Season: All year, but best in containers in summer. Protect from temperatures below 40 degrees.
Light: Full sun.
Water: Medium.
Salt tolerance: Medium.
Wind tolerance: Medium.
Zone: 10b to 11 in the ground. In cooler zones, move containers inside if cold threatens.
Pest problems: None known.

Also see pages 46, 47, 68, and 132 in this book. For info about copperleafs in the landscape, "Best Garden Color for Florida", pages 110-115.

Plant Profiles: The High Performers

Corn Plant *(Dracaena fragrans 'Massangeana')*

Characteristics and Care

Use: Centerpiece plant.

Growth rate: Slow.

Size: Each cane in this pot is a separate plant of a different height; this range of 2 to 8 feet is typical of corn plants in containers.

Colors: Green with some lighter green stripes in the leaves.

Average life: 15 to 20 years. Grows for about 2 years in the same container before requiring transplanting.

Cautions: None known.

Care: Very easy. Plant with slow-release fertilizer, and leave them alone! Fertilize again in 2 or 3 months. Trim off brown leaf tips with scissors.

Corn plants are one of the easiest indoor plants. They not only adapt well to the dense shade of interiors but also offer the advantage of a vertical growth habit, which is very useful in corners and in front of columns. Corn plants grow outdoors in tropical areas and produce a flower with a wonderful scent. Look for plants with multiple trunks of varying heights, like the one pictured.

Companions: Other house plants, like pothos and Chinese evergreen.

Growing Conditions

Season: All year, but protect from frost.

Light: Dense, medium, or light shade.

Water: Low. Water only when the soil feels dry, which could be every 10 days inside.

Salt tolerance: Low.

Wind tolerance: Unknown.

Zone: 10b to 11 outside. Used throughout the world as an indoor plant.

Pest problems: None known.

Croton *(Codiaeum variegatum)*

Characteristics and Care

Use: Centerpiece or mounding plant.

Growth rate: Medium.

Size: Varies greatly by variety, from dwarfs to small trees.

Colors: Shades of red, yellow, green, pink, grey, black, and orange.

Average life: 15 to 20 years. Plant in your garden (in frost-free areas) when it outgrows your container. Lasts about 1 year in the same pot.

Cautions: Milky sap irritates skin and stains clothes.

Care: Very easy. Plant with slow-release fertilizer, and repeat every 3 months.

Crotons are one of the easiest plants for containers in Florida. They are happy in the same pot for years on end and require little care. Crotons not only offer constant color but also look good all year, provided they are protected from cold.

Companions: Plant crotons with leaf or flower color that looks good with their leaves. I use red and yellow crotons, (like the stoplight, above) with the same color flowers, or contrast it with dark purple leaves, like Persian shield. pink crotons, like the icetone, look great with pink butterfly pentas and golden shrimp plants.

Growing Conditions

Season: All year. Protect from frost.

Light: Medium shade to full sun.

Water: Medium.

Salt tolerance: Medium.

Wind tolerance: Medium.

Zone: 10a to 11 in the ground.

Pest problems: Occasional scale, mealybugs, and spider mites.

**Also see pages 42, 82, 83, 84, 109, 132, 138, 139, 144, 173, 182, 223, 227, 248, and 249 in this book. To learn how to grow crotons in the landscape, see "Easy Gardens for Florida" and pages 126 to 131 in "Best Garden Color for Florida."

For container sources, go to www.easygardencolor.com

Crown of Thorns *(Euphorbia milii)*

Characteristics and Care

Use: Centerpiece or mounding plant.
Growth rate: Slow.
Size: Varies by variety, from tiny dwarfs to larger ones that grow to 3 feet tall.
Colors: Red, pink, peach, or yellow.
Average life: About a year in the same container. 10 to 15 years in the ground in frost-free areas.
Cautions: Sharp thorns and toxic, milky sap.
Care: Very easy. Plant with slow-release fertilizer, and leave them alone! Fertilize again in 2 or 3 months. Trim back hard in summer if it gets leggy.

Crown of thorns is one of the better container plants for tough situations, like low water, high salt, and high wind. Look for newer, better cultivars at your garden center. The "Rosy" has been around for a long time and performs well in containers. The new Thai hybrids (pictured) have not only larger flowers but also a choice of different colors. But the Thai hybrids have very visible thorns, which are more hidden from view in the "Rosies." All of the Thai hybrids we tested did well in containers, but some of them died in the ground.
Companions: Crown of thorns looks good alone in a bright pot or mixed with low-water succulents.

Growing Conditions

Season: All year. Protect from frost.
Light: Full sun.
Water: Low, but adapts to watering of up to 3 times a week.
Salt tolerance: High.
Wind tolerance: High.
Zone: 10b to 11. Leaves darken or fall off in response to temperatures in the mid-to-high 30's.
Pest problems: Fungus, shown by black spots and yellow leaves.
Also see page 273 in this book. See "Easy Gardens for Florida" for information about using the "Rosy" crown of thorns in the landscape.

Daisy, California Bush *(Gamolepis chrysanthemoides)*

Characteristics and Care

Use: Centerpiece or mounding plant.
Growth rate: Medium.
Size: About 18 inches tall by 12 inches wide.
Colors: Yellow.
Average life: Looks good for about 6 months in the same container. Goes into a slow decline after that. Will not do too well in the ground after 6 months in a pot.
Cautions: None known.
Care: Very easy. Plant with slow-release fertilizer, and leave them alone! Fertilize again in 2 or 3 months. Blooms more if old blooms are removed.

California bush daisy (yellow flower, above) is one of the highest performing daisies for Florida. The flowers are not as large as the cape or marguerite daisies, but the plant lasts longer than they do. It blooms almost continuously. The plant also performs well in the ground, but don't expect more than about six months' use.
Companions: Since California daisies look great with reds and blues, the above mixed arrangement is ideal. Also, try it with other shapes and sizes of flowers, like salvias, geraniums, and pentas.

Growing Conditions

Season: Cool season. Avoid planting from July through September.
Light: Full sun.
Water: Medium.
Salt tolerance: Medium.
Wind tolerance: Medium.
Zone: Although this plant is used as a perennial in other warm parts of the world, it performs best as an annual in Florida. Protect from frost.
Pest problems: Spider mites occasionally. I have never had a pest on this plant in my gardens.

Plant Profiles: The High Performers

Daisy, Cape *(Osteospermum spp.)*

Characteristics and Care

Use: Most are mounding or centerpiece plants. Some of the newer cultivars trail slightly.
Growth rate: Medium.
Size: About 12 inches tall by 8 inches wide.
Colors: White, orange, purple, yellow.
Average life: Blooms for about 2 months. Lives for a few months longer without flowers.
Cautions: None known.
Care: Plant with slow-release fertilizer. They look better and will bloom more with the old flowers removed.

Growing Conditions

Season: Spring.
Light: Full sun.
Water: Medium.
Salt tolerance: Unknown.
Wind tolerance: Unknown.
Zone: 10 to 11. Use as an annual. They occasionally live for a few years, blooming in spring and remaining green the rest of the time. Protect from frost.
Pest problems: Wilt, powdery mildew and aphids.

Cape daisies are similar to marguerites and quite useful for spring displays. Although the bloom period is relatively short, about 2 months, they are attractive enough to make them worthwhile. In many parts of the world, they are perennials but are best used as annuals in Florida.

Companions: Since these flowers have a country garden look, use them mixed with other cottage garden flowers. Try them with other short-lived flowers that bloom at the same time, like lobelia, dahlberg daisies, and fuschias. They also look good with lamium for leaf color.

Daisy, Dahlberg *(Thymophylla tenuiloba)*

Characteristics and Care

Use: Mounding plant.
Growth rate: Medium
Size: 6 to 12 inches tall and equally as wide.
Colors: Yellow.
Average life: 2 to 3 months.
Cautions: None known.
Care: Plant with slow release fertilizer and repeat in 3 months if the plants are still alive. This plant looks better and blooms more if the dead flowers are removed.

Growing Conditions

Season: Cool season. Avoid planting from July through September.
Light: Full sun.
Water: Medium. Withstands periods of drought.
Salt tolerance: Unknown.
Wind tolerance: Unknown.
Zone: Use as an annual. I have heard of cases in which it returned the following year, but that has not been my experience.
Pest Problems: None known.

Dahlberg daisies are still mysterious to me - some years they've thrived and others, not done so well. But I keep trying them because of their profuse blooms and unique texture - the leaves and flowers are tiny, which makes them quite useful to contrast with larger flowers. Understand that they are short-lived, just a few months.

Companions: Use this daisy with bright-colored flowers that are different in texture. Bright red geraniums and purple petunias make an eye-catching display when paired with this daisy.

Daisy, Marguerite 'Butterfly' *(Argyranthemum frutescens 'Butterfly')*

Characteristics and Care

Use: Mounding or centerpiece plant. I found some gorgeous specimens last winter that made instant, full centerpieces.
Growth rate: Medium.
Size: About 12 inches tall by 8 inches wide.
Colors: Yellow, white, purple, pink.
Average life: 3 to 4 months.
Cautions: None known.
Care: Plant with slow-release fertilizer, and repeat in 2 or 3 months. Looks better and blooms more if the spent flowers are removed.

Growing Conditions

Season: Spring. This plant requires low temperatures to begin flowering and is an ideal early spring plant for Florida.
Light: Full sun.
Water: Medium.
Salt tolerance: Medium.
Wind tolerance: Medium.
Zone: 8 to 11. Use as an annual.
Pest problems: Crown gall and leaf miner.

Marguerite daisies are new to me - I've only had one season's experience. Even though they didn't live as long as the California daisy, they are quite useful because their flower is a lot larger, giving a different look. Their larger size makes them much showier than the California daisy. The 'Butterfly' (above) is supposed to be one of the most heat-tolerant types, but it didn't last past June in our trials.

Companions: Use this daisy with bright-colored flowers that are different in size and shape. Petunias and salvia are ideal. Variegated mint is a good foliage companion.

Daisy, Outback Jumbo *(Brachyscome 'Jumbo Mauve')*

Characteristics and Care

Use: Mounding plant that looks great alone in a yellow pot.
Growth rate: Medium.
Size: In the top of a container, grows 6 to 8 inches tall.
Colors: Purple, rose and yellow.
Average life: 2 to 3 months.
Cautions: None known.
Care: Plant with slow-release fertilizer, and leave them alone! They produce a lot more flowers if you deadhead them. Water when soil feels dry to the touch

Growing Conditions

Season: Cool season. Avoid planting from March through May.
Light: Light shade to full sun. Blooms more in full sun.
Water: Medium. We watered the pots shown every third day in bright sun.
Salt tolerance: Unknown.
Wind tolerance: Unknown.
Zone: Use as an annual in Florida.
Pest problems: Mildew if leaves stay too wet.

Jumbo outback daisies are a new plant for me that I only tried for one season. I loved the purple flowers with their bright yellow centers. They grew from March until May, with their short bloom period extending just about two months in spring. Even though their bloom period is short, their beauty and low cost make them worth the effort.

Companions: Use with flowers that are very different like sweet alyssum, marigolds, and petunias. Interesting with red salvia and geraniums for the color contrast.

Plant Profiles: The High Performers

Diascia, Twinspur *(Diascia spp.)*

Characteristics and Care

Use: Mounding or semi-trailing plant.
Growth rate: Medium.
Size: 4 to 6 inches tall by about 8 inches wide.
Colors: Red, rose or peach.
Average life: 3 to 5 months.
Cautions: None known.
Care: Very easy. Plant with slow-release fertilizer, and leave them alone! Fertilize again in 2 or 3 months. Trim off the tips if the plants become too large.

Diascias: We were quite impressed by the Diascia 'Miracle' we tested from Bodger Botanicals (through Michell's). It started blooming at the start of the cool season and continued right on through late spring with tremendous color. We had great luck with it both in containers and in the ground. This plant should become easily available in Florida because it is such a high performer.
Companions: Use this plant by itself, as shown above, or mix it with blues and yellows. It looks good with blue daze, yellow daisies, and lobelia.

Growing Conditions

Season: Cool season. Avoid planting from July through September. Protect from freezes.
Light: Light shade to full sun.
Water: Medium. We watered the pots shown every third day.
Salt tolerance: Medium.
Wind tolerance: Medium.
Zone: Used as an annual throughout the world. Protect from freeze.
Pest problems: None known.

Dieffenbachia *(Dieffenbachia spp.)*

Characteristics and Care

Use: Centerpiece plant.
Growth rate: Medium.
Size: Most average about 2 feet tall in a container.
Colors: Leaves are variegated in shades of bright green, lime green, and white.
Average life: Lives many years in containers if root-pruned annually.
Cautions: Highly toxic. Sap is a skin irritant. Poisonous if eaten.
Care: Very easy. Plant with slow-release fertilizer, and leave them alone! Fertilize again in 2 or 3 months. Trim off brown leaves. Trim back branches if plant becomes leggy.

Dieffenbachia is one of the easiest house plants around. It also does well outside, although the leaves burn when the temperatures dip below 45 degrees. It grows well in dense shade, one of the few that will. Be sure to handle with gloves and long sleeves because this is a very toxic plant.
Companions: Use dieffenbachia for texture, mixing it with other plants that have interesting leaves. Combined with the little 'Fiber Optic Grass', it's quite attractive (see page 48). It also looks great grouped with palms. *(Pot and photo from Lechuza)*.

Growing Conditions

Season: All year, but protect from temperatures as low as the mid-40's.
Light: Medium to dense shade.
Water: Medium.
Salt tolerance: Low.
Wind tolerance: Low.
Zone: Used throughout the world as a house-plant. Outdoors, zone 11 is the safest. I used it outdoors in zone 10a for several years with no problems, but a cold spell finally damaged them.
Pest problems: Mites, mealybugs and aphids. Also see pages 18, 19, 48, 49, 132, 144, 145, 155-156, and 177 in this book.

For container sources, go to www.easygardencolor.com

Dracaena 'Lemon Lime' *(Dracaena deremensis 'Lemon-Lime)*

Characteristics and Care

Use: Centerpiece.
Growth rate: Medium.
Size: Up to 6 feet tall in a large container. Size is proportional to container size.
Colors: Leaves are striped with different shades of green.
Average life: 10 to 15 years outside in the landscape. Lives for up to a year in the same container before requiring root pruning or a larger pot.
Cautions: None known.
Care: Very easy. Plant with slow-release fertilizer, and leave them alone! Fertilize again in 2 or 3 months.

Dracaenas are one of the most common indoor plants. They work well outdoors as well, provided they are protected from frost. Most plants that grow in dense shade are dark green, so the 'Lemon Lime' dracaena is a welcome newcomer, with its unique leaf color. It is one of the few indoor plants that gives a significant amount of color and lasts for years on end.

Companions: In dense shade, mix this plant with peace lilies and pothos. Outdoors (in frost-free areas), it looks good with bright reds and dark purples, like ti plants, crotons, purple queen, and coleus.

Growing Conditions

Season: All year. Protect from frost.
Light: Light, medium, or dense shade.
Water: Medium.
Salt tolerance: Unknown.
Wind tolerance: Medium.
Zone: 10 to 11. Protect from freezes in cooler area if used outdoors.
Pest problems: Scales and mealybugs, particularly if used indoors or under screening.

Dracaena Reflexa *(Dracaena reflexa 'Song of India')*

Characteristics and Care

Use: Centerpiece plant.
Growth rate: Slow.
Size: Grows to 8 feet tall in a large container. Its size is proportional to the container size.
Colors: Green and yellow stripes.
Average life: Lives for more than 10 years in the landscape. In containers, root prune or plant in a larger container annually.
Cautions: None known.
Care: Very easy. Plant with slow-release fertilizer, and leave them alone! Fertilize again in 2 or 3 months. Trim if the plants become too large.

Dracaena reflexas are great plants for containers, both indoors and out. They are not only quite easy but also offer some color in dense shade, which is unusual. The 'Song of India' (above) is a variegated variety that grows slower that the green one. This plant is commonly used outdoors with good results in frost-free areas of Florida.

Companions: Use 'Song of India' to set off dark or bright leaves or flowers. See it on page 109 surrounded by the darker foliage of mammey crotons.

Growing Conditions

Season: Year-round in frost-free conditions.
Light: Deep shade to full sun.
Water: Low, but tolerates water up to 4 times per week.
Salt tolerance: Medium.
Wind tolerance: Medium.
Zone: 10a to 11. Bring it inside if a freeze threatens.
Pest problems: None known.

See pages 172 and 254 in this book. Also see pages 146-147 in "Best Garden Color for Florida" to learn about using this plant in the landscape.

Plant Profiles: The High Performers

Elephant Ear *(Alocasia or Colocasia spp.)*

Characteristics and Care

Use: This one works well as a center focal point. Doesn't shed much.

Growth rate: Medium.

Size: Size varies by type, from 1 to 8 feet tall.

Colors: Various shades of green and black.

Average life: Depends on the cultivar, but some of mine have been going 5 years.

Cautions: Sap can irritate skin. Don't let children eat this one.

Care: Very easy. Plant with slow-release fertilizer, and apply again in 2 or 3 months. Trim off the dead leaves.

Elephant Ears - Two popular types (*Alocasia spp.* and *Colocasia spp.*) behave similarly in the landscape. There are many different sizes and shapes, from tiny foliage to umbrella-sized monsters from Costa Rica. The one I used the most was this Colocasia 'Black Magic' from Proven Winners, which performed extremely well. I have some that have lasted two years so far in the same container.

Companions: Looks best with tropical plants in lime greens (coleus, sweet potato vines, 'Goldilocks'), whites (scaevola, verbena, petunias) and reds (coleus and crotons).

Growing Conditions

Season: All year.

Light: Medium shade to full sun.

Water: Medium. Water when you see signs of wilt. Can be daily in summer.

Salt tolerance: Unknown.

Wind tolerance: Low.

Zone: 8 to 11.

Pest Problems: None known.

Also see pages 56 and 57 in this book.

Ficus Tree *(Ficus benjamina)*

Characteristics and Care

Use: Centerpiece.

Growth rate: Fast.

Size: Containers keep these trees smaller than the huge ones that grow outdoors in the southern part of Florida. The size of the tree is proportional to the container size.

Colors: Green.

Average life: Lasts up to 2 years in the same container without transplanting, although if outside, the roots can break through the bottom of the container and grow into the ground.

Cautions: Roots can cause considerable damage if planted outside.

Care: Very easy except for leaf drop.

Ficus trees are excellent indoor plants because they are easy to grow and adapt well to indoor conditions. They drop leaves as a response to a new situation, however, so expect a mess while your new tree adapts to its new home. Avoid planting them outside unless you have about an acre for it to spread because the roots cause damage and mature trees blow over <u>very</u> easily, crushing everything and everyone in their way.

Companions: For an attractive indoor grouping, use a ficus tree with blooming bromeliads planted at the base of the tree. Dieffenbachia and pothos are also good companions.

(Pot and photo from Lechuza.)

Growing Conditions

Season: Year round. Protect from frosts.

Light: Dense shade to full sun. If you move one suddenly from shade to sun, the leaves will burn while it adapts.

Water: Medium.

Salt tolerance: Medium.

Wind tolerance: Low.

Zone: 10 to 11. Protect from freezes.

Pest problems: Lobate lac scale is a serious threat outdoors in south Florida. Other types of scale infest this plant occasionally, particularly if it is inside a building or screened area.

Firecracker *(Russellia equisetiformis)*

Characteristics and Care

Use: Semi-trailing plant.
Growth rate: Medium.
Size: Firecrackers grow to 4 feet tall in the ground. In containers, the size is proportional to the size of the container.
Colors: Red, peach, or yellow flowers.
Average life: Lives in the same container for up to 1 year. In the garden, lives a few years in frost-free areas.
Cautions: None known.
Care: Very easy. Plant with slow-release fertilizer, and leave them alone! Repeat in two or three months. Trim off dead branches from time to time.

Firecracker plants are good container plants that take tough conditions, like salt and wind. They also are one of the few plants that bloom constantly. When they outgrow their containers, you can plant them in the ground in frost-free areas. But, they only last a few years (if that long) in Florida soils.

Companions: Firecrackers look good planted alone in bright-colored containers. They also look good planted along the edge of containers with palms or elephant ears in the center.

Growing Conditions

Season: All year. Protect from frost.
Light: Full sun.
Water: Low.
Salt tolerance: High.
Wind tolerance: High.
Zone: 10b to 11 in the ground. Protect from frost in containers.
Pest problems: Nematodes when planted in the ground.

Also see page 233 in this book

Geranium, Trailing *(Pelargonium x hortorum)*

Characteristics and Care

Use: Trailing plant.
Growth rate: Slow.
Size: Trails 6 to 8 inches over the side of the container.
Colors: Red, pink, white, burgundy.
Average life: 5 to 6 months.
Cautions: None known.
Care: Very easy. Plant with slow-release fertilizer, and then follow up every 2 to 3 months. Geraniums do better if you deadhead the flowers and brown leaves.

Geraniums do well in our dry, cool season but do not thrive during summers. Both the brown leaves and spent flowers require deadheading. These trailing varieties are relatively new in Florida. I bought the plant in November, and it grew so slowly they didn't get many blooms until March. Once it got going, I was quite happy with it. Many other trailing geraniums have leaves that look more like ivy.

Companions: I liked it mixed with dark burgundy leaves, like coleus and Perilla 'Magilla.'

Growing Conditions

Season: Cool-season annuals. Plant from October to March, and move inside if a freeze threatens.
Light: Light shade to full sun.
Water: Medium. I water mine every 3 days.
Salt tolerance: High.
Wind tolerance: Medium.
Zone: In zones 9 to 11, sometimes lives for a year or two with freeze protection. Takes a light frost.
Pest problems: None known.
See pages 64-65 in this book. Also see pages 44-45 in "Best Garden Color for Florida" to learn about growing this plant in the landscape.

Plant Profiles: The High Performers

Geranium, Upright *(Pelargonium x hortorum)*

Characteristics and Care

Use: Most commonly used as a centerpiece.
Growth rate: Medium.
Size: 12 to 14 inches tall.
Colors: Many shades of red, pink, peach, white, and lavender.
Average life: 5 to 6 months.
Cautions: None known.
Care: Plant with slow-release fertilizer, and fertilize again in 2 or 3 months. Geraniums look better with the dead flowers removed, which can be tedious. I sometimes let them go and am surprised at how well they do!

Geraniums: Geraniums do well in the cool, dry weather of Florida's cool season. They thrive in containers and are one of our best choices for that time of year. Since they look better when dead headed (removing spent flowers), it is easier to use a few in an easy-to-reach pot than hundreds in the landscape. They have a sense of fit in terra cotta pots placed around our Mediterranean homes with barrel tile roofs.
Companions: I like them with other winter flowers, especially ones with different shapes, like salvias and petunias. Geraniums, petunias, and alyssum are one of my favorite combinations.

Growing Conditions

Season: Cool-season annuals. Plant from October to March, and move inside if a freeze threatens.
Light: Light shade to full sun.
Water: Medium.
Salt tolerance: Medium.
Wind tolerance: Medium.
Zone: Use as an annual. Tolerant of light frost but not a freeze.
Pest problems: Fungus.

Also see pages 52, 109, 122, 123, 134, 135, 196, and 273 in this book and pages 44-45 in "Best Garden Color for Florida."

Grass, Fiber Optic *(Scirpus cernuus (a.k.a Isolepsis cernuus)*

Characteristics and Care

Use: Mounding plant that works well in the center or along the edges of any pot.
Growth rate: Medium.
Size: In my trials, grew to about 6 inches tall by equally as wide.
Colors: Green.
Average life: Looked good for about 6 months in a container.
Cautions: None known.
Care: Very easy. Plant with slow-release fertilizer, and leave them alone! Fertilize again in 2 or 3 months.

Fiber optic grass features tiny, grass-like leaves with minute yellow spikes on the tips of each leaf, giving the illusion of a fiber optic lamp. And talk about easy! They required no care other than water and an occasional fertilization. Although fiber optic grass did beautifully in our container trials, it didn't fare well in the ground. Thanks to Proven Winners for introducing us to this great plant.
Companions: I found occasional uses for fiber optic grass as a centerpiece, as shown above. But, I found it much more useful as a mounding plant contrasted with different textures, as shown on pages 48-49.

Growing Conditions

Season: All year.
Light: Medium to light shade.
Water: Adapts to somewhat dry or very wet conditions.
Salt tolerance: Medium.
Wind tolerance: Medium.
Zone: 8 to 11. Tolerant of light frost.
Pest problems: Unknown.

Also see pages 47-49, 193, and 263 in this book.

Grass, Fountain *(Pennisetum spp.)*

Characteristics and Care

Use: Centerpiece.
Growth rate: Medium.
Size: In the top of a container, grows about 3 feet by 2.5 feet wide.
Colors: Green, bronze, gray.
Average life: 6 months.
Cautions: None known.
Care: Very easy. Plant with slow-release fertilizer, and leave them alone! Fertilize again in 2 or 3 months. Trim the occasional dead stalk; replace them when they start to look messy.

Fountain grass has tall, colorful seed fronds that look fabulous in large pots. And, they are easy to care for - not much fertilizer, not much water, no trimming in pots. Eventually, they get a lot of brown leaves and are traditionally cut back to the ground if they are planted in the landscape. Since it takes quite a while for them to recover, it is inexpensive to simply replace them if they are in containers when this occurs.

Companions: While they look very dramatic alone in huge pots, I love grasses with flowers. They look good with pentas, lantana and verbena.

Growing Conditions

Season: All year.
Light: Light shade to full sun.
Water: Low. In the summer, they can make it on rain water in a large pot. Otherwise, water every 3 to 5 days.
Salt tolerance: Medium.
Wind tolerance: Medium.
Zone: 5 to 11.
Pest problems: None known in pots.

Also see pages 21, 193, and 214-215 in this book.

Grass, 'Frosted Curls' *(Carex comans 'Frosted Curls')*

Characteristics and Care

Use: Slightly trailing.
Growth rate: Slow.
Size: About 12 inches over the edge of the pot at maturity.
Color: Greyish green.
Average life: 6 to 8 months in our Florida container trials.
Cautions: Unknown.
Care: Hardly any. Plant with slow-release fertilizer, and leave them alone! Fertilize again in 2 or 3 months.

New Zealand hair sedge offers a unique trailing habit that is quite unusual for grasses, which are normally upright. It's wonderful for adding texture to a wide range of container arrangements. After a few months, it trails a full foot down the edge of a pot. Thanks to Proven Winners for introducing us to this useful plant.

Companions: It looks great with copperleaf, coleus, earth-toned plants and "Goldilocks."

Growing Conditions

Season: All year.
Light: Light shade to full sun. Untested in more shady conditions.
Water: We watered ours every 3 days, but it seems pretty adaptive.
Salt tolerance: Unknown.
Wind tolerance: Unknown.
Zone: 7 to 11.
Pest problems: Unknown.

Also see pages 46 and 193 in this book.

Plant Profiles: The High Performers

Heliconia *(Heliconia spp.)*

Characteristics and Care

Use: Centerpiece plant.
Growth rate: Fast.
Size: Many different types available, from 1 to 9 feet tall.
Colors: Orange, red, or yellow.
Average life: Stays in the same container for about 8 months. Lives in the landscape for 5 to 10 years, at least.
Cautions: None known.
Care: Very easy for short-term use. Plant with slow-release fertilizer, and leave them alone! Fertilize again in 2 or 3 months. Groom the plant as needed, cutting off dead flowers, stems, and leaves. Transplant to a frost-free garden after it outgrows the pot.

Heliconias are one of the best container plants I know for summer, particularly the small, orange one. They are easy to grow and add a tropical touch to the landscape. The taller ones (like 'Lady Di') tended to fall over in our trial containers by the end of summer. Although they grow in frost-free landscapes, many (of the 400 types available) can become a pain in the neck in the landscape because of their fast-spreading habit.

Companions: Heliconias show best when highlighted with adjacent plants that have leaf color, exotic flowers, or very different textures.

Growing Conditions

Season: Summer.
Light: Light shade to full sun.
Water: Medium. We watered the pots shown every third day.
Salt tolerance: Medium.
Wind tolerance: Low.
Zone: 10a to 11. Use as an annual further north.
Pest problems: Fungus or spider mites occasionally.

Also see pages 66,133, 216, 223, and 227 in this book. To learn how to grow this plant in the landscape, see pages 152-153 in "Best Garden Color for Florida."

Impatiens *(Impatiens wallerana)*

Characteristics and Care

Use: Mounding plant that works well alone or mixed with other bright colors.
Growth rate: Fast.
Size: Generally, in containers, they get 12 inches by 12 inches.
Colors: Red, salmon, orange,white, purple or pink
Average life: 3 to 5 months.
Cautions: Very high water use.
Care: Medium. Plant with slow release fertilizer and leave them alone! Fertilize every 2 months. Trim off the tips if leggy, but will take 3 to 4 weeks to recover.

Impatiens: Although you may be tired of seeing so many impatiens, they are one of the most dependable cool-season flowers. They literally bloom their heads off from the day you put them in till the day you take them out. And they thrive in the sides of hanging baskets.

Companions: Mix them with other cool season annuals, particularly petunias, salvias, and begonias. Or combine bright colored impatiens with other bright colors in the sun. The whites and pale pinks are best in shade or areas where you can view them at night.

Growing Conditions

Season: Winter and spring. Avoid planting from July through September.
Light: Medium shade to full sun.
Water: High (as much as twice daily) in full sun, medium in shade.
Salt tolerance: Medium.
Wind tolerance: Low.
Zone: Use as annual. Very susceptible to frost.
Pest Problems: Fungus and slugs.

Also see pages 17, 78, 83, 109, 111, 117, 122, 123, 144, 170, 206 in this book. See pages 34-39 in "Best Garden Color for Florida" to learn how to grow impatiens in the landscape.

Impatiens, Double (Impatiens spp.)

Characteristics and Care

Use: Mounding plant that works well alone or mixed with other bright colors.

Growth rate: Fast.

Size: Mounds to 18 inches round.

Colors: Red, pink, purple, orange, peach, and white.

Average life: 3 to 5 months.

Cautions: None known.

Care: Very easy. Plant with slow-release fertilizer, and repeat every 2 months. No deadheading required so there's no special care required other than frequent waterings.

Double impatiens are spectacular. They are one of the top ten container plants on the market today, providing all the advantages of the regular impatiens with prettier flowers. The flowers look like roses. They bloom non-stop, so you can count on them looking great all the time. About the only disadvantage is they do shed a lot in containers.

Companions: Be careful what you put around them because they are fairly aggressive growers. I show them alone, and I prefer to pair them with dark Persian shield, wax begonias and dragon wing begonias.

Growing Conditions

Season: Cool season. Avoid planting from July through September.

Light: Medium shade to full sun in the cool season, but burns out in the really hot weather.

Water: Medium in shade and very high in sun - as much as twice a day.

Salt tolerance: Low.

Wind tolerance: Low.

Zone: Very sensitive to the lightest frost so bring them indoors.

Pest problems: Fungus and slugs.

Also see pages 100, 141, 177, 196, and 204-205 in this book and pages 34-35 in "Best Garden Color for Florida."

Impatiens Little Lizzie (Impatiens Little Lizzy)

Characteristics and Care

Use: Mounding plant that works well in the center or along the edges of any pot as well as in the sides of hanging baskets.

Growth rate: Medium.

Size: In the top of a container, grows 6" tall. Smaller if planted in the side of a basket, about 4" tall.

Colors: Red, pink, orange, purple, white.

Average life: 6 months.

Cautions: None known.

Care: Very easy. Plant with slow-release fertilizer, and leave them alone! Fertilize again in 2 or 3 months. Trim off the tips if the plants become too large.

Impatiens 'Little Lizzy' don't take over all the other plantings in a container like the larger varieties of impatiens. They also love being planted in the sides of the hanging baskets. I did not test them in the ground, but have heard that they work well there, too. Different colors are also reported to perform differently so let me know your results. www.easygardencolor.com. My thanks to Bodger Botanicals (through Michell's) for introducing us to this plant.

Companions: Use them with larger flowers, like petunias, geraniums, and pansies.

Growing Conditions

Season: Cool season. Avoid planting from July through September.

Light: Medium shade to full sun in the cool season but burns in the summer sun.

Water: Medium. We watered the pots shown every third day.

Salt tolerance: Medium.

Wind tolerance: Low.

Zone: Use as an annual. Tolerant of light frost but not a freeze.

Pest problems: Occasional fungus, caterpillars, or snails.

Also see pages 78, 98, 99, 101, and 204 in this book.

Plant Profiles: The High Performers

Impatiens, New Guinea *(Impatiens x New Guinea Hybrids)*

Characteristics and Care

Use: Mounding plant that works well in the center or along the edges of any pot as well as in the sides of hanging baskets.
Growth rate: Medium.
Size: About 8 inches tall in the top of a container, smaller in the sides of a basket.
Colors: Iridescent pinks, oranges, reds, purples, peaches, whites, and multi-colored.
Average life: 4 to 6 months.
Cautions: None known.
Care: Very easy. Plant with slow-release fertilizer, and leave them alone! Fertilize again in 2 or 3 months.

New Guinea impatiens have more color impact than any other plant you can use in a container. Both their flowers and leaves are colorful, with the most color coming from the flowers. They do extremely well in containers, even in the sides of hanging baskets. These impatiens are very easy to grow, not requiring quite as much water as regular impatiens.
Companions: One great and easy idea is to use these at the base of bromeliads. Another dramatic combination is to use them as the centerpiece plant surrounded by the lime-green sweet potato, in a dark container.

Growing Conditions

Season: Cool season. Plant from October to March, and bring inside if a frost threatens.
Light: Medium shade to full sun.
Water: High, but not as much as regular impatiens.
Salt tolerance: Medium.
Wind tolerance: Medium.
Zone: Use as an annual. Very sensitive to the slightest frost.
Pest problems: Fungus and slugs.
Also see pages 16, 20, 21, 62, 109, 197, and 207 in this book. See pages 38-39 in "Best Garden Color for Florida" to learn more about these plants in the landscape.

Ivy *(Hedera helix)*

Characteristics and Care

Use: Trailing plant.
Growth rate: Slow.
Size: Trails about 12 inches over the sides of a pot.
Colors: Green or variegated.
Average life: 1 to 3 years in the warmer parts of Florida, longer in the cooler areas of the state.
Cautions: None known.
Care: Very easy. Plant with slow-release fertilizer, and leave them alone! Fertilize again in 2 or 3 months. Trim off the tips if the plants become too large.

Ivy is one of the best trailing plants, especially because most garden centers stock it in small hanging baskets, with vines are already ten to twelve inches long. Pull them apart (at the roots) into small sections and use them around your container for instant trailers.
Companions: Pair the ivy with almost any other plant - from flowers like impatiens to formal topiaries. Many new, variegated ivy plants are appearing on the market each season to supplement the traditional, dark green types.

Growing Conditions

Season: All year.
Light: Sun to dense shade in winter. Shade in summer.
Water: Low. Very adaptable to what is needed by the plants around it.
Salt tolerance: Low.
Wind tolerance: High.
Zone: Throughout Florida.
Pest problems: Scale and mold.

Also see pages 54, 78, 122, 123, 133, 144, 172, 196, 232, 254, and 273 in this book.

For container sources, go to www.easygardencolor.com

Jatropha *(Jatropha integerrima 'Compacta')*

Characteristics and Care

Use: Centerpiece plant.
Growth rate: Medium.
Size: 3 to 8 feet tall in a container.
Colors: Red and pink.
Average life: Lives in the same container for up to 6 months. In the garden, lives 10 to 30 years in frost-free areas.
Cautions: Poisonous; sap stains clothing.
Care: Plant with slow-release fertilizer, and repeat in 2 or 3 months. Trim back hard once a year. This plant takes a few months to look good after a hard cut-back.

Jatrophas are easy to grow, bloom all the time, and attract butterflies. This plant is particularly useful as a centerpiece plant in summer because it loves heat and humidity. Jatropha is available as a shrub or small tree. I leave mine in containers until they start to look leggy and then transplant them into my garden.
Companions: I like to mix it with bright colors. It looks gorgeous with small mammey crotons around the base of the container (see page 249). It also mixes well with shrimp plants, plumbago, and pentas for great summer container arrangements.

Growing Conditions

Season: All year in frost-free zones.
Light: Light shade to full sun.
Water: Medium. We watered the pots shown every third day.
Salt tolerance: Medium.
Wind tolerance: Medium. If grown as a small tree, keep it staked for better wind tolerance.
Zone: 10a through 11
Pest problems: Scale, leaf miners occasionally.
Also see pages 42-43, and 248-249 in this book. See "Easy Gardens for Florida" to learn more about using this plant in the landscape.

Kalanchoe *(Kalanchoe blossfeldiana)*

Characteristics and Care

Use: Centerpiece or mounding plant along the edge of a pot.
Growth rate: Medium.
Size: About 6 to 8 inches tall.
Colors: Red, salmon, yellow or pink.
Average life: 6 months, blooming on and off during that time period.
Cautions: Poisonous.
Care: Very easy. Plant with slow-release fertilizer, and leave them alone! Fertilize again in two or three months.

Kalanchoe provides very intense color in shade or sun. It also performs well in high salt and wind situations. However, many of the hybridized varieties don't last well from one season to the next. Nor do they bloom continually during a single season. They flower for a month or so, rest, and bloom again a month later. Blooming increases if you remove the dead flowers.
Companions: Mix different colors of kalanchoe together in a bright pot for easy, color impact (see page 69). Kalanchoes also work well planted around larger plants, as shown on page 268.

Growing Conditions

Season: Cool season. Avoid planting from July through September.
Light: Medium shade to full sun.
Water: Low.
Salt tolerance: High.
Wind tolerance: High.
Zone: 10a to 11. Use as an annual. Tolerant of light frost but not a freeze.
Pest problems: Occasional crown rot, slugs and snails. Do not over water.

Plant Profiles: The High Performers

Lamium 'White Nancy' *(Lamium maculatum 'White Nancy')*

Characteristics and Care

Use: Trailing plant that works best cascading down the edges of a container or planted in the sides of a hanging basket.

Growth rate: Medium.

Size: Trails about 8 inches down the side of a pot.

Colors: Green and white leaves with small, white flowers. Use this plant for its leaves.

Average life: 6 months.

Cautions: Unknown.

Care: Very easy. Plant with slow-release fertilizer, and repeat in 2 or 3 months. Trim off the tips if the plant become too large.

Lamium is a favorite in northern gardens. We were thrilled with the results here in Florida with the samples that Proven Winners sent us. As a trailing plant, it worked beautifully to define other plants like verbena and petunias. Lamium adds a distinct texture and feel to hanging baskets. We did not test it in the ground.

Companions: Use with other trailing plants like verbena and petunias. I particularly like this one with different shades of purple.

Growing Conditions

Season: Cool season. Avoid planting from July through September.

Light: Medium shade to full sun in the cool season, but burns in the summer sun.

Water: Medium. We watered the pots shown every third day.

Salt tolerance: Unknown.

Wind tolerance: Unknown.

Zone: Used as a groundcover up north. I only tested it as annual in Florida.

Pest problems: Unknown.

Also see page 94 in this book.

Lantana spp. *(Lantana spp)*

Characteristics and Care

Use: Trailing or mounding varieties

Growth rate: Fast.

Size: Expect trailers to grow 6 inches down the edge of the pot. The upright variety will grow 2 feet tall.

Colors: Yellow, purple, red, orange, and white.

Average life: 2 to 4 months in container.

Cautions: Poisonous to humans and pets. Can cause serious illness or death.

Care: Very easy. Plant with slow release fertilizer and leave them alone! Fertilize again in 2 or 3 months. If it looks weedy, cut it way back.

Lantana: I found the yellow and purple (both trailing varieties) to be the most dependable bloomers. I encountered a lot of problems with other varieties, which would go out of bloom for as long as two months. These are mainly useful in high-salt situations and a great plant for butterflies.

Companions: For salt and wind situations, combine lantana with pentas and blue daze. Or, plant it at the base of oleander along with scaevola 'Blue Wonder' for an amazing combination that also works well for salty locales.

Growing Conditions

Season: Purple peaks in dry season; yellow peaks in summer.

Light: Full sun.

Water: Medium.

Salt tolerance: High.

Wind tolerance: High.

Zone: Yellow 9b to 11; purple 9 to 11. Purple will grow back after freeze. Use as summer annual in Zone 8.

Pest problems: Occasional fungus, and whitefly.

Also see pages 44 and 91 in this book. See pages 100-103 in "Best Garden Color for Florida" to learn more about lantana in the landscape.

Licorice, White *(Helichrysum petiolare 'White Licorice')*

Characteristics and Care

Use: Trailing plant.
Growth rate: Medium.
Size: 8 to 12 inches tall and wide.
Colors: Silvery gray.
Average life: 6 months.
Cautions: None known.
Care: Very easy. Plant with slow-release fertilizer, and leave them alone! Fertilize again in 2 or 3 months. Trim as needed to keep it looking good.

Growing Conditions

Season: Fall, winter, and spring. Protect from frost.
Light: Tested only in full sun.
Water: Medium.
Salt tolerance: Unknown.
Wind tolerance: Unknown.
Zone: Use as an annual. Tolerant of light frost but not a freeze.
Pest problems: Whiteflies, crown and stem rot in cool, damp conditions.

White licorice: Talk about a winner! Pinder's Nursery (wholesale) in Palm City gave me some to try and I was thrilled with its performance. It mixed beautifully with hot pink periwinkles, and we found that this combination stands up to our heat in early summer very well. I don't know how it's going to do long-term because I've only used it for one year, but I'm very excited about the color - a wonderful, silver-frosted foliage.

Companions: Used with dark burgundy or pink flowers; with foliage like coleus and Perilla 'Magilla', it looks great. It also shows well with hot pink periwinkles and snowbush (see pages 228 and 229).

Lysimachia 'Goldilocks' *(Lysimachia mummularia)*

Characteristics and Care

Use: Trailing plant for the edges of any container, hanging basket, wall pot, or window box.
Growth rate: Fast.
Size: Trails over the edge of the pot to at least 18 inches.
Colors: Lime green.
Average life: We kept them in pots up to 6 months.
Cautions: None known.
Care: Very easy. Plant with slow-release fertilizer, and leave them alone! Fertilize again in 2 or 3 months. Trim the tips as needed.

Growing Conditions

Season: All year.
Light: Medium shade to full sun. Burns a bit in constant sun in the hottest part of summer.
Water: Medium.
Salt tolerance: Unknown.
Wind tolerance: Medium.
Zone: Use as an annual in Florida.
Pest problems: No pests bothered our 'Goldilocks.' According to Euro American growers, watch for aphids and whiteflies. Foliage easily damaged by sprays.

Also see pages 42, 43, 46, 78, 109, 182, and 232 in this book.

'Goldilocks' is one of the best trailing plants for containers. Most long trailers are either so fast-growing that they take over the whole pot, like the sweet potato vines, or so slow that the other plants in the pot are dead by the time they reach an acceptable size. Not so for 'Goldilocks.' It is easy to grow - and quick to reach a good size without overwhelming the arrangement. My thanks to Proven Winners for introducing us to this plant.

Companions: This plant works beautifully in almost any style. It not only compliments cottage flowers but tropical arrangements as well.

Plant Profiles: The High Performers

Lysimachia 'Outback Sunset' *(Lysimachia 'Outback Sunset')*

Characteristics and Care

Use: Trailing plant.
Growth rate: Medium.
Size: Grows about 8 inches down the sides of a pot.
Colors: Yellow and green leaves with yellow flowers.
Average life: 4 to 6 months.
Cautions: None known.
Care: Very easy. Plant with slow-release fertilizer, and leave them alone! Fertilize again in 2 or 3 months. Trim off the tips if the plants become too large.

Lysimachia: I first tried a lysimachia 'Golden Globes' with solid green leaves, which had a very short bloom time (see page 97). However, I was thrilled with the 'Outback Sunset' because the leaves give color all the time, even when the flowers are dormant. The bright color of the leaves is quite showy, and this plant is very easy to grow, performing well in our trials.

Companions: Use it with plants that have dark flowers or leaves. It's dynamite with New Guinea impatiens, crotons, ti plants and trailing torenia.

Growing Conditions

Season: I tested this plant in the cool season and have no data about its performance in summer.
Light: Medium shade to full sun in the cool season, but burns in the summer sun.
Water: Medium.
Salt tolerance: Unknown.
Wind tolerance: Unknown.
Zone: Used as a perennial in some northern regions. I tested it as an annual.
Pest problems: Unknown.

Also see pages 62 and 78 in this book.

Mandeville Vine *(Mandevillea spp.)*

Characteristics and Care

Use: Trailing plant.
Growth rate: Fast.
Size: From 6 to 36 inches, depending on variety.
Colors: Pink or white.
Average life: 6 to 12 months if protected from frost.
Cautions: Parts of the plant are poisonous if eaten.
Care: Very easy. Plant with slow-release fertilizer, and leave them alone! Fertilize again in two or three months. Trim if the plants become too large.

Mandeville vines are commonly used throughout the world as summer annuals. They die in winter in north Florida. In south and central Florida, it is dormant in winter, and sometimes does not return the following spring. I find it most useful in hanging baskets or growing up a trellis in the summer. Or, place an obelisk in the middle of a large pot and let the vine twine its way to the top.

Companions: I mix them with bright colors like melampodium, trailing torenia, and periwinkles. They also look good in a separate pot but part of the same grouping with heliconia.

Growing Conditions

Season: Summer.
Light: Full sun.
Water: Medium.
Salt tolerance: Unknown.
Wind tolerance: Unknown.
Zone: Use as an annual. Tolerant of light frost but not a freeze.
Pest problems: Leaf miners occasionally.

For container sources, go to www.easygardencolor.com

Marigold *(Tagetes spp.)*

Characteristics and Care

Use: Mounding plant or centerpiece.
Growth rate: Medium.
Size: From 6 to 30 inches tall, depending on variety.
Colors: Yellow, orange, burnt orange, white, and burgundy.
Average life: 2 months.
Cautions: None known.
Care: Plant with slow-release fertilizer, and remove the spent flowers. Fertilize again in 2 or 3 months if the plants are still alive.

Marigolds were not my favorite yellow plant during our container trials. They didn't last anywhere near as long as other yellows we tried, like melampodium during the warm season, or violas during the cool season. And most of them require deadheading, or removing of the spent blooms, which is too time consuming for my low-maintenance garden. But, so many others seem to have such great luck with them that I will keep trying!

Companions: I mix them with bright colors like petunias and salvia. I love red salvia, yellow marigolds and the dark purple petunias planted together.

Growing Conditions

Season: Cool season. Avoid planting from July through September.
Light: Full sun.
Water: Medium.
Salt tolerance: Medium.
Wind tolerance: Medium.
Zone: Use as an annual. Protect from freezes.
Pest problems: Occasional spider mites, particularly in dry weather.
Also see pages 44, 79, 98, 122, 123, 125, 127, and 189 in this book. See pages 60-61 in "Best Garden Color for Florida" to learn how to use this plant in the landscape.

Melampodium *(Melampodium paludosum)*

Characteristics and Care

Use: Mounding plant that works well as a centerpiece or along the edges of a container. Does not work in the sides of a basket.
Growth rate: Fast.
Size: About 12 inches tall.
Colors: Golden yellow.
Average life: 5 to 6 months.
Cautions: None known.
Care: Easy, except they like a lot of water, particularly in hot weather. Plant with slow-release fertilizer, and repeat in 2 or 3 months. No trimming or deadheading required.

Melampodium is one of my favorite yellow-flowering container plants. It blooms well all summer - one of the few annual plants that will. The daisy-like flowers add a mass of yellow to any arrangement. But, avoid using them in the sides of hanging baskets or during the cool season.

Companions: An easy summer arrangement includes melampodium with red or hot pink pentas and trailing blue torenia. They also are a great accent for crotons and ti plants.

Growing Conditions

Season: Summer. It does not like temperatures lower than 50 degrees.
Light: Medium shade to full sun. Needs much less water in shade.
Water: Medium to high. In a pot, it can require daily watering when in sun.
Salt tolerance: Medium.
Wind tolerance: Medium.
Zone: Summer annual throughout Florida.
Pest problems: Occasional fungus.
Also see pages 68 and 90-91 in this book. See pages 42-43 in "Best Garden Color for Florida" to learn more about growing this plant in the landscape.

Plant Profiles: The High Performers

Mint, Variegated *(Plectranthus coleoides 'Variegata')*

Characteristics and Care

Use: Great trailing plant; grows as a mounding plant if trimmed.
Growth rate: Medium.
Size: Trails 36" over the edge of a pot.
Colors: Light green and white.
Average life: 6 months.
Cautions: None known.
Care: Very easy. Plant with slow-release fertilizer, and leave them alone! Fertilize again in 2 or 3 months. Trim or not, depending on how you want to use the plant. Pinching back makes them bushier.

Variegated mint is a fabulous plant. Proven Winners sent us samples to try, and the plants thrived. This plant really likes Florida so it may be one of our best trailers. Variegated mint will eventually trail 18 to 24 inches over the sides of a basket, but it takes a while. I've had it in the same basket for six months and it still looks fantastic.

Companions: I count on this foliage plant because it defines the colors around it and goes with almost anything. Use it with brighter colors, like brilliant reds, purples, and yellows in petunias, melampodium, or verbenas.

Growing Conditions

Season: All year.
Light: Medium shade to full sun in winter. Medium to light shade in summer.
Water: Low.
Salt tolerance: Unknown.
Wind tolerance: Unknown.
Zone: Use as an annual in Florida.
Pest problems: Whiteflies.

Mona Lavender *(Plectranthus plepalila 'Mona Lavender')*

Characteristics and Care

Use: Centerpiece.
Growth rate: Medium.
Size: Size is proportional to the container, ranging from 16 to 36 inches tall.
Colors: Light purple spiky flowers; dark green leaves with solid purple undersides.
Average life: 6 months.
Cautions: None known.
Care: Very easy. Plant with slow-release fertilizer, and leave them alone! Fertilize again in 2 or 3 months. I never trimmed mine.

Mona Lavender did very well in our container trials. Although it was one of the better centerpiece plants for cool-season containers, it did poorly in the ground. So, stick to good potting soil and containers with this plant and you will be quite happy. Mona Lavender required no maintenance at all once it was planted, other than watering.

Companions: This plant looks fabulous with other purples, like verbena, petunias, and lamium. Or, plant it with bright-colored flowers, like petunias and daisies.

Growing Conditions

Season: Cool season. Avoid planting from July through September.
Light: Medium shade to full sun in the cool season, but burns in the summer sun.
Water: Medium. We watered the pots shown every third day.
Salt tolerance: Unknown.
Wind tolerance: Unknown.
Zone: 9b to 11. Use as an annual. Tolerant of light frost but not a freeze.
Pest problems: We had no pests on ours.

Also see pages 51, 79, 90, 91, 94, 95, 182, 190-191, and 196 in this book.

For container sources, go to www.easygardencolor.com

Moss Rose and Purslane *(Portulaca spp.)*

Characteristics and Care

Use: Mounding plant that trails slightly over edge of pot.
Growth rate: Fast.
Size: 4 to 8 inches tall.
Colors: Bright pinks, oranges, yellows, purples, and whites.
Average life: 2 to 3 months for moss rose and 4 to 6 months for purslane.
Cautions: Shorter-lived than most other summer annuals. Flowers only open in sunny weather.
Care: Very easy. Plant with slow-release fertilizer, and leave them alone! Fertilize again in 2 or 3 months if the plants are still going.

Moss Rose Purslane

Moss rose and purslane: Technically, moss rose (*Portulaca grandiflora*) and purslane (*Portulaca oleracea*) are two different plants, the latter lasting longer and the former offering more attractive flowers. The good part about both portulacas is that they love the heat of summer in Florida. Another great advantage of these two in containers is their drought tolerance. However, they close up when the weather is cloudy or they're not getting enough sun.

Companions: Use with other summer bloomers, particularly tropical plants, like crotons and tis.

Growing Conditions

Season: Summer.
Light: Full sun.
Water: Low.
Salt tolerance: High.
Wind tolerance: High.
Zone: Grown all over the world as a summer annual. Occasionally lasts longer in zones 9 to 11.
Pest problems: Occasional snails or mites.

Also see pages 222, 226, and 258-259 in this book. See pages 50-53 in "Best Garden Color for Florida" to learn about how to grow this plant in the landscape.

Mussaenda, Dwarf *(Mussaenda philipinenss)*

Characteristics and Care

Use: Centerpiece plant or accent.
Growth rate: Medium.
Size: Proportional to the container - from 12 inches tall in a small container to 6 feet tall in a large one.
Colors: Yellow and white flowers.
Average life: Remains in the same size container for about 6 months. Lives in the ground for years in frost-free areas.
Cautions: Unknown.
Care: Very easy. Plant with slow-release fertilizer, and leave them alone! Fertilize again in 2 or 3 months.

Mussaendas: The dwarf varieties of mussaenda are a great choice for summer color. The bloom offers two colors, with non-stop flowers that thrive in the worst of Florida's heat and humidity. Be sure to plant these where you can see them from above because the flowers will not show if you locate the pot above eye level. Hence, not good as centerpiece for hanging baskets.

Companions: When used as a centerpiece plant, they look really good with dwarf chenille or trailing torenia around them. They can also be used as mounding plants around small flowering trees, as shown on page 31.

Growing Conditions

Season: Summer.
Light: Medium shade to full sun.
Water: Medium, but may need daily watering in full sun in August.
Salt tolerance: Unknown.
Wind tolerance: Unknown.
Zone: 10a to 11 in the landscape. Use as an annual in central and north Florida.
Pest problems: I have grown this plant for years without seeing any pests.
See pages 216-217 in this book. See "Easy Gardens for Florida" to learn how to grow this plant in the land-scape.

Plant Profiles: The High Performers

Mussaenda, Salmon *(Mussaenda phillippica 'Aurorae')*

Characteristics and Care

Use: Centerpiece.
Growth rate: Medium.
Size: Proportional to the container - from 2 feet tall in a medium container to 6 feet tall in a large one.
Colors: Salmon. Other similar varieties are lighter peach or white.
Average life: Lives in the same container for up to 6 months. In the garden, lives 10 to 30 years in frost-free areas.
Cautions: Unknown.
Care: Plant with slow-release fertilizer, and leave them alone! Fertilize again in 2 or 3 months.

White Mussaenda

Peach Mussaenda

Salmon Mussaenda

Growing Conditions

Season: Summer.
Light: Full sun.
Water: Medium.
Salt tolerance: Unknown.
Wind tolerance: Unknown.
Zone: 10a to 11 in the landscape. For the rest of Florida, this one is worth bringing indoors during freezes.
Pest problems: Unknown.

See page 217 in this book. Also see pages 162-163 in "Best Garden Color for Florida" to learn how to grow this plant in the landscape.

Salmon mussaenda and cousins (the white and peach) are some of our most spectacular summer plants and deserve much more attention throughout Florida. They do well planted in the ground in zones 10 to 11 but are completely leafless in the winter. In summer, they are nothing short of spectacular, even in the worst heat of August, in any spot in Florida.
Companions: These plants are so spectacular they show well alone. If you want companions, try summer annuals like melampodium and torenia.

Orchid, Ground *(Spathoglottis spp)*

Characteristics and Care

Use: Centerpiece plant.
Growth rate: Medium.
Size: Varies by type, from 8 to 24 inches tall.
Colors: Lavender, yellow, or dark purple.
Average life: 3 to 8 years if kept in frost-free areas.
Cautions: None known.
Care: Plant in spring or summer with slow-release fertilizer. Fertilize again in two or three months. Trim off dead leaves and flowers. Plants look great in the warm months but go out of bloom and get brown splotches on their leaves in the cool months.

Spathoglottis 'Grapette'

Spathoglottis plicata

Growing Conditions

Season: Warm months.
Light: Light shade to full sun. The ideal light is partial shade.
Water: Medium.
Salt tolerance: Unknown.
Wind tolerance: Unknown.
Zone: 10a to 11. Protect from frost.
Pest problems: None serious in our trials.

See pages 133, 162, 216, and 224-225 in this book. Also see pages 104-105 in "Best Garden Color for Florida" to learn more about how to grow this plant in the landscape.

Ground orchids are one of our best container plants for the warm season. Although the flowers are smaller than some of the more spectacular orchids, they bloom much longer, a full 6 months in warm weather. While many orchids require different soils and containers than the rest of your plants, these orchids grow in regular potting soil and containers.
Companions: Normally, I use these alone. I really like to see ground orchids in gorgeous pots, where they can come into their own.

Orchid, Epiphytic (those that grow in trees)

Characteristics and Care

Use: Too beautiful to use as anything other than focal points by themselves.
Growth rate: Slow.
Size: Varies greatly by species, from tiny dwarfs to large hedges.
Colors: Every color in the rainbow.
Average life: Many years if protected from frost.
Cautions: None known.
Care: Varies by species.

Dendrobiums, cattleyas, and oncidiums are good choices because they are fairly easy to grow outdoors in Florida. Phalaenopsis is the most common orchid indoors. Since the prices of orchids have dropped considerably, many people use them for a month or so indoors and then discard them. See pages 158 to 169 for detailed information.
Companions: Most orchids stand alone. Occasionally, I have seen them mixed with bromeliads (see page 171) to create spectacular arrangements.

Growing Conditions

Season: All year.
Light: Medium shade to full sun, depending on the variety.
Water: Overwatering is the number one way to kill all orchids. Allow roots to dry out between waterings.
Salt tolerance: Medium to high.
Wind tolerance: Medium.
Zone: Varies by species.
Pest problems: Occasional fungus, bacteria and scale.

Also see pages 158 to 169 in this book.

Palm, Alexander *(Ptycosperma elegans)*

Characteristics and Care

Use: A beautiful palm for containers.
Growth rate: Medium.
Size: Grows to 10 feet or more, depending on the size pot you plant it in.
Colors: Lime green.
Average life: Leave in the same large container (at least 20" diameter) for up to 3 years. Then, trim the roots or plant in your garden in frost-free areas.
Cautions: None known.
Care: Easy. Plant with slow-release fertilizer, and repeat two or three times a year.

Alexander palms do extremely well in containers. They are attractive, relatively inexpensive, and easy to grow. While they reach twenty feet tall in the landscape, the size of the pot you put them in will determine how big they get in containers. They do not do too well indoors because of spider mite attacks.

Companions:
Alexander palms look best planted in very large containers, with diameters of at least 20 inches. This size gives you the space to underplant the palms with smaller plants, like bromeliads or annuals.

Growing Conditions

Season: All year.
Light: Medium shade to full sun.
Water: Low.
Salt tolerance: Medium.
Wind tolerance: Medium.
Zone: 10b to 11.
Pest problems: Occasional mites, scale or aphids, particularly if the palm is indoors or under screening. This palm is not recommended for indoors.

For information about growing this plant in the landscape, see "Easy Gardens for Florida."

Plant Profiles: The High Performers

Palm, Areca *(Dypsis lutescens)*

Characteristics and Care

Use: Centerpiece plant.
Growth rate: Medium.
Size: Proportional to the container - from 2 feet tall in a small container (10" diameter) to 8 feet tall in a large one (24" diameter). Grows to 20 feet tall in the ground.
Colors: Green.
Average life: Stays in a very large container (20" diameter or more) for 3 years without requiring root-pruning. Transplant into a larger pot or into a frost-free garden at that time.
Cautions: None known.
Care: Very easy. Plant with slow release fertilizer and repeat every 3 months. Trim as needed to remove brown fronds.

Areca palms are quite inexpensive, do well in containers, and tolerate deep shade outdoors. They are not an ideal choice for indoors, however, because of a tendency to thin out and attract spider mites. Bamboo palms (*below*) look similar to arecas and do much better inside. Arecas are particularly useful as screening plants outdoors because larger ones are quite dense and inexpensive as well.
Companions: Used with pothos and bromeliads (like this picture), areas are quite tropical in appearance.

Growing Conditions

Season: All year.
Light: Dense shade to full sun.
Water: Low.
Salt tolerance: Medium.
Wind tolerance: Medium.
Zone: 10b to 11. Bring inside if frost threatens.
Pest Problems: I have never had a pest outside, but they are somewhat susceptible to ganoderma. Under screening, watch out for caterpillars, mealybugs, and scale.
See page 239 in this book. Also see "Easy Gardens for Florida" to learn how to grow this plant in the landscape.

Palm, Bamboo *(Chamadorea spp)*

Characteristics and Care

Use: Centerpiece.
Growth rate: Medium.
Size: Proportional to the container - from 2 feet tall in a small container (10" W) to 6 feet tall in a large one (24" W). Grows to about 8 feet tall in the ground.
Colors: Green.
Average life: Stays in a very large container (20" W) for 3 years without requiring root-pruning. Transplant into a larger pot or into a frost- free garden at that time.
Cautions: Seeds or fruit are irritants.
Care: Very easy. Plant with slow-release fertilizer, and leave them alone! Fertilize again in 3 to 4 months. Remove dead fronds.

Bamboo palms are one of the best and easiest indoor palms you can buy. They have been popular for generations and are sometimes called parlor palms because they used to grace the sun porches in Victorian houses. The bamboo palm is taller and thinner than its relative the cat palm. It also adapts to dense shade in the landscape, provided it is protected from frost.
Companions: Underplant them with pothos, dwarf spathophyllum, dwarf chenille or cast iron plants. This palm also looks good by itself.

Growing Conditions

Season: All year.
Light: Dense to medium shade.
Water: Medium.
Salt tolerance: Low.
Wind tolerance: Unknown.
Zone: 10b to 11.
Pest problems: Mites, mealybugs, and scale.

See "Easy Gardens for Florida" for more information about growing this plant in the landscape.

Palm, Cardboard or Zamia *(Zamia furfuracea)*

Characteristics and Care

Use: Centerpiece.
Growth rate: Slow.
Size: Proportional to the container - from 18 inches tall in a small container (10" diameter) to 4 feet tall in a large one (24" diameter).
Colors: Green.
Average life: Stays in a very large container (20" W) for 3 years without requiring root-pruning. Transplant into a larger pot or into a frost-free garden at that time.
Cautions: Poisonous.
Care: Very easy. Plant with slow-release fertilizer, and repeat in 2 or 3 months. No need to trim this plant.

Cardboard palms are prehistoric cycads that are slowly replacing the sago palm, which has fallen victim to the cycad scale. It's a wonderful plant when you want tropical foliage with almost no care. For high salt-and-wind situations, cardboard palms stand up admirably, like the one shown that was photographed next to the ocean at the Breakers Resort in Palm Beach.
Companions: Underplant with a cascading plant, like dwarf chenille plants.

Growing Conditions

Season: All year.
Light: Medium shade to full sun.
Water: Low.
Salt tolerance: High.
Wind tolerance: High.
Zone: 9b to 11.
Pest problems: Few pests outdoors; occasional scale and mealybug, especially under screening.

Also see "Easy Gardens for Florida" for more information about using this plant in the landscape.

Palm, Cat *(Chamadorea cataractum)*

Characteristics and Care

Use: Centerpiece.
Growth rate: Medium.
Size: Proportional to the container - from 2 feet tall in a small container (10" W) to 6 feet tall in a large one (24" W). Grows to about 8 feet tall in the ground.
Colors: Green.
Average life: Stays in a very large container (20" diameter or more) for 2 years without requiring root-pruning Transplant into a larger pot or into a frost-free garden at that time. It lives for many years in the landscape.
Cautions: Irritant.
Care: Very easy. Plant with slow-release fertilizer, and leave them alone! Fertilize again in 2 or 3 months.

Cat palms look good, with their dark green fronds and full appearance. Like areca palms, their growth habit is shrub-like, with suckers (baby plants) growing from the base. Their fronds are more attractive than areca palms, but their shape is different - shorter and stouter. This palm is easy to grow in containers, provided it is outside or under screening. It doesn't do well inside a building.
Companions: Use this palm alone in a container.

Growing Conditions

Season: All year.
Light: Light to medium shade. Bleaches out somewhat in full sun.
Water: Low.
Salt tolerance: Low.
Wind tolerance: Low.
Zone: 10b to 11 outdoors. Further north, bring inside if a frost threatens.
Pest Problems: Spider mites or mealybugs indoors or under screening. Few pests outside.

Also see "Easy Gardens for Florida" for more information about using this plant in the landscape.

Plant Profiles: The High Performers

Palm, Fishtail *(Caryota mitis)*

Characteristics and Care

Use: Centerpiece.
Growth rate: Medium.
Size: Proportional to the container - from 2 feet tall in a small container (10" W) to 6 to 8 feet tall in a large one (24" W). Grows to about 18 feet tall in the ground.
Colors: Green.
Average life: Stays in a very large container (20" diameter or more) for 2 years without requiring root-pruning. Transplant into a larger pot or into the ground in a frost-free garden at that time. It lives for many years in the landscape.
Cautions: Seeds are a severe skin irritant.

Fishtail palms are another excellent indoor plant, although they require a little more light than the kentia, lady, or bamboo palm. They also thrive outdoors, provided they are protected from frost. Their attractive leaves really do resemble fishtails. Take care not to handle the seeds without gloves as they are a strong skin irritant, one of the worst of our commonly-used plants. They also have really aggressive roots; I saw them break through a concrete planter once.
Companions: These palms look good planted alone in a container.

Growing Conditions

Season: All year.
Light: Medium shade to full sun.
Water: Medium.
Salt tolerance: Low.
Wind tolerance: Low.
Zone: 10b to 11. Protect from frost.
Pest problems: Moderately susceptible to lethal yellowing and leaf spots caused by fungus.
Care: Very easy. Plant with slow release fertilizer and leave them alone! Fertilize again in 2 or 3 months. Trim off dead leaves.

Palm, Kentia *(Howea forsteriana)*

Characteristics and Care

Use: Centerpiece.
Growth rate: Slow.
Size: Proportional to the container - from 4 feet tall in a medium container (14" W) to 8 to 10 feet tall in a large one (24" W). Grows to about 30 feet tall in the ground.
Colors: Green.
Average life: Stays in a large container (20" diameter or more) for years without requiring root-pruning. Transplant into a larger pot or into the ground at that time. It lives for many years in the landscape (zones 9b-11).
Cautions: None known.
Care: Very easy.

Kentia palms are one of the best indoor plants on the market, period. They not only adapt well to low light, dust, and air-conditioning, but also require very little care. Their slow growth allows them to remain in the same container for years, and their graceful fronds are just beautiful, working well indoors as well as outside in zones 9b to 11. Kentia palms thrive in low-light situations but take some sun after they are at least five years old. Give them some shade outdoors, however, or they begin to look a bit straggly.
Companions: For an easy indoor grouping, arrange pots of chinese evergreen and pothos at the base of this palm.

Growing Conditions

Season: All year.
Light: Dense to light shade. Indoors, place them in a location where there is enough light to read by.
Water: Medium. Do not overwater this plant, as that causes fungus, which is its biggest problem. Let the soil dry out between waterings.
Salt tolerance: Low.
Wind tolerance: Medium.
Zone: 9b to 11. Tolerant of light frost (26 to 28 degrees) but not a freeze.
Pest problems: Spider mites, scale, lethal yellowing, leaf spot diseases.

Palm, Lady *(Rhapis excelsa)*

Characteristics and Care

Use: Centerpiece.
Growth rate: Slow.
Size: Proportional to the container - from 2 feet tall in a small container (10" W) to 6 feet tall in a large one (24" W). Grows to about 8 feet tall in the ground.
Colors: Green.
Average life: Stays in the same container for 2 years without requiring root-pruning. Transplant into a larger pot or into the ground in a frost-free garden at that time. It lives for many years in the landscape.
Cautions: None known.

Lady palms are so well-adapted to indoor situations that they have become one of the world's most popular indoor palms. They also adapt very well to outdoor conditions in zones 9 to 11. Lady palms grow quite slowly, which cuts down on their care needs but increases their price.
Companions: Combine lady palms with other low-light indoor plants with different textures, like pothos and snake plants. *(Container and photo from Lechuza.)*

Growing Conditions

Season: All year.
Light: Dense to light shade. Leaves turn yellow in too much light.
Water: Medium.
Salt tolerance: Medium.
Wind tolerance: Medium.
Zone: 9 to 11.
Pest problems: Occasional scale and mealybugs.
Care: Easy. Plant with slow release fertilizer and repeat in two or three months. Trim off brown leaves.
See pages 145 and 157 in this book. Also see "Easy Gardens for Florida" to learn how to grow this plant in the landscape.

Palm, Pygmy Date *(Phoenix roebellini)*

Characteristics and Care

Use: Centerpiece.
Growth rate: Slow.
Size: Proportional to the container - from 2 feet tall in a medium container (14" W) to 6 feet tall in a large one (24" W). Grows to about 10 feet tall in the ground.
Colors: Green.
Average life: Stays in the same container for 2 years without requiring root-pruning. Transplant into a larger pot or into the ground in a garden (zones 9b-11) at that time. It lives for many years in the landscape.
Cautions: Dangerous spines.

Pygmy date palms are commonly used in exterior landscaping in south and central Florida. Although they do fairly well indoors, not many are used in confined spaces because of dangerous spines on the fronds.
Companions: Tropicals, like ti plants, crotons, and golden shrimp plants. *(Container and photo from Lechuza.)*

Growing Conditions

Season: All year.
Light: Medium shade to full sun.
Water: Low.
Salt tolerance: Low.
Wind tolerance: High.
Zone: 9b to 11.
Pest problems: Leaf-spotting disease.
Care: Very easy. Plant with slow-release fertilizer, and repeat in two or three months. Trim off brown, drooping fronds using gloves and long loppers to keep from getting hurt from the thorns.
Also see "Easy Gardens for Florida" for information about use in the landscape.

Plant Profiles: The High Performers

Palm, Thatch *(Thrinax radiata)*

Characteristics and Care

Use: Centerpiece.
Growth rate: Slow.
Size: Proportional to the container - from 2 feet tall in a small container (10" diameter) to 8 feet tall in a large one (24" diameter). Grows to 20 feet tall in the ground.
Colors: Green.
Average life: Stays in the same container for 2 years without requiring root-pruning. Transplant into a larger pot or into the ground in a garden (zones 10b-11) at that time. It lives for many years in the landscape.
Cautions: None known.

Thatch palms require more light than most of the palms in this book, so this Florida Keys native works better outside than it does indoors. Its very attractive, fan-like (palmate) fronds give it an interesting appearance. This is a palm you can put in a pot and leave for years because it's that slow-growing. This slow growth cuts down on their care needs but increases their price. Thatch palms are ideal for someone who wants a really low-maintenance container plant outdoors.

Companions: Use with dark coleus, crotons or ti plants because its lime green color contrasts well with bright or dark colors.

Growing Conditions

Season: All year.
Light: Medium shade to full sun.
Water: Low.
Salt tolerance: High.
Wind tolerance: High.
Zone: 10b to 11. Tolerant of light frost but not a freeze.
Pest problems: None known.
Care: Very easy. Plant with slow release fertilizer and repeat in 2 or 3 months. Trim brown fronds, but do not trim any green fronds that extended higher than horizontal.
Also see "Easy Gardens for Florida" for more information about this plant in the landscape.

Palm, Xmas *(Adonidia merrillii)*

Characteristics and Care

Use: Centerpiece.
Growth rate: Medium.
Size: Proportional to the container - from 4 feet tall in a medium container (14" W) to 8 feet tall in a large one (24" W). Grows to about 15 feet tall in the ground.
Colors: Green.
Average life: Stays in the same container for 2 years without requiring root-pruning. Transplant into a larger pot or into the ground in a garden (zones 10b-11) at that time. It lives for many years in the landscape.
Cautions: High susceptibility to lethal yellowing.

Christmas palms (or dwarf royal palms) are one of our most popular palms because of their small stature and their attractive appearance. They do very well either in the ground or in containers, indoors or out. Use them in containers only in zones 8 or 9 because they need to be brought inside during freezes.

Companions: Christmas palms look best when underplanted with smaller plants, as shown with these foxtail ferns from Universal Studios. Bromeliads are an ideal companion in shade.

Growing Conditions

Season: All year.
Light: Medium shade to full sun.
Water: Medium.
Salt tolerance: Medium.
Wind tolerance: High.
Zone: 10a to 11.
Pest problems: Lethal yellowing.
Care: Very easy. Plant with slow-release fertilizer, and repeat in two or three months. Trim off brown, drooping fronds but be careful not to take any that are horizontal or higher.
Also see "Easy Gardens for Florida" to learn how to grow this plant in the landscape.

For container sources, go to www.easygardencolor.com

Pansy *(Viola spp.)*

Characteristics and Care

Use: Mounding plants that trail slightly over the edge of the pot.
Growth rate: Medium.
Size: 4 to 6 inches tall by about 6 inches wide.
Colors: White, yellow, purple, brown, blue, or red.
Average life: 2 to 4 months in containers.
Cautions: None known.
Care: Plant with slow-release fertilizer, and repeat in 2 or 3 months. No trimming required, but they look better if you remove the dead blooms and leaves.

Pansies are just great for winter containers, where you can see the detail of those wonderful faces you often miss when they're planted in the garden. They did not work in the sides of our hanging baskets, however. Put them in a small bowl, and they look pretty for months. Biggest bonus: They'll last in north Florida outside all winter!
Companions: Yellow pansies look great with red salvia and purple petunias. I use the yellow the most because we don't have that many yellow flowers that bloom in winter. You can also plant different colored pansies in the same container for a great look.

Growing Conditions

Season: Plant from December through February.
Light: Light shade to full sun.
Water: Medium.
Salt tolerance: Medium.
Wind tolerance: Low.
Zone: Grown throughout the world. Tolerant of all the winter cold that Florida has to offer.
Pest problems: Occasional slugs or aphids.

Also see pages 64-65 in "Best Garden Color for Florida" for more information about using this plant in the landscape.

Pentas, Butterfly *(Pentas lanceolata)*

Characteristics and Care

Use: Centerpiece. Do not use in the sides of hanging baskets.
Growth rate: Medium.
Size: 12 to 18 inches tall in containers.
Colors: Red, white, purple, or pink.
Average life: 3 to 5 months.
Cautions: None known.
Care: Plant with slow-release fertilizer, and repeat in 2 to 3 months. Blooms more if dead flowers are removed.

Pink Butterfly Pentas   Red Butterfly Pentas

Butterfly Pentas are one of twenty different penta varieties. Like the 'New Look' pentas, the 'Butterfly' pentas are annuals that live only one season. However, the 'Butterfly' pentas don't have the fungus problems that the 'New Looks' have. Other taller varieties, like 'Cranberry' pentas, are perennials that last for a few years planted in the ground but only about six months in containers. I like the 'Butterfly' pentas better than the 'Cranberry' pentas in containers because they stay short and full longer. But, the 'Cranberry' bloom constantly while the 'Butterflies' bloom very profusely and then stop for a time. They resume blooming faster if you remove the dead blooms.
Companions: Use pentas with other flowering annuals that give a country garden look, like torenia and salvia.

Growing Conditions

Season: All year if they are protected from frost.
Light: Light shade to full sun.
Water: Medium.
Salt tolerance: Medium.
Wind tolerance: Medium.
Zone: Grown all over the world as a summer annual. Frost sensitive.
Pest problems: Mites.

Also see pages 34-37, 40, 52-53, 182, and 216-217 in this book. To learn more about pentas in the landscape, see both "Easy Gardens for Florida" and 'Best Garden Color for Florida."

Plant Profiles: The High Performers

Perilla 'Magilla', Shiso *(Perilla frutescens 'Magilla')*

Characteristics and Care

Use: Centerpiece.
Growth rate: Medium.
Size: In the top of a large (17"D) container, has grown 4 feet tall in about 6 months. Stays shorter in smaller pots.
Colors: Burgundy leaves with hot pink centers.
Average life: Unknown, but going strong after 8 months in my frost-free garden.
Cautions: Poisonous if eaten.
Care: Very easy. Plant with slow release fertilizer, and repeat in 2 or 3 months. After 4 months, we trimmed ours in half, and it came back quite well.

Perilla 'Magilla' is a rising star for Florida gardens, growing extremely well with minimal care. Use perilla as you would a large coleus, taking advantage of its burgundy leaves with hot pink veins. It looks like a coleus, but it's larger, doesn't snap off as easily, and has a denser form.
Companions: Perilla looks great with white licorice for a nice contrast. I also used it successfully with trailing geraniums, trailing purple torenia, and lime green (sweet potato, coleus or 'Goldilocks').

Growing Conditions

Season: All year. Protect from frost.
Light: Medium shade to full sun in the cool season. Likes some break from the sun in summer.
Water: Medium.
Salt tolerance: Unknown.
Wind tolerance: Unknown.
Zone: Used primarily as an annual.
Pest problems: None in our trials.

Also see pages 58, 63-64, 85, 133, and 196 in this book.

Persian Shield *(Strobilanthus dyeranus)*

Characteristics and Care

Use: Works well as a center focal point.
Growth rate: Fast.
Size: In the top of a container, grows about 24 inches tall by 18 inches wide.
Colors: Purple.
Average life: 6 months.
Cautions: None known.
Care: Very easy. Plant with slow-release fertilizer and, leave them alone! Fertilize again in 2 or 3 months. Give it room to grow because it grows very quickly. If it gets leggy, trim it hard because it will recover quickly.

Persian shield is a spectacular container plant. The leaves are so gorgeous they almost look artificial. Their iridescence gleams in arrangements. This plant is short-lived when planted in the ground in Florida but perfect for about six months in a container.
Companions: Use Persian shield with either bright colors or other shades of blue and purple.

Growing Conditions

Season: All year, but looks best in winter.
Light: Medium shade to full sun in the cool season; light to medium shade in summer.
Water: High.
Salt tolerance: Unknown.
Wind tolerance: Low.
Zone: 10 to 11; protect from freezes elsewhere in Florida.
Pest problems: We had none in our trials.

Also see pages 59, 101, 133, 196, and 226 in this book.

Petunia *(Petunia spp.)*

Characteristics and Care

Use: Mounding or trailing plant that works well in the center or along the edges of any pot.
Growth rate: Medium.
Size: 6 to 18 inches tall.
Colors: Red, purples, white, yellow or pink.
Average life: 4 to 5 months.
Cautions: None known.
Care: Plant with slow-release fertilizer. Apply a fungicide if the plant has spots on the leaves or wilts when the soil is moist. Fertilize again in 3 or 4 months. Trim the plant as needed. Remove dead blooms if you have the time!

Petunias are easy, very colorful, and deserve much more use in Florida. Some are small, clumping plants, and others cascade down the sides of a pot. They are easier to grow in containers than in the ground in Florida because of nematodes and soil pH. However, hundreds of new cultivars are being sold in Florida. Some do well, others don't. We had consistent success with Proven Winners' Supertunias.
Companions: Use with snapdragons, salvias, pansies and geraniums. They also look wonderful mixed with other colors of petunias.

Growing Conditions

Season: Cool season. Avoid planting from July through September.
Light: Full sun.
Water: Medium.
Salt tolerance: High.
Wind tolerance: High.
Zone: 9 to 11. Tolerant of light frost but not a freeze.
Pest Problems: Fungus and whiteflies.

See pages 28, 51, 79, 90-91, 122-123, 182, 189-190, 195-196 in this book. To learn how to grow this plant in the landscape, see pages 48-49 in "Best Garden Color for Florida".

Philodendron *(Philodendron spp.)*

Characteristics and Care

Use: Centerpiece, mounding, or trailing plant.
Growth rate: Medium to fast, depending on type.
Size: Varies by type.
Colors: The leaves are white, orange, yellow or green.
Average life: About a year in the same container; many years in the ground in frost-free areas.
Cautions: Poisonous.
Care: Very easy. Plant with slow release fertilizer and leave them alone! Fertilize again in 2 or 3 months. Trim off the tips if the plants become too large.

Philodendron is a huge plant genus consisting of hundreds of different species ranging from small to quite large. They have done quite well in containers for generations. Many take low light well, a real plus for using them indoors. The 'Kalaidoscope' (above) is one of my favorites.
Companions: Plant the 'Kalaidoscope' with varied textures and colors. I like it with small textures, like peacock spike moss or pilea, and similar colors, like coleus 'Crime Scene."

Growing Conditions

Season: All year. Protect from frost.
Light: Deep shade to full sun, depending on type. Most prefer some shade.
Water: Low. Some philodendrons (like the 'Xanadu') get fungus with too much water.
Salt tolerance: Varies by species.
Wind tolerance: Varies by species.
Zone: 10 to 11 outdoors.
Pest problems: Fungus if overwatered; occasional mealybug, especially if used indoors.

Plant Profiles: The High Performers

Phlox *(Phlox spp.)*

Characteristics and Care

Use: Mounding plant or centerpiece.
Growth rate: Medium.
Size: Varies by type from quite small to over 3 feet tall.
Colors: White; shades of pink and purple.
Average life: About 4 months in a container.
Cautions: None known.
Care: Very easy. Plant with slow-release fertilizer, and leave them alone! Fertilize again in 2 or 3 months. Trim off the tips if the plants become too large.

Purple and white phlox planted as the centerpiece; pink calibrachoa and ivy cascading down the sides.

White Phlox

Growing Conditions

Season: Cool season. Avoid planting from July through September.
Light: Light shade to full sun. Flowers most in full sun.
Water: Medium.
Salt tolerance: Medium.
Wind tolerance: Unknown.
Zone: 5 to 11.
Pest problems: Occasional spider mites, snails, thrips.

Phlox are better known up north where they're grown as both annuals and perennials. I tested many annual phlox; the flowers bloomed profusely but went out of bloom while new flowers were forming. They give a really unique bit of color if you're trying to create a cottage garden look.

Companions: Plant with other winter flowers, including impatiens, snapdragons, petunias, and pansies.

Plumbago *(Plumbago auriculata)*

Characteristics and Care

Use: Centerpiece plant.
Growth rate: Medium.
Size: In the top of a container, grows 3 feet tall and wide.
Colors: Blue or white.
Average life: 10 to 15 years in landscape, but it can remain in the same container for up to a year.
Cautions: None known.
Care: Very easy. Plant with slow-release fertilizer, and again in 2 or 3 months. Don't trim the tips. Give it an occasional hard cutback and leave alone the rest of the time.

Growing Conditions

Season: All year, but seldom blooms in winter.
Light: Light shade to full sun, but flowers best in summer sun.
Water: Low, once it's established in landscape. Medium in pots.
Salt tolerance: Medium.
Wind tolerance: Medium.
Zone: 9b to 11.
Pest problems: Occasional scale or mites. Develops fungus and root rot if kept too wet.

Also see pages 36-37 in this book. To learn more about using this plant in the landscape, see "Easy Gardens for Florida."

Plumbago is a great plant for Florida, although it's not my favorite in containers. It works well if you need a plant that lasts a long time because it takes all the climate abuse that zones 9 and 10 have to offer. Plumbago sheds a lot and blooms intermittently.

Companions: For a cottage garden look, mix it with other flowers that look like summer wildflowers, like melampodium and pentas.

For container sources, go to www.easygardencolor.com

Polka Dot Plant *(Hypoestes phyllostachya)*

Characteristics and Care

Use: Mounding plant that works well in the center or along the edges of any pot.
Growth rate: Fast.
Size: About 8 inches tall by 5 inches wide.
Colors: Green and pink or green and white leaves.
Average life: 3 to 6 months.
Cautions: None known.
Care: Very easy. Plant with slow-release fertilizer and leave them alone! Fertilize again in 2 or 3 months. Shape it if it becomes too leggy.

Polka dot plants: I count on this plant for its fabulous, clear, pink color during the winter months. Don't plant it in the garden unless you want thousands of polka dot plants because it self-seeds. It's also available in white and green. Understand that this plant gets leggy fairly quickly outdoors.
Companions: Use it with other plants that have the same colors as the leaves. The green and white variety looks good in all white arrangements that include white caladiums, variegated mint, and ivy. The pink variety looks stunning with pink begonias, anthuriums, and pink-flowered bromeliads.

Growing Conditions

Season: Year round.
Light: Medium shade to light shade.
Water: Medium.
Salt tolerance: Low.
Wind tolerance: Low.
Zone: 9a to 11. Tolerant of light frost but not a freeze.
Pest Problems: Aphids.

Also see pages 32, 54, and 55 in this book.

Pothos *(Epipremnum aureum)*

Characteristics and Care

Use: Trailing plant.
Growth rate: Fast.
Size: There may not be any limit as to the lengths their runners will grow. They can spread over an entire window ledge. The leaves grow much larger if the vine grows up instead of down.
Colors: Green and variegated.
Average life: Years!
Cautions: Poisonous.
Care: Very easy. Plant with slow-release fertilizer, and leave them alone! Fertilize again in 2 or 3 months. Trim if the plants become too large.

Pothos is a workhorse houseplant. It survives more neglect than possibly any other indoor plant. Take care not to plant it (in the ground) outside because it is invasive in frost-free Florida and can actually smother and kill our trees. It's impossible to pull out once it's established. Having said that, it beats all other trailing plants in low-light situations indoors or restricted to containers.
Companions: Use pothos as a trailing plant with other shade lovers. It works really well with orchids and bromeliads.

Growing Conditions

Season: All year.
Light: Dense, medium, or light sun.
Water: Medium.
Salt tolerance: Medium.
Wind tolerance: Medium.
Zone: 10b to 11. Tolerant of light frost but not a freeze.
Pest problems: None known.

Also see pages 145, 173, and 206 in this book.

Plant Profiles: The High Performers

Purple Queen *(Tradescantia pallida 'Purpurea')*

Characteristics and Care

Use: Mounding or trailing plant.
Growth rate: Medium.
Size: In a container, it grows 6" tall by 6" wide.
Colors: Purple, with tiny, pink flowers.
Average life: Grows for about 5 years in the ground. Requires transplanting after about 6 to 12 months in a container.
Cautions: Poisonous sap irritates skin.
Care: Very easy. Plant with slow-release fertilizer and leave them alone! Fertilize again in 2 to 3 months. Trim it to keep the plant neat.

Purple Queen has its uses, especially because it it so salt-and-heat tolerant. It is ideal for tough situations and survives well in the sides of hanging baskets. The form of it is a bit awkward - somewhere between a trailing plant and a mounding plant. Grooming is key to this plant - like giving it a good haircut. Wear gloves when handling purple because its sap can cause dermatitis. Don't get it near your face.
Companions: For high salt situations, pair it with silver buttonwood as your centerpiece and hot pink periwinkles as your edge plants.

Growing Conditions

Season: All year.
Light: Light shade to full sun.
Water: Low.
Salt tolerance: High.
Wind tolerance: High.
Zone: 9 to 11. It is damaged by frost but will recover in warm weather.
Pest Problems: Occasional fungus.

See "Easy Gardens for Florida" to learn more about growing this plant in the landscape.

Purslane *(Portulaca oleracea)*

Characteristics and Care

Use: Trailing plant.
Growth rate: Medium.
Size: In a container, grows about 3 inches tall by 8 inches wide. Trails down the side about 6 inches.
Colors: Red, pink, purple, yellow, orange, white.
Average life: 6 months.
Cautions: None known.
Care: Very easy. Plant with slow-release fertilizer, and leave them alone! Fertilize again in 2 or 3 months. Seldom requires trimming, but if it looks scraggly it will take a hard cut-back.

Purslane is not my favorite plant in containers because the flowers close up in shade and evening light, but it's very useful for salt and low-water situations. Its flowers are quite colorful when they are open, however.
Companions: Use this with other high-salt tolerant plants like purple queen, silver buttonwood, and agaves. It looks good alone in pots because it will cascade over the edges. In medium salt situations, try it with crotons.

Growing Conditions

Season: Spring, summer, fall.
Light: Full sun.
Water: Low.
Salt tolerance: High.
Wind tolerance: High.
Zone: Grown all over the world as a summer annual. Occasionally lasts longer in zones 9 - 11.
Pest problems: Occasional fungus, caterpillars, or snails.

See pages 222, 226, and 258 in this book. Also see pages 52-53 in "Best Garden Color for Florida" to learn how to use purslane in the landscape.

Salvia, Annual *(Salvia spp.)*

Characteristics and Care

Use: Mainly as a centerpiece.
Growth rate: Medium.
Size: In the top of a container, the blue grows 12 to 18 inches tall. The red grows about 6 to 8 inches tall.
Colors: Many shades of white, red, peach, and purple.
Average life: 5 to 6 months.
Cautions: None known.
Care: Very easy. Plant with slow-release fertilizer, and leave them alone! Fertilize again in 2 or 3 months.

'Victoria Blue' Salvia   Annual Red Salvia

Annual salvias are some of the most useful centerpiece plants for cool-season containers in Florida. They not only bloom for five to six months without stopping but also offer spiky flowers. This vertical shape contrasts well with round flowers, adding textural interest to container arrangements. 'Victoria Blue' salvia is used as a perennial up north but works best as an annual in Florida.
Companions: Use with round flowers like petunias and pansies. Add a cascading plant with small leaves and/or flowers, like sweet alyssum or 'Goldilocks.'

Growing Conditions

Season: Cool season. Avoid planting from July through September.
Light: Light shade to full sun.
Water: Medium.
Salt tolerance: Medium.
Wind tolerance: Medium.
Zone: Used throughout the world as annuals.
Pest problems: I have never seen a pest on these plants but have heard of occasional thrips, mites, caterpillars, and slugs. Also see pages 8, 35, 52, 96, 121, and 191 in this book. For information about using salvia in the ground, see pages 54-57 in "Best Garden Color for Florida."

Salvia, Perennial *(Salvia spp.)*

Characteristics and Care

Use: Centerpiece plant.
Growth rate: Medium.
Size: Varies by type. Most grew to about 2 feet tall in our container trials.
Colors: Red, salmon, pink, blue, purple, yellow.
Average life: 4 to 6 months in a container. Years in the ground.
Cautions: None known.
Care: Very easy. Plant with slow-release fertilizer, and leave them alone! Fertilize again in 2 or 3 months. Trim off the tips if the plants become too large.

Perennial salvias grew quite large quickly in our container trials. Some so fast they looked too tall and out of proportion to the pot. Our favorite was Mexican sage (*Salvia leucantha*) because it developed a weeping habit, falling over the edges of the pot. It only blooms for a few months, but the gorgeous effect is worth the effort.
Companions: Use this salvia alone in a tall urn or surround it with trailing plants. Yellow lantana is a good choice (shown above), as are trailing petunias and calibrachoa.

Growing Conditions

Season: Fall and beginning of winter.
Light: Medium shade to full sun. Blooms more with more light.
Water: Medium.
Salt tolerance: Medium.
Wind tolerance: Medium.
Zone: 9 to 11.
Pest problems: None known.

For information about using this plant in the ground, see pages 176-179 in "Best Garden Color for Florida."

Plant Profiles: The High Performers

Sedum *(Sedum spp.)*

Characteristics and Care

Use: Mounding plant.
Growth rate: Slow.
Size: About 3 inches tall by 6 to 8 inches wide.
Colors: Lime green.
Average life: 6 months.
Cautions: None known.
Care: Very easy. Plant with slow-release fertilizer, and leave them alone! Fertilize again in 2 or 3 months. I never trimmed them.

Sedum is the plant I use whenever I am stumped over what to put in a pot. When I got down to the final touches and needed just one more plant, sedum always worked. This succulent never lasted too long for me in the ground, but in containers it was fantastic, lasting six months with no problems.

Companions: This plant is so versatile that I've used it with just about everything. Whenever I did mixed arrangements, I found it added a needed splash of lime green. Its fuzzy texture added interest, too.

Growing Conditions

Season: All year. but protect from frost.
Light: Full sun.
Water: Low.
Salt tolerance: Medium.
Wind tolerance: Medium.
Zone: 3 to 11.
Pest problems: Occasional aphids.

Also see pages 41 and 57 in this book.

Shrimp Plant, Golden *(Pachystachys lutea)*

Characteristics and Care

Use: Centerpiece plant or accent.
Growth rate: Fast.
Size: In the top of a container, grows 1 to 3 feet tall.
Colors: Yellow.
Average life: 5 to 10 years in the ground. A few months in a container.
Cautions: None known.
Care: Very easy. Plant with slow release fertilizer, and leave them alone! Fertilize again in 2 or 3 months. Be sure to underplant this plant with something full to cover the bottom stalks; when it grows, it gets leggy.

Golden shrimp plants are one of the few plants that bloom all the time, which is perfect for containers. The spiky shape of the flowers is also an excellent textural addition to many arrangements. And, this plant thrives in Florida - all seasons, and in sun or shade. Plant it in the ground when it outgrows the container if you live in zones 9 to 11.

Companions: Use shrimp plants with other bright colors. It looks great with red and purple. I particularly like shrimp plants with pentas, coleus, and bright-colored crotons.

Growing Conditions

Season: All year, but protect from frost.
Light: Medium shade to full sun. Happier with some break from noon sun in summer.
Water: Medium to high.
Salt tolerance: Medium.
Wind tolerance: Low.
Zone: 9 to 11.
Pest problems: Caterpillars and snails.

Also see pages 35, 37, 43, 45, 112, 116, 138, 144, 223, and 227 in this book for more container ideas with shrimp plants. To learn more about growing this plant in the ground, see "Easy Gardens for Florida" and "Best Garden Color for Florida."

Snake Plant, Sanseveria *(Sanseveria spp.)*

Characteristics and Care

Use: Centerpiece plant.
Growth rate: Slow.
Size: Many types available ranging from tiny dwarfs to 3 feet tall.
Colors: Green.
Average life: 20 years in landscape. Lives for years in the same container.
Cautions: Poisonous to eat. Also causes dermatitis.
Care: One of the easiest plants in the world. Plant with slow-release fertilizer, and leave them alone! Fertilize again in 2 or 3 months, although it might not notice if you miss one!

Snake plants are one of the easiest plants in the world. They grow well in frost-free locations outdoors and thrive in even difficult indoor conditions. Many sizes are available - from tiny dwarfs to the more common variety shown at left. Use them for their sculptural quality in contemporary containers, or mix them with trailing plants for a more casual look.
Companions: Use them with other easy indoor plants shown on page 145.
(Pots and photo from Lechuza.)

Growing Conditions

Season: All year.
Light: Full sun to dense shade.
Water: Low.
Salt tolerance: High.
Wind tolerance: High.
Zone: 10b to 11. Protect from frost.
Pest problems: None near the ocean, but sooty mold, scale and mites occur very occasionally inland.

Also see page 254 in this book.

Snapdragon *(Antirrhimum majus)*

Characteristics and Care

Use: Centerpiece plant.
Growth rate: Medium.
Size: In the top of a container, the tall ones grow to 36 inches tall. The dwarf variety grows to 6 inches tall.
Colors: Red, white, purple, orange pink, salmon, and yellow.
Average life: 2 to 3 months.
Cautions: None known.
Care: Easy. Plant with slow-release fertilizer, and leave them alone! Fertilize again in 2 or 3 months. These do much better if you deadhead the spent flowers.

Snapdragons are one plant I didn't like as well in containers as I do in the ground because they went out of bloom on me. The tall snapdragons are perfect as centerpiece plants because of their size and their stately appearance, but they bloom for a month and then stop for a month.
Companions: Mix these with flowers of different shapes like petunias, geraniums, and pansies. The variety of colors available in snapdragons gives you lots of options.

Growing Conditions

Season: Cool season annuals. Plant from October to January.
Light: Light shade to full sun. Flowers more in full sun.
Water: Medium. We watered the pots shown every third day.
Salt tolerance: Medium.
Wind tolerance: Medium.
Zone: Summer annual in cooler areas of the world. Winter annual in South and Central Florida. Tolerant of light frost but not freeze.
Pest problems: Occasional caterpillars.

Also see pages 28-29, 44, 79, and 100 in this book.

Plant Profiles: The High Performers

Succulents

Characteristics and Care

Use: Centerpiece plant or accent.
Growth rate: Slow.
Size: Many different types, from tiny dwarfs to large specimens.
Colors: Different shades of green. Some flower, but it is usually insignificant.
Average life: Years in the same containers.
Cautions: Some are poisonous.
Care: Easy. Plant with slow-release fertilizer, and leave them alone! These are some of the easiest plants we tried.

Succulents really surprised me during our plant trials. I had expected them to fill up with water and die when the summer rains hit. They didn't, living for over a year in the same container with no care at all - no water, no trimming, no fertilizer. They even loved our toughest salt and wind environments.
Companions: I like seeing succulents used together. Vary the sizes and textures of a few different types in the same pot.

Growing Conditions

Season: All year.
Light: Varies by type. Most like sun.
Water: Low, but the ones we tried also adapted well to the high water of our wet season.
Salt tolerance: High.
Wind tolerance: High.
Zone: Varies by type.
Pest problems: We had no pests on the succulents outdoors in our trials. I have heard of problems with mealy bugs, spider mites, scale, snails, white flies, and aphids.
Also see pages 132, 256-257, and 271 in this book for more ideas with succulents.

Sweet Potato, 'Black Heart', Margarita, and 'Tricolor' *(Ipomea batatas)*

Characteristics and Care

Use: Trailing plant.
Growth rate: Fast.
Size: They know no bounds...literally they'll shoot out fifty feet. Luckily, they don't live that long in Florida or they'd take over the state!
Colors: Lime green, purple, and pink.
Average life: 6 months.
Cautions: Poisonous if leaves are eaten.
Care: Very easy. Plant with slow-release fertilizer, and leave them alone! Fertilize again in 2 or 3 months. You will have to trim these to keep them from taking over your arrangement.

Sweet Potatoes are the best and the worst of plants. They are definitely the fastest growing trailing plant we have in this book. While that's an advantage, it's also a pain when they grow so fast they overtake other plants in the arrangement. But, the new color varieties are fabulous, definitely worth using. Plant them with snail bait because these are snail candy, and they'll look ragged in no time unless you protect them.
Companions: See the many arrangements in this book (page numbers, right) for lots of companion ideas.

Growing Conditions

Season: All year. Protect from frost.
Light: Medium shade to full sun.
Water: High.
Salt tolerance: Medium.
Wind tolerance: Medium.
Zone: 10 to 11. Protect from frost.
Pest problems: Snails, snails, and more snails! Fungus, aphids, and white flies occasionally.

Also see pages 47, 56-57, 78, 96, 98-99, 100, 118-119, 125, 127, 138-139, 144, 151, 182, 207, 216, 227, 232, and 227 in this book.

Syngonium, Nephthytis *(Syngonium spp.)*

Characteristics and Care

Use: Trailing plant.
Growth rate: Varies with type, from quite slow to fast.
Size: Will trail several feet down the side of a container.
Colors: Different shades of green and pink.
Average life: Years in the same container.
Cautions: Invasive in the landscape. Contact with sap can cause pain and swelling.
Care: Very easy. Plant with slow-release fertilizer, and leave them alone! Fertilize again in 2 or 3 months. Trim as needed.

Syngonium has been commonly-used as a houseplant for generations. It is easy to grow and many new types are introduced each year. Avoid planting the common green variety outside in the south Florida landscape because it is invasive and can even smother whole trees! I have only tested a few of the newer cultivars, like the 'Bold Allusion' shown above. It did quite well in containers but died after about six months in the ground.
Companions: Use this plant to trail over the edges of container combinations with a tropical look.

Growing Conditions

Season: All year, if you protect them from frost.
Light: Dense, medium, or light shade.
Water: Medium.
Salt tolerance: Low.
Wind tolerance: Unknown.
Zone: 10b to 11. Protect from frost.
Pest problems: Few problems outdoors. Scale, mealy bugs, aphids, and spider mites can be problems indoors.

Also see page 245 for syngonium in a mixed container.

Ti Plant *(Cordyline fructicosa)*

Characteristics and Care

Use: Centerpiece plant.
Growth rate: Medium.
Size: Varies by type. Most grow to about 3 feet tall in a container.
Colors: Shades of red, pink, and green.
Average life: 6 months in a container. Transplant it to a larger container or into the ground for another 5 or 10 years of life if you live in zones 10 to 11.
Cautions: None known.
Care: Very easy. Plant with slow-release fertilizer, and leave them alone! Fertilize again in 2 or 3 months. Remove unsightly leaves throughout the year.

Ti Plants are one of the most useful centerpiece plants for container gardens. Their upright, spiky form contrasts well with round leaves and flowers. Ti plants are also easy to grow in Florida as long as you protect them from frost. They eventually develop trunk-like stems that are not attractive in containers. Trim them in April, staggering the cuts on the different stalks for a layered effect. Stick the cuttings in the soil nearby, and about half of them will root.
Companions: Use ti plants as the centerpiece of arrangements with a tropical look.

Growing Conditions

Season: All year, though they look better in the warm months.
Light: Medium shade to full sun, depending on variety.
Water: Medium.
Salt tolerance: Low.
Wind tolerance: Low.
Zone: 10 to 11. Protect from frost.
Pest problems: If holes appear in the leaves, it is probably snails.
Also see pages 38-39, 102, 105, 133, 138, 144, and 248 in this book for more container ideas.
See pages 132-137 in "Best Garden Color for Florida" to learn more about growing ti plants in the ground.

Plant Profiles: The High Performers

Torenia, Trailing *(Torenia fournieri)*

Characteristics and Care

Use: Trailing plant.
Growth rate: Medium.
Size: Grows about 6 to 12 inches down the side of a container.
Colors: Shades of blue, purple, and red.
Average life: Up to one year.
Cautions: None known.
Care: Very easy. Plant with slow-release fertilizer, and leave them alone! Fertilize again in 2 or 3 months. Trim off the tips if the plants become too large.

Torenia comes in either upright or trailing varieties. The trailing torenia is one of the top performers from our container trials. They are not only very easy to grow but also bloom all year in frost-free parts of Florida, even in the hottest parts of summer. We use them in the ground - as well as in containers - with equal success in both locations. The dark purple torenia (shown above, right) did the best in our trials, although all the colors did well.

Companions: Trailing torenia is one of the most useful container plants. See the pages shown at right (in blue type) for lots of companion ideas.

Growing Conditions

Season: All year if protected from frost.
Light: Light shade to full sun.
Water: Medium.
Salt tolerance: Medium.
Wind tolerance: Medium.
Zone: 10 to 11. Use as an annual. Tolerant of light frost but not a freeze.
Pest problems: None known.
Also see pages 45, 59, 62-63, 73, 78, 144, 216, 223, 232, for more information in this book and pages 62-63 in "Best Garden Color for Florida" to learn how to grow this plant in the ground.

Torenia, Upright *(Torenia fournieri)*

Characteristics and Care

Use: Mounding plant that works well alone or mixed with other bright colors. Works very well in sides of baskets.
Growth rate: Medium.
Size: Mounds to about 8 inches tall and equally as wide.
Colors: Blue, pink, purple, white, red and multi. All have yellow centers.
Average life: 2 months in containers; 3 to 4 months in the landscape.
Cautions: None known.
Care: Easy. Plant with slow-release fertilizer, and leave them alone! Fertilize again in 2 or 3 months. Seldom requires trimming.

Torenia did well in our trials except they didn't last that long. They did great in the sides of the baskets, looking fabulous on planting day. However, they disappeared after a month or so. The other plants then filled in, so it was still a useful flowering plant.

Companions: Use wherever you need a small clump of color. I used the white torenia in all white arrangements, like caladiums and variegated mint. In summer, they look good with melampodium and pentas. They also look fabulous with coleus and dragon wing begonias.

Growing Conditions

Season: Spring, summer, fall.
Light: Light shade to full sun.
Water: Medium. We watered the pots shown every third day.
Salt tolerance: Medium.
Wind tolerance: Medium.
Zone: Summer annual in many parts of the world. Won't tolerate temperatures below 50 degrees.
Pest problems: Powdery mildew.

Also see pages 216-217 in this book and pages 62-63 in "Best Garden Color for Florida."

Verbena *(Verbena canadensis)*

Characteristics and Care

Use: Trailing or mounding plant.
Growth rate: Medium.
Size: The trailing form trails about 12 inches down the sides of pots. The upright variety grows about 6 to 8 inches tall.
Colors: Lilac, white, pink, purple, and red.
Average life: 3 to 4 months.
Cautions: None known.
Care: Very easy. Plant with slow-release fertilizer and leave them alone! Fertilize again in 2 or 3 months. Trim off the tips if the plants become too large.

Verbena is a plant of great extremes in our trials. The trailing verbenas did the best, especially Proven Winners' 'Superbena Large Lilac Blue' show above. But, it didn't flower for as long as many other plants we tried. The upright verbenas have not worked as well for me, dying after about two weeks.
Companions: Verbena works well with other cool-season annuals that have different textures. The purple looks great with other blues and purples, like torenias and ajuga.

Growing Conditions

Season: Cool season. Avoid planting from July through September.
Light: Full sun.
Water: Medium. We watered the pots shown every third day.
Salt tolerance: Medium.
Wind tolerance: Medium.
Zone: 7 to 11. Use as an annual. Tolerant of light frost but not a freeze.
Pest problems: Powdery mildew.

Also see pages 79, 192, and 208-209 in this book.

Viola *(Viola spp)*

Characteristics and Care

Use: Mounding plant that works well in the center or along the edges of any pot as well as in the sides of hanging baskets.
Growth rate: Medium.
Size: 4 to 6 inches tall and equally as wide.
Colors: Lavender, blue, purple, red, brown and yellow.
Average life: 2 to 4 months.
Cautions: None known.
Care: Very easy. Plant with slow-release fertilizer, and leave them alone! Fertilize again in 2 or 3 months. Deadhead for best blooming.

Violas are similar to pansies except the flowers are smaller. They do well during the coldest times of the years, and thrive in containers. Although they produce enough color to glow from a distance, the flowers are so detailed that I like to plant them in containers that I can see from a close distance.
Companions: Violas look great planted in mixed colors. They also look good mixed with other flowers, particularly in differing sizes. Alyssum is a good companion with smaller flowers and petunias are great choices for larger flowers.

Growing Conditions

Season: Cool season. Avoid planting from July through September.
Light: Light shade to full sun in the cool season, but burns in the summer sun.
Water: Medium. We watered the pots shown every third day.
Salt tolerance: Medium.
Wind tolerance: Medium
Zone: Use as an annual. Tolerant of light frost but not a freeze.
Pest problems: Occasional aphids or snails.

Also see pages 28, 44, and 79 in this book.

Other Plants That Deserve Mention: *Notes from our ongoing trials*

Ageratum houstonianum
Ageratum

This annual is primarily useful for its interesting texture and pretty color. We used it from March until June. My one complaint is that it stopped blooming periodically, taking rests for brief periods. Prefers sun.

Ajuga repens 'Black Scallop'
Ajuga 'Black Scallop'

What a surprise! I didn't expect this plant to do well this far south, but it excelled from January until July! It grows low, only to about 3" tall in containers, and worked in sun or shade. Use as an annual in Florida. Lasts about 6 months.

Angelonia spp.
Angelonia

Everyone I know loves angelonia except me. Its flowers are gorgeous but intermittent. I tried it in all four seasons and couldn't get it to bloom for more than about a month running. Many experts love it, so I will keep trying!

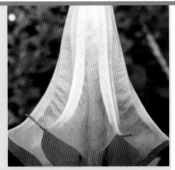

Brugmansia spp.
Angel's Trumpet

Spectacular flowers on a plant that is highly poisonous, so be careful with this one. See "Best Garden Color for Florida," pages 210-211 to learn more. I prefer this plant in the ground because it looks a bit straggly in a pot.

Schefflera arboricola
Arboricola

This plant takes it all - dense shade, hot sun, high salt and wind. It grows to about 5' tall in a container. Zones 10 to 11 or protect from frost. Read more about this plant in "Easy Gardens for Florida."

Rhododendron spp.
Azalea

One of the most popular plants in the deep south. Does better the further north you go in Florida but does poorly in south Florida as a long-term plant. Great for short-term container color. See pages 212-213 for more ideas.

Begonia 'Sinbad'
Begonia 'Sinbad'

Another winner from Proven Winners, this begonia grows like a small angelwing. It lasted about a year in south Florida, growing to about 1' tall. Use as an annual in areas that freeze. Prefers light to medium shade.

Begonia odorata alba
Begonia, White 'Odorata'

One of my favorite landscape plants for south Florida, this one is not my favorite in containers because it doesn't grow evenly. Read more in "Best Garden Color for Florida," pages 84-85. Blooms for about 8 months each year. Zones 10 to 11.

Evolvulus glomeratus
Blue Daze

I used this plant a lot in containers until I discovered trailing torenia, which performs much better. Blue daze is useful in salt situations. Grow as an annual. Short-term perennial in the ground in south Florida. Medium to light shade.

Cactus spp.
Cactus

I had rotten luck with cactus in the ground and great luck in containers, even indoors! Hundreds of types available. Skin irritant. *(Photo and container from Lechuza).*

Aspidistra eliator
Cast Iron Plant

Tough plant that likes light to dense shade. Grows 12" to 14" in a container, lasting years. Green and variegated forms.

Cleome hasslerana
Cleome

Beautiful flower traditionally used in the deep south with few problems. New to Florida. It bloomed beautifully in spring for about 6 weeks, which is short for an annual, but the beauty of this one makes it worth it.

Cosmos spp.
Cosmos

Cosmos is a terrific annual for Florida. It blooms in winter and spring. I have not tried it much in containers, but will. See "Best Garden Color for Florida," pages 30-31, for more information.

Crossandra spp.
Crossandra

Attractive peach flowers. Erratic performer, blooming a full summer some years and only a few weeks the next. Occasionally keeps going as a perennial shrub in south Florida, but not too often. Sun or shade. Reseeds.

Curcuma 'Purple Prince'
Curcuma 'Purple Prince'

Glamorous, tropical plant that loves summer heat and grows 12" to 18" tall in a container, blooming for one to two months. Dormant (no leaves!) in winter. Zones 10 to 11 or protect from frost.

Adenium obesum
Desert Rose

A succulent that grows slowly into a shrub of 6' to 10' in the ground. Very low-water. Zones 10 to 11. Inconsistent results - some do beautifully, and some die for no known reason.

Pedilanthus spp.
Devil's Backbone

Shrubby succulent that grows to about 18" tall in a container. Use it for its interesting, variegated texture. Does not like a lot of water, and prefers light shade. Zone 10 to11 or protect from freezes.

Dianthus spp.
Dianthus

Many professionals swear by dianthus, but I haven't found any great ones yet. I use them in containers for their showy flowers, knowing they will bloom for a month, go out of bloom, and resume in another month or two.

Mandevilla spp.
Diplademia

Bright pink flowers in summer, this is an excellent vine or small shrub for containers. It takes all the heat you can give it and looks great for months on end. Some live for a year or so but consider it an annual in Florida. Full sun.

Senecio cineraria
Dusty Miller

This plant did very well in our trials and is easy to grow, both in the ground and in containers. Use it from October to May. Protect from frost. Grows to about 12" tall in a container. Use as an annual in Florida.

Acorus gramineus
Dwarf White Stripe Sweet Flag

Did very well in our trials, preferring light shade. Tolerates wet conditions. Grows to about 12" tall in a container. Zones 5 to 11. Lasts about 6 months in a container.

Eugenia spp.
Eugenia

Eugenia is a large genus of green shrubs that are most often used as topiaries in containers. Look for *Eugenia compacta*, a slow-growing variety that doesn't require as much trimming as many others.

Selaginella uncinata
Fern, Blue Peacock or Moss, Peacock Spike

Very useful filler for pots. Grows quickly. Quite low in form. Best in light to medium shade. Zones 9b to 11. Shown on pages 49, 218, and 249 in this book.

Nephrolepis biserrata 'Furcans'
Fern, Fishtail

An excellent fern for the landscape because it doesn't spread as quickly as many others. Good for containers in medium to light shade. Zones 10 to 11 or protect from frost.

Microsorum scolopendrium
Fern, Wart
A tough fern for the landscape or containers. The leaves are thicker than most ferns, giving it a more tropical appearance. Grows to about 12" to 18" tall in light to medium shade. Zones 10 to 11 or protect from frost.

Ficus lyrata
Fiddle-Leaf Fig
An easy tree for containers but don't plant it in the ground because it quickly grows into a monster tree with damaging roots. Leaves shaped like a fiddle. Medium shade to full sun. Frequently used indoors. Zones 10 to 11 or protect from frost.

Fittonia verschaffeltii
Fittonia, Red Ann
I found this plant in the house-plant section of a garden center and used it in the arrangement of page 40. It takes medium to light shade, grows to about 6" tall, and lives for about 6 months in a container in fall, winter, or spring. Protect from frost.

Dianella ensifolia
Flax
Excellent results from our south Florida trials so far. Untested further north. Variegated groundcover with a tropical look. About 2' tall by 2' wide. Does better in shade. Low maintenance. Separate clumps every 5 years or so. Tiny yellow flowers.

Plumeria spp.
Frangipani
An excellent tree because it blooms when it is quite small, just the right size for containers! Most bloom in summer and are bare in winter, but a few are evergreen. Salt-tolerant, zones 10 to 11, sun. See "Best Garden Color for Florida," pages 242-243.

Fuchsia spp.
Fuchsia
Yes! Fuchsias grow in our winters quite well! They are making their way into our garden centers all over the state. I have very little data about how one compares with another, but all the ones we tried lived for 4 to 6 months in sun or light shade without frost.

Gaillardia spp.
Gaillardia or Blanket Flower
Worked as an annual during the dry months in our south Florida trial gardens, but only lasted a month or so. Somewhat messy-looking but improved by dead-heading.

Gomphrema globosa
Globe Amaranth
Winter and spring annual (protect from frost) that does quite well in containers, where it grows to about 8" tall. Prefers full sun. Use this plant with flowers of different sizes and textures.

Duranta repens
Golden Dewdrop
Used primarily as a standard (shrub trimmed into a small tree) in containers. Blooms about half the year in sun in zones 9b to 11. See "Best Garden Color for Florida," pages 216-219, for detailed information.

Hibiscus spp.
Hibiscus
Although this shrub/small tree is commonly used throughout the world in summer containers, we can find better choices in Florida. Hibiscus thins out quickly in a container. See "Best Garden Color for Florida."

Helichrysum thianschanicum
Icicles
A filler plant that did quite well in our winter and spring trials. We didn't try it in summer. Grows to about 5" tall in a container. Use as an annual in Florida. Prefers light shade.

Dietes vegetata
Iris, African
Seldom bloomed in our south Florida trials, but the spiky texture of the leaves is very useful in containers. Flower is lovely during its brief appearances. Zones 8 to 11. Sun to light shade.

Trimezia martinensis
Iris, Walking
An excellent plant for container centerpieces because of its vertical leaves and capacity to bloom in deep shade. Grows to about 2' tall in a container in dense to light shade. Zones 10 to 11. Also see "Easy Gardens for Florida."

Trachelospermum asiaticum 'Vareigatum'
Jasmine, Variegated
A variegated vine with small leaves that does well in containers, lasting up to 1 year. Sun to medium shade. Zones 8 to 11. Low water.

Talinum paniculatum
Jewel of Opar
Low-growing ground cover that adds texture to an arrangement because of its variegated leaves. Lasts about 6 months in a container in sun (winter only) to light shade in summer. Zones 9 to 11. Wispy flowers sporadically.

Juniper conferta
Juniper, Shore
A tough groundcover that takes salt, wind, sun, and heat. It eventually cascades down the sides of containers, as shown above. Zones 6 to 10b. Grows about 6" tall in a container.

Kalanchoe thursifolia
Kalanchoe Thursifolia
Very interesting texture in this succulent plant. Easy to grow. I keep it for about 6 months in a container, until it gets tall and lanky. Full sun and low water. Zone 10 to 11 or protect from frost.

Lobelia erinus
Lobelia
I have had mixed results with lobelia. Some bloom constantly for months, and others sporadically. But, it is so beautiful I will always have some in my cool-season containers. It likes winter sun or light shade. Grows to about 6" tall. Annual.

Lysimachia 'Golden Globes'
Golden Globes
This plant produces green vines that easily grow about 12" down the sides of containers in sun or light shade. They only bloom occasionally, and the Lysimachia 'Outback Sunset' is a better bet. See page 304 in this book.

Selaginella uncinata
Moss, Peacock Spike, or Fern
Very useful filler for pots. Grows quickly. Quite low in form. Best in light to medium shade. Zones 9b-11. Shown on pages 49, 218, and 249 in this book.

Bismarckia nobilis
Bismarckia Palm
One of our finest palm specimens for making a strong statement. Requires a large container (see page 233). Avoid root pruning, or it could shock. Zones 10a to 11. See "Easy Gardens for Florida."

Ravenala madagascariensis
Palm, Travelers
Similar to a white bird of paradise when small, which is easier to keep in a container for a longer time. Grows to about 20' tall in the ground. Medium shade to full sun in zones 10b to 11.

Spathiphyllum spp.
Peace Lily
Tropical plant often used indoors all over the world. Blooms in deep shade in south Florida but is almost always plagued by snails eating the leaves when it is planted outdoors. Very cold-sensitive.

Peperomia 'String Bean'
Peperomia 'String Bean'
I heard about this one from Karen O'Brien (see page151). It has an interesting texture and works well in shady conditions. It lives for about 6 months in a container, staying under 6" tall.

Peperomia variegata
Peperomia, Variegated

Although I had bad luck with this plant in the ground, it thrived in containers. Grows to about 6" tall in a pot. Prefers medium to light shade. Zones 10 to 11 or protect from frost. Very susceptible to snail damage. Low water.

Catharanthus roseus
Periwinkle

White, pink, or purple flowers that do best in sun. Some have naturalized, like wildflowers, and come back each year. These are strong but short-lived plants. Many hybrids have serious fungus problems in our rainy season.

Pilea microphylla
Pilea or Artillery Fern

An old Florida favorite, groundcover that is very easy to grow in full sun or light shade in zones 10 to 11. Good filler when you need light texture in a container. Grows about 8" tall, and trails slightly over the edge of a container.

Podocarpus spp.
Podocarpus

Excellent plant for formal shapes in containers. Prefers light shade to full sun. Zones 7 to 11. Slow-growing, so easy to maintain. See "Easy Gardens for Florida" for more information.

Rosa spp.
Rose

Since rose bushes look thin in Florida, I didn't include these in my container trials. I grow these plants in the landscape for cut flowers. See "Best Garden Color for Florida", pages 174-175, for more information.

Ficus elastica
Rubber Tree

This tree is good for indoor use or areas that need salt tolerance. Don't plant it in the ground because of invasive roots. Sun or shade. Protect from frost. *(Photo from Lechuza.)*

Scaevola 'Whirlwind White'
Scaevola 'Whirlwind White'

Did well in our trials, blooming for about 4 months straight in winter. Its relative, Scaevola 'Blue Wonder,' is better known in Florida and does well in sun and salt situations. Grows about 6" tall in a container, and cascades a bit. Use as an annual in Florida.

Breynia disticha
Snowbush

I use this plant most in summer to accent a pot that includes red or pink flowers (see page 228). It is not an ideal container plant because it thins out in pots. Zones 10b to 11 or protect from frost. Very susceptible to caterpillars in spring.

Anthericum sanderii
Star Grass

Grows to about 2' tall in a container. Takes sun and heat. Keep it on the dry side, and fertilize regularly. Has tiny flowers in spring, summer, and fall.

Trifolium repens 'Dark Dancer'
Trifolium 'Dark Dancer'

This plant did very well in our trials. We used it in winter and spring, so we don't know its heat tolerance. Sun to light shade. Use as an annual in Florida.

Vinca minor 'Illumination'
Vinca 'Illumination'

This small vine worked very well in our winter and spring trials. Its variegation and texture add interest to arrangements. It grew slowly, trailing down the side of a pot about 6" to 8". Lasted about 6 months. Use as an annual here.

Zinnia spp.
Zinnia

Commonly planted in commercial gardens. I have had a lot of fungus problems with zinnias but like them so much that I keep planting them anyway. New, narrow-leafed types show promise of high performance.

Want to experiment with a lot of plants from this chapter? The three-tiered planter, shown both empty and full, gives you a wonderful opportunity to plant a lot of different plants in a small space. Check out pages 243 and 207 to see this versatile container planted with other arrangements.

I found the two containers shown below at the Falls Country Club in Lake Worth. They are planted with some of our best cool-season color - petunias, lobelia, geraniums, alyssum, diascia, 'Goldilocks', and dragon wing begonias.

Chapter 15

Planting & Maintenance

As I say in the beginning of the book, skim this chapter before planting your first container. It will save you a lot of time, money, and trouble - and make container gardening a lot easier for you.

On the whole, container gardens are more maintenance than gardens planted in the ground because they are an unnatural condition for a plant. Plants are used to having a lot of space for their roots, and that space is limited in a container.

Plants cannot stay in the same container forever. When the roots reach the sides, most need a larger container. Or, you can prune the roots and put the plant back into the same one.

Plants need more water in containers because their roots, which store water, are limited in size.

However, many more plants thrive in containers in Florida than in the ground. In our trial gardens, only about one out of a hundred new landscape plants we try does really well. I was quite surprised and delighted to find that most of the container plants we tried did beautifully. However, we were happy if it lasted three or four months, and we didn't expect many to make it through our hot, rainy summer.

I find container gardening a lot easier than growing plants in the ground when I want small, quick projects. Landscaping a home is hard, back-breaking work. Going to a garden center on a Saturday afternoon and picking up a few small plants for a container is a delight!

Buying Plants, Soil, and Fertilizer

Buy Quality Plants

1. Look at the two plants shown above, left. Which one would you buy? Many people would choose the leggy plant on the right because it is taller. But, you'll be much happier in the long run with the shorter, fuller plant on the left. The leggy plant needs trimming immediately, and it will look bare for a few weeks while it re-grows. Chances are, it's root-bound as well. The shorter plant will look full and healthy the day you plant it. Also, plants do not have to be in flower when you purchase them. It is much more important to buy a full, healthy specimen.

2. It's easy to check the roots on a small plant in the garden center. Simply turn the plant upside down and lift off the pot, as shown on the page 344, step 3. If is difficult to remove, choose another plant because chances are the tightly-potted plant is root-bound. Root-bound plants have outgrown their pots. Since the roots have nowhere else to go, they grow in circles or tangled masses. Most severely root-bound plants won't grow well. Slightly root-bound plants do alright if the roots are separated prior to planting.

3. Avoid buying plants with leaf damage. Sometimes it can be the result of something quite harmless, but why take a chance? If you see signs of pests after your new plant has been planted, they probably came from your garden instead of the garden center. Newly-planted plants send out a signal that attracts some pests. If the damage is slight, ignore it. If it is severe, take a leaf to a garden center so they can identify the bug. Ask them for the least toxic alternative. The goal is to minimize pests, not eradicate every insect in the garden and poison yourself as well!

Potting Soil

Don't skimp on your potting soil. Good potting soil (called potting 'mix') is a mixture of peat moss and perlite, and it is expensive. Do not buy topsoil for containers. It is too heavy, and the plants may rot.

Look for a brand name you trust. Peters, Miracle Grow, Lambert's and Fafard (along with many others) offer top-quality potting soil.

Look for a potting soil with fertilizer and/or water saving polymers mixed in. This will save you some time.

Fertilizer

Don't skimp on fertilizer, either! I use timed-release, like the photo shows. Liquid (like Miracle Grow and Peters) is better for the plants but must be applied weekly, whereas the timed release lasts 2 to 3 months and works just about as well. Once again, use a brand you trust. Osmocote, Dynamite, and Nutricote are all fine choices for containers.

Follow the instructions on the box carefully! If you use too much, you could burn the plant. Too little, and the plant won't thrive.

Preparing & Displaying Containers

Preparing Pots for Planting

Check all your pots before planting to be sure they have holes in the bottom. If they don't, the water cannot drain out of the pot and the plant will drown and rot. The only exception to this rule is the indoor, decorative container that often has another plastic pot inside that is removed for watering. The plastic pot has the holes.

Many garden centers will drill holes in your containers before you buy them. If you need to drill them yourself, it's easy. Just turn the container upside down on a soft surface so you don't damage the rim. Use a drill bit that is appropriate for the material - masonry bit for clay, wood bit for wood, etc. Drill a few holes about 1/2 inch in diameter. I like these small holes because they aren't large enough for the potting soil to fall through.

I used to put gravel in the bottom of my pots to make them drain better but found it didn't make any difference. I now put the soil directly in the pot. However, if the drainage hole is very large, I put something over it that allows it to drain but doesn't let the dirt go through it. A piece of screening works well. Don't try newspaper because it keeps the water from draining properly until it rots.

If you are using huge pots, it might cost less to fill the bottom of it with mulch instead of potting soil. I prefer soil, however, because a lot of soil allows the roots of the plants to really spread and need less watering. Soil is also heavier, which is a benefit if you don't want the container to blow over but a disadvantage if you want to decrease the weight. You can use styrofoam packing peanuts to fill the bottom, but be sure to secure them in a plastic bag. Most of the newer packing peanuts are biodegradable - they break down when exposed to moisture.

If weight is a safety concern, like on a roof garden or balcony, you can opt for lightweight fiberglass containers, which are much lighter than cast stone or terra cotta. However, be careful that they aren't so light that they blow over in the wind!

If you need to add weight to a container for stability in wind, simply put a few bricks in the bottom of it before you plant.

We clean our containers after using them. Glazed clay is really easy to clean - just mild soap and water. If containers are mildewed, I use a mildew-killing spray. Be sure to test a small, inconspicuous area first to determine if the spray hurts the finish on the pot. Terra cotta pots are a pain in the neck to clean if they have developed that white, crusty substance on their sides. The better quality terra cottas don't develop it as much as the cheaper types.

Displaying Containers

I seldom use saucers under my pots. They hold water and sometimes keep the plant too wet. I will occasionally bring them out to use in very hot weather, however, because I'm not worried about too wet but rather too dry in our summer heat.

It's a good idea to use little 'pot feet' or some sort of stand to keep the pot off the ground. I don't worry about this with pots in the garden but like them when pots are on hardscapes, such as wood, brick, or concrete. Sometimes I can't find one that looks good with the pot and in that case, I don't worry about it. I am noticing wood rot on my wood deck where I have had large containers directly on the wood for a few years.

Low plant stands on wheels are very useful. They keep the pot off the ground and make it easy to move. If pots are against a building or wall, they need to be turned so that all sides get some light. Wheels make this quite easy, especially with heavy pots.

Watering...

General

Watering takes the most time of any container garden chore. Plants in containers need more water than plants in the ground because their root systems are smaller, and the roots are where plants store most of their water. The root system of a plant in the ground is three times the diameter of the plant. Not so for container plants - the roots are only as large as the container.

Factors that Affect Water Use

1. **Sun or shade.** Plants use half as much water in shade than in full sun.

2. **Temperature.** Plants use more water when the temperatures are high than in the winter. I do not have many containers out in the bright sun in July and August because I can't keep up with the watering.

3. **Wind.** Plants in windy areas require more water than plants in calm areas.

4. **Reflections from walls.** If you have a light-colored wall facing south with no shade, you may have to plant succulents to take the reflected heat.

5. **Soil.** Good-quality potting soil (mix) usually includes peat moss, which holds water better than cheaper, sandy soils.

6. **Plant type.** Plant species vary in their need for water. Impatiens, for example, need much more water than cactus.

7. **Container size.** Large containers with small plants require much less water than small containers filled to the brim with large plants.

8. **Container type.** We didn't notice too much difference between the materials that a container is made of and water use.

9. **How long the plant has been in the container.** As plants age in containers, their roots fill the pot, leaving less space for water.

How to Tell When a Plant Needs Water

Water when you see signs of wilt, or the soil feels dry to the touch. Use your finger to test the soil. Push it into the soil about an inch or so. Low-water plants like cacti and succulents, need less water and can go longer with dry soil. **Knowing when to water is very important because many container plants die from overwatering.** If the plant looks wilted and the soil has been wet for several days, the plant has drowned and will probably die. It has a fungus. You might try a fungicide if the plant is very important to you.

How Much Water to Apply

Water thoroughly with each application. The biggest watering mistake people make is to give the plant *just a little bit of water*. That is the same as giving a person who is dying of thirst just a teaspoonful of water! Soak the plant thoroughly until you see a steady stream of water coming out of the bottom of the pot. A slow soaking is better than a fast hit with the hose because it allows the roots time to absorb the water.

For container sources, go to www.easygardencolor.com

An Important Part of Container Gardening

Water Needs Change as a Plant Ages

Plants need a lot of water right after they are planted. Then, as the roots grow, the plant needs less water. Once the roots fill the pot, the plant needs more water again!

Watering Methods

1. Hand watering takes the most time. But, it allows you total control over how much water each plant receives and when they receive it. Be sure to use a watering can or hose attachment that delivers a fine spray of water because this gentle spray cannot damage the roots, leaves, or flowers. High-pressure hose nozzles can wash the plant right out of the container! And, be sure to water evenly and thoroughly, so you don't miss half of the root ball!

2. Drip irrigation hooks up to your hose or sprinkler system and has an emitter for each pot. Systems are easily available in kit form and fairly easy to install, or your sprinkler repairman can install them for you. These systems greatly reduce the time spent watering but do require some maintenance because the emitters can fall out of the pots or become clogged. There are many different types of emitters available, so be sure yours fit the size of your pot. Some emitters are designed for very small pots, for example, and won't deliver enough water for a large container.

Drip systems are designed to water a lot of pots at once, which can be a disadvantage if only one plant needs it and the others don't.

3. Your garden sprinklers. Most of the containers that are on the ground or on posts in our gardens get water from our automatic sprinkler system, which goes on twice a week if we don't get rain. This is enough for many of our containers, particularly when the weather is cool and the containers are established but not pot-bound. Our shade containers are particularly happy with just water from the sprinklers until it gets really hot. We supplement waterings as needed with a hose.

What to Do When You're Out of Town

If you have a sprinkler system, put your containers in the shade somewhere in your yard where the sprinklers will hit them. If you are a snowbird and gone for months at a time, consider annual flowers (that just last one season) for your containers. They are inexpensive, and you can plant them when you arrive in fall or early winter, leaving your pots empty for the summer.

Watering and Replacing Plants

Water-holding Polymers

Many companies are developing water-holding gels (like Terrasorb or Hortasorb) to hold water in containers longer. These materials look like rock salt when they are dry. They absorb water and expand into a jello-like substance when soaked in water. A tablespoon of polymer expands to about a quart of wet material. It is added to the potting soil before planting. Desire Foard, owner of Gardenstyle and creator of the beautiful container gardens along the streets in Naples, uses these materials in most of her containers. They cut her watering chores down by about a third. She saturates the material in water for 10 to 15 minutes before adding it to the potting soil. It is very important to wet it before you add it to the soil. One lady told me that all her plants died after she tried the polymers. My guess is that she either added it dry or added too much. Be sure to follow the instructions on the box to the letter.

Re-Hydrating *Really* Dry Plants

Plants in a severe state of wilt that look like they are near death may benefit from a bottom-soaking. The soil is dry and has shrunk away from the sides of the pot, and when you water from the top, the water just washes down between the sides of the pot and the soil. The soil feels hard, like a chunk of wood, and is not absorbing the water. If this is the case, put the whole pot on top of a container of water - a saucer is ideal. I have used a frying pan before. Leave it overnight. The water is absorbed by the soil like a sponge, and your plant will probably be quite healthy in the morning!

Plant One Inch Below the Rim to Make Watering Easier

Watering is easier if you have some room between the top of the soil and the edge of the pot. Water can pool in this space and drip into the soil slowly so you don't have to stand there giving the plant a little bit of water at a time until you see it drain out of the bottom. This is easy to do in large pots but harder in small ones that are packed full of plants.

Replacing Plants

Before

During

After

Sometimes one plant dies in a mixed container while the others are still thriving. Simply remove it, and replace it with a new one. Even though this unsightly plant is not quite dead, it needs replacing.
First, wet the soil and try to gently remove the roots with your hand. If the roots resist, get a small trowel and gently cut around the roots of the plant. Try not to disturb the roots of the other plants any more than is necessary.
Second, plant the new plant in its place. Fertilize with your slow-release fertilizer. Look at the difference in the before and after photos! One unsightly plant had completely ruined the look of this container.

Pinching, Trimming & Root Pruning

Pinching and Trimming

Bulge

Before Pinching

Pinching to Smooth Bulge

After Pinching

If plants look leggy or uneven, pinch or trim off the unwanted portions. Use your finger or pruning shears (if the stem is too thick). See the plant profiles for individual pinching and cutback requirements. The plant in the first photo has a bulge on the right side near the top. It is easy to pinch the plants to even it out.

Root Pruning

Root prune a plant to keep it in the same container after its roots have outgrown it. It is usually done with large plants, like palms, that are in large containers for many years. Be sure to check the plant profiles to see if the palm can take it. Bismarckia palms, for example, go into shock with root-pruning.

1. Remove the plant from its container, and lay it on its side.

2. Untangle the roots with your hand. If they are too large, use clippers.

3. Trim off about one third of the roots.

4. Re-plant in the original container, adding more soil as needed.

5. Trim off about one-third of the top growth, unless it is a palm. Leave all palm fronds on.

6. The plant is smaller afterwards, but can stay in the same container for a long time to come.

Bromeliads, Gravel and Pest Control

Separating Bromeliads

After a bromeliad flowers, it produces offshoots (baby bromeliads) at the base. The mother plant dies when the babies are grown. When the babies are half as big as the mother plant, they can be separated. It is easy!

1. Remove the bromeliad clump from its container.

2. Cut them apart. This is really fool-proof. I have never lost one by doing this step incorrectly!

3. Even if they have no roots, most will survive.

4. The three plants are ready for planting.

5. Here are the plants in their containers. When they are this small, I store them in an out-of-the-way place until they grow large enough to make attractive, full plants.

Mulching with Gravel

I don't like seeing bare dirt in container arrangements. Gravel is a useful and decorative alternative. The black Mexican beach pebbles (shown, left) are polished so they keep a nice shine. I got them at Giverney Garden Center in Jupiter. I have heard you can spray gravel with Min-wax and it will retain a shine. I've never tried it. A store called Bushel Stop is another great source for both containers and decorative gravel. They have multiple locations in Broward, Palm Beach, Martin, and St. Lucie counties. Check your local yellow pages for more. Be sure to avoid gravel that is used on roads and for drainage as it can actually hurt your plants.

Pest Control

I seldom use pesticides on container plants. Many pesticides are quite toxic and are capable of killing you as well as the pest. Before using any pesticide, type the name of it into an internet search engine and push 'go.' Read about it to understand its risks. Occasionally, I use fungicide after rainy periods and I routinely use snail bait with sweet potato vines. If I see holes in the leaves, I leave the plant alone unless it becomes severe. Holes are normally caused by snails or caterpillars, which feed at night when you can't see them. Take the leaf to your garden center and ask them for the least-toxic alternative. Be sure the plant is not a larval food plant for butterflies.

For container sources, go to www.easygardencolor.com

Root Balls and Vegetables

Splitting Root Balls

Vining plants with roots that clump can often be split or pulled apart so you can use one plant in several different locations. I frequently split pots of 'Goldilocks', ivy, and white licorice. Ivy can also be pulled apart by the roots into even smaller pieces.

1. After removing the plant from its container, soak the roots in water until it is really soaked.

2. Gently pull the roots apart. (Once, before I knew better, I cut a root ball in two with a steak knife, and it worked just fine!)

3. Now you have two plants instead of just one!

Soaking Root Balls to Make Them Smaller

Throughout this book, you see containers that are very full. One of the professional tricks to filling a container to the brim on planting day is to soak the roots of the plants in water prior to planting them. This soaking allows you to squeeze them into smaller shapes.

This can be hard to get used to for the novice. I talk a lot about proper spacing with plants in the landscape in my "Easy Gardens for Florida" book. Generally, you leave quite a bit of space between the plants to give them room to grow when planting them in the ground. This is very important for long-term landscapes.

But most container gardens are designed for short-term, maximum impact. Most people don't want to wait six months for the container on their front steps to look good. Soaking the roots can assist in yielding instant, full results.

Vegetables in Containers

It is easier to grow vegetables in Florida in containers than in the ground. Most vegetables like neither our native soils nor the nematodes and other destructive critters that live there. Although south Florida farms produce huge crops of winter vegetables, they use seven times the national average of fertilizer!

Vegetables grow at different times in different parts of Florida. For example, most vegetables in south Florida grow in winter. If you try to grow tomatoes in July, you won't be happy with the results! For more information about growing vegetables in Florida, see two other valuable books, *Vegetable Gardening in Florida* by James M. Stephens and *Florida Vegetables: How to Grow Them* by Lewis S. Maxwell and Betty M. Maxwell.

The best book I know of for growing vegetables in containers (although not specifically for Florida) is *McGee & Stuckey's Bountiful Container* by Rose Marie Nichols McGee and Maggie Stuckey.

Planting a Bowl
(See this demo on the companion DVD. Watch how long it takes - only 5 minutes!)

1. Put some soil in the bottom of a pot with holes in it to ensure drainage. Without drainage, most plants die. If the holes are large, cover with a layer of rock or plastic screen to keep potting soil from escaping.

2. To see how much more soil you'll need, hold the largest plant in the center so the top of the soil line is about an inch below the top of the new pot. Remove the plant, and adjust the soil to reach that level.

3. To take the plant out of its pot, hold it upside down, and pull the pot off the root ball. If it resists, squeeze the sides of the pot and try again, or cut the pot off with garden shears.

4. If the roots are tightly wound in a circle, the plant is root-bound. It will grow better if you separate the roots.

5. Untangle the roots slightly by breaking the tight circle apart. Repeat this action all around the root ball.

6. Place the centerpiece plants in the middle of the container. These three dianthus make a full grouping. They are placed very close together, with root balls touching.

For container sources, go to www.easygardencolor.com

Important note: While the full-size root balls of these plants fit easily into this bowl, this is not the norm. We reduced the size of the root balls of many of the plants in this book prior to planting to make it easier to fill the pots. See page 343 for instructions.

7. Place two smaller plants (in this case, yellow coleus) on opposite sides of the pot. Lean them out slightly, so you won't see soil from the top edge when the pot is done.

8. Place two other plants (in this case, pink and green coleus) opposite each other in the same manner. Add more soil under these plants, if necessary, to keep all the root balls even on top.

9. Fill in with four other plants (blue torenia here). Be sure to tilt all of them, and keep the tops of their root balls even with the centerpiece. If they are not perfectly filled in, they will grow quickly!

10. Once all the plants are placed, fill in any open spots with soil. Keep the soil loose around the sides of the root balls. If soil gets on top of the root balls or near the stem, the plants could die.

11. Sprinkle slow-release fertilizer on top of the soil. Apply the amount specified on the fertilizer box. Too much can burn the plant, and too little can starve it.

12. Water the container thoroughly and evenly in a gentle stream with a watering can until you see water coming out of the drainage holes. After the pot has drained, add soil wherever it has settled.

Planting a Large Hanging Basket

Before

45 minutes later!

If you haven't watched the companion DVD, now is the time! I made the DVD because of the difficulty I had understanding hanging basket demos in books. The DVD hanging basket demo will make this one easier to understand, although this demo includes more details. Learn the basics from the DVD and the details from this book.

1. After hanging the basket from a swivel hook (see page 352), remove the coco fiber liner. This rigid liner is almost impossible to plant through. However, you want to keep it just in case you decide to create a different arrangement some day just by planting the top of this basket.

2. Use loose coco fiber to create the sides and bottom of this basket. Sphagnum moss holds so much water that the stems of the plants can rot, so don't use it.

3. Line the bottom and sides of the pot with coco fiber, up to the middle of the first square. Don't fill the basket with coco fiber. You need it to hold the plants and soil in place on the sides and bottom of the basket.

For container sources, go to www.easygardencolor.com

4. Spin the pot, making sure you don't see any light. Wherever you see light peeking through the area you've lined, add more coco fiber. Just lay it in loosely. It does not have to be perfect.

5. Add potting soil (see page 336 for type). Fill it to the top of the coco fiber. Don't press it down; you want the soil to remain light.

6. Add the correct amount of slow-release fertilizer (see page 336). Be sure you follow the instructions on the box. Mix it in gently with your hands.

7. To take the plant out of its pot, hold it upside down, and pull the pot off the root ball. If it resists, squeeze the sides of the pot and try again. If it still won't come out, cut the pot off with garden shears.

8. If the roots are tightly wound in a circle, the plant is root-bound. It will grow better if you separate the roots. Untangle the roots slightly by breaking the tight circle apart. Repeat this all around the root ball.

9. Because this root ball is a little too big for the squares in the basket, I am soaking it in water so it is easy to squeeze into the size of the opening.

Step by Step: How It's Done

10. Once the roots are soaked, remove them from the water and squeeze the ball, so it is small enough to go through the sides of the basket.

11. Push the roots through the side. The plant should be sideways, with the roots inside the basket and the plant outside. It is important that the stem rest on the coco fiber and not on the soil, which could rot it.

12. Continue planting every other square in the bottom layer. Here, I am alternating four different colors of coleus.

13. Push down slightly on the root balls to make sure they are secure. Check to be sure the plants are facing out, not down.

14. The plants look a big leggy to me, so I pinch off the tips. This makes them fuller as they grow in. It also keeps them from hanging upside down.

15. Check underneath each stem to be sure the coco fiber is next to it, rather than soil or the metal bar. Soil on the stem will rot it.

For container sources, go to www.easygardencolor.com

16. The first layer of plants is finished. Now it is time to repeat the process on the next layer. Add more coco fiber, starting with small pieces on top of each stem.

17. Keep adding the coco fiber until it reaches about halfway up the top square. Spin the pot, and look for light. Wherever you see light peeking through the area you've lined, add more coco fiber.

18. Add more soil, almost up to the top of the coco fiber.

19. Add more fertilizer.

20. Insert the plants in every square of this layer. Be sure the stems are next to the coco fiber and the roots are next to the soil.

21. Push down slightly on the root balls, so the plants themselves are facing out and not down.

It takes about an hour...

22. Now that the soil and coco fiber are just below the top rim of the basket, you are ready to plant the top layer of plants. Notice that there is a depression in the center of the basket.

23. Before I place my centerpiece plant, I check to make sure I don't see bare soil or daylight anywhere around the edges of my basket.

24. I've chosen a golden shrimp plant as my centerpiece because it's colorful enough to stand up to all the bright coleus. I carefully place it in the depression I left in the center of my basket.

25. It's now time to fill in the area around my centerpiece with soil to hold it in place. I leave room for the plants that I will be planting around the centerpiece.

26. Again, I add exactly the amount of fertilizer that's recommended on the package.

27. Now, I am ready to put the final layer of plants along the edge of the basket. Checking the last layer, I see which plants I've placed where on the other layers; this way, I can stagger the last ones.

For container sources, go to www.easygardencolor.com

and the plants cost less than $40.

28. I stagger the different colors of coleus around the edge of the basket, leaning them out slightly. I don't want them upright because the wire will show through when the arrangement is finished.

29. These lime green coleus are too tall, relative to my centerpiece plant, so I pinch them back as I place them in.

30. Check to make sure the soil is level with the tops of the roots of the final plants. Add small amounts where needed. Do not cover the stems of the plants with soil!

31. One final bit of fertilizer, and I'm almost done.

32. I'm done! It took me less than an hour to create my instant masterpiece, and all forty plants cost me less than $40. It weighs 40 pounds.

33. I will not water this arrangement for about three days because I soaked it thoroughly during planting. I'll stick my finger in the soil to make sure it's dry before watering again.

Basket Basic: Mounting and Hanging

Hanging the Baskets

IMPORTANT: Before moving or hanging any basket that has a detachable hanger, check the integrity of the connection. It is easy for the hook to fail if it is not properly tightened with pliers prior to hanging. I lost a whole, planted, gorgeous, 20" basket once because one side fell down (and emptied on the ground) when I started to rotate it so the back side would get light. The hook had come partially undone when we previously moved it, and the slight movement of the rotation caused the whole thing to fall!

Above: The white hook connects the chain to the 20" basket. Use pliers to close it so that it doesn't fall. The green hook connects the 16" basket to its hanger. Be sure it is completely closed. Below: The swivel hook I use to turn the baskets.

Large baskets are heavy, and you need to know how much they weigh in order to choose the correct hardware. Average basket weights for the ones we planted are: 16", 20 pounds; 18" Imperial and 20" basket, 40 pounds each.

I always have someone help me decide how to hang the basket, someone who knows more than I do about loads. The chain department at your local home improvement or hardware store is a wealth of information. The chains are rated by weight, which helps a lot. That is where I found this hook (left), which swivels. Take this book so you can show the salesperson exactly what you want. It is much easier to plant the basket with one of these hooks, so you can turn it as you plant. And, it makes them easier to maintain because you need to turn them every few days if they are planted in an area of uneven light, such as adjacent to a solid wall.

Baskets on Posts

The most popular feature of our trial gardens is our baskets on posts. They elicit more comments and questions than any other plant or garden accessory we have - and lots of oohs and aahs!

Think about it - flowers in most gardens are on the ground, quite a distance from your eyes! By raising them to eye level, you see them more closely. Another layer is added to the garden.

All of our baskets on posts get water from our garden sprinklers! We water twice a week if it doesn't rain, which is all the large ones need for much of their lifespan (more about water on page 354).

Installing Baskets on Posts

We used wooden posts to support our baskets. If wood comes into contact with soil, it rots, so we put a 4" x 4" cedar post on the stake (shown on the opposite page on top). The sharp part is pounded (or dig a hole and plant it!) into the soil, up to the level of the square top. This can be hard if you are working in soil with a lot of roots or rock, but it is easier than digging and then pouring concrete! The rest is simple. Just place the post in the square holder and tighten the screws. Since the post is in contact with metal instead of soil, we didn't think it would rot.

We were wrong. Water collected in the square section of the metal holders and the wood started to rot at the end of eighteen months. We also found the 4" x 4" posts too flimsy for the 20" baskets - two out of six fell.

Above: Use only baskets that are flat on the bottom to mount on posts.

   For container sources, go to www.easygardencolor.com

Basket Basic: Light and Plant Replacement

Installing Baskets on Posts (continued)

Above, left: This stake makes it possible to install a post without concrete. Above, right: After the stake is pounded into the ground, insert the post in the square section that remains above ground. The wooden posts we tried in these stakes began to rot on the bottom after about 18 months, so use them for short-term use only.

It is safer to use larger posts (at least 6" x 6") for the 20" baskets and 4" x 4" posts for the 16" baskets. Sink the posts securely in a hole lined with concrete for security.

I like the posts at 3', 4', and 5' heights - that is, the above-ground height. And give them plenty of space. At first, we put the posts too close together. The baskets on pages 92-93 eventually grew together with posts spaced two feet apart. Leave about 3 to 4 feet in between your posts for the larger, 20" baskets.

Once you have the post in the ground, cut a piece of marine plywood the same size as the flat bottom of your basket. Nail it to the top of the post. Drill small holes in the top for you to run wires to connect the container to the post. You'll need four wires to hold it securely.

Use your imagination! Decorative columns would look great, or iron plant stands, as long as they are secure with the weight of the baskets. I would love to see your creations. Email me photos at info@easygardencolor.com; you may see them in a book someday!

Be sure to find a spot with good light all around your basket because I haven't yet figured out how to rotate them after they are wired into place.

Side-Planted Baskets Need More Light than Other Containers

Above, top: These coleus are suffering from too little light. Bottom: Variegated ivy is a good choice for shady spots.

The plants at the bottom of the sides of the baskets do not get as much light as the plants in the top. My baskets did not do well in too much shade, even planted with shade plants, like coleus or torenia. Check out 'Assessing Shade' on pages 142-143, and stick to spots that are light shade or brighter for most plants.

Baskets do better if they are in the open and receive light from all sides. If you hang them with one side against your house, that side will not receive light unless you turn it. If you will never see that side, don't worry about it. However, if the basket is viewed from all sides, like outside a screened porch where it is seen from inside and out, be sure to hang it with one of the swivel hooks shown on page 352 and turn it every few days.

Ivy is a good choice for the bottom layer of baskets that may be in too much shade. The variegated ivy shows up better in shade than the dark green ivy. And, ivy is very easy to use. I buy it in a small hanging basket from the garden center. After removing the root ball from the pot, simply pull small pieces of ivy off the root ball. Tuck these pieces around the bottom of the basket.

Check out page 173 to see a basket specifically designed for shade.

Replacing Plants

If a plant dies that was planted in the top of the basket, it is easy to replace (see page 340). Replacing dead plants from the sides of the basket is a bit more of a challenge. Luckily, if you stick to the ones I suggest on pages 78-79, it won't happen often. If it does, pull it out and force another one in the same hole as best you can. Be sure to soak the roots in water first to make it easier to fit in the small hole. I have never had a replacement plant die!

Basket Watering

Watering

Above: Be sure to water the basket thoroughly and evenly, until the water comes out of the bottom. This wand that fits on the end of a hose is great for watering baskets.

Above: Our baskets on posts get water from the sprinklers that water the garden. We supplement with hand watering as needed because the baskets sometimes need more water than the landscape plantings.

Watering

The most common reason for plant death in hanging baskets is overwatering. The plants placed through the sides of the basket retain water longer than the plants placed on the top. When we first planted these baskets, we had them in a section of the nursery that gets daily water. After a few weeks of this drenching, many of the plants placed on the sides of the baskets died. When I checked them with my finger, the soil around them was completely soaked, and I realized I had drowned the poor things. We replaced the dead plants and moved the baskets to another area where we could water less frequently. I began to check the soil under the coco fiber at the base of the side plantings before watering. We had no more unexpected plant fatalities.

The baskets we planted in March on average needed water every three days when they were placed in light shade. As the plants grew and the days warmed, we increased the water to every other day. In the heat of summer, when the plants are fully grown, plan on daily watering if the plants are in the sun. Some of the thirstiest plants, like sweet potato vines, need water twice a day in full sun in the summer. It's best to stick to shade baskets for summer, like the one shown on page 173.

Baskets in very windy locations are hard to manage. The wind dries them out quickly, so be prepared to water often before making the decision to use them in a windy spot.

If your plant shows signs of wilt, water it. Otherwise, use your finger to see if the soil is dry before watering.

We used three different systems for watering our baskets: hand watering, drip irrigation, and in-ground sprinklers (the same ones that water the garden). Hand watering is the most time consuming. The drip system worked pretty well. My friend, Tim Hadsell, installed it, and it didn't take too long. He ran a black flexible pipe from my hose bib to the pots. Tiny black tubes (I call them spaghetti tubes) ran from the larger pipe to the pots. Little emitters were attached to the tubes and stuck into the pot. Different kinds of emitters fit different pots. We hooked it to a timer, which I found difficult to use, so, I just turned on the hose when I wanted to water, and all the pots connected to the drip system got watered at the same time.

I found a few disadvantages to the drip system. You need to check the emitters from time to time to be sure that work because they can get clogged. Well water clogs them up more than city water. Also, sometimes an emitter would fall out of a pot, and I would not notice it until the plant wilted. Another disadvantage is that all the plants on the same system get watered at the same time. Some may need it when the rest don't.

Our baskets on posts get water from our sprinkler system most of the time. We water our gardens twice a week if it isn't raining. When the weather is hot and the basket is big, twice a week is not enough, so we supplement with hand watering.

For container sources, go to www.easygardencolor.com

Planting & Mounting Epiphytic Orchids

Planting an Orchid in a Slatted Basket

1. Put some coco-fiber in the bottom and along the sides of the basket to keep the potting mix from falling out.

2. Be sure to use orchid potting mix instead of regular potting mix. It is available at most garden centers.

3. Remove the orchid from its plastic pot, and clean the old mix off the roots.

4. If roots are discolored, they are bad. Cut them off.

5. Put some planting mix in the container. Add the orchid. Pat more mix around it, and anchor it with a clip or wooden stake if it is wobbly.

6. Add the hangers, and put it on a tree. Since this is a phalaenopsis orchid, it is tilted so the water won't remain in the crown (p. 166).

Mounting an Orchid on a Tree

1. Clean the old potting mix off the roots, and cut off any bad roots, as shown in step 4 above.

2. Hold the roots against the tree. This is a 2 person job. Have someone else do the tying.

3. Secure the roots with stretchy tape or anything that will hold the orchid well and not cut into the tree.

Planting an Instant Wall Pot

1. Hang your wall pot (16" round hayrack) first. It is quite difficult to plant otherwise. The wires measure 2" apart at the top. This is about the minimum size in which to put plants with 4.5" root balls.

2. This pot is easy to secure to lattice. We used simple wire, twisting it behind the lattice.

3. Fill the bottom and the back with coco fiber, up to about four inches from the bottom.

4. Look for light through the coco fiber. Add more where needed. Remember, the purpose of the fiber is to keep plants and soil inside the container, not to fill it up.

5. Fill the hollowed fiber with loose, good-quality potting soil. See page 336 for more information about potting soil.

6. Add slow-release fertilizer, being careful to follow the instructions on the box. If you add too much, the plants could burn. Not enough, and they will not thrive.

For container sources, go to www.easygardencolor.com

If you haven't watched the enclosed DVD, now is the time! I made the DVD because of the difficulty I had understanding hanging basket demos in books. The DVD hanging basket demo will make this arrangement easier to understand, although this demo below includes more details.

7. To take the plant out of its pot, hold it upside down and pull the pot off the root ball. If it resists, squeeze the sides of the pot and try again, or cut the pot off with garden shears.

8. Check to make sure the roots are not growing in a tight circle inside the pot. If they are, loosen them and break away the ones on the bottom of the root ball.

9. Since this root ball is too big to fit through the wires of this pot, I soak it in water so I can squeeze it down to size.

10. Once the roots are soaked, remove them from the water and squeeze the ball flat (between your palms) so that it is small enough to go through the sides of the basket.

11. In order to fit it easily through the slats, it should be flat, like a sandwich. The sides of this basket are smaller than the hanging basket in the previous chapter, so the root balls must be smaller.

12. Slide the root ball through the slats, so the roots are on top of the soil, the stem is next to the coco fiber, and the leaves are outside the container.

Planting an Instant Wall Pot

13. Now, rotate the root ball so the flat side faces down.

14. Alternate your plants on this layer. I planted every other slot. This is what your pot should look like from the outside after you have inserted all the plants. Expect the roots to be close! This is a lot of plant material for this size pot, but you will like the final result, and the coleus take the crowding just fine.

15. Add coco fiber until it extends about one inch above the top.

16. Your pot should now look like this one at this point.

17. Position your centerpiece (a one-gallon ti plant) as close to the back of the pot as possible. Its roots should be soaked and reduced, like the other plants.

For container sources, go to www.easygardencolor.com

If you haven't watched the enclosed DVD, now is the time! I made the DVD because of the difficulty I had understanding hanging basket demos in books. The DVD hanging basket demo will make this one easier to understand, although this demo does include more details.

18. Time to add some soil and fertilizer. Add just enough soil to bring the tops of the root balls of the next layer of coleus even with the top of the root ball of the ti plant.

19. Plant the top layer of coleus. Tilt the plants slightly, so that they cover the black wire.

20. Fill in <u>lightly</u> with soil. Do not pack it down. Cover up any bare roots you see without getting any soil close to the stems. Fill in between the plants.

21. Add the final bit of fertilizer.

22. Admire your masterpiece, but don't even think about watering it! The roots are soaked! Wait until you see signs of wilt or when the soil feels dry after you have tested it down to about 1/2 inch with your finger. Overwatering is the most common cause of plant death in these baskets. In most situations, they will only need water every 2 to 3 days until they are quite large. Fill in the bare spots with soil after the first watering.

Bibliography

Armitage, Allan. *Armitage's Garden Annuals.* Portland, Oregon: Timber Press, 2004.

Batchelor, Stephen. *Your First Orchid.* Delray Beach, Florida: American Orchid Society, 2001.

Broschat, Timothy K. and Meerow, Alan W. *Betrock's Reference Guide to Florida Landscape Plants.* Hollywood, Florida: Betrock Information Systems, 1999.

Luebbermann, Mimi. *Easy Orchids.* San Francisco, California: Chronicle Books, 1996.

MacCubbin, Tom, and Tasker, Georgia. *Florida Gardener's Guide.* Franklin, Tennessee: Cool Springs Press Inc., 2002.

Morton, Julia. *Plants Poisonous to People.* Miami, Florida: Hallmark Press. 1995.

Noble, Mary. *You Can Grow Orchids.* Jacksonville, Florida: Mary Noble McQuerry Publisher, 1985.

McDonald, Elvin. *Ortho's All About Orchids.* Des Moines, Iowa: Meredith Corportation, Ortho Books, 1999.

Ross, Susan, and Schrader, Dennis. *Hot Plants for Cool Climates.* New York: Houghton Mifflin Company, 2000.

Smith, P. Allen. *Container Gardens.* New York, New York: Clarkson Potter/Publishers, 2005.

The South Florida Orchid Society. *An Introduction to Orchids.* Edited by Julie Rosenberg. Miami, Florida: The South Florida Orchid Society, 2005.

Williams, Paul. *Container Gardening.* New York, New York: DK Publishing, 2004.

Index

Index

Index

Index

Index

For container sources, go to
www.easygardencolor.com

The Florida Gardening Series...

Florida Gardening Series, Volume 1

EASY GARDENS for SOUTH FLORIDA

- companion to *Best Garden Color for Florida*
- simple landscape plants and gardens
by Pamela Crawford

Volume 1 -
Easy Gardens for South Florida

This book is the first of a series of books designed to educate both gardeners - and the professionals who work with them - about the keys to achieving an easy, beautiful landscape. It describes in detail the first (and easiest) 100 plants that survived decades of extensive trials and includes chapters on garden planting and maintenance that are critical for the success of the Florida garden. It tells you how to water, plant, fertilize, control pests, mulch, trim, and control weeds. These maintenance instructions will keep people from making all the mistakes the author made when she began gardening here. She shares years of research and experience that will save you years of mistakes and frustration.

Florida Gardening Series Volume 2

Best Garden Color for Florida

- primarily for USDA Zones 9 through 11 in Florida
- best annuals, perennials, flowering shrubs, & trees
- companion to "Easy Gardens for Florida"
by Pamela Crawford

Volume 2 -
Best Garden Color for Florida

This book is a must-have for Florida gardeners and professionals who love garden color! It is not only loaded with 575 spectacular photos, but also includes reams of easy-to-understand information about use and care of 150 terrific Florida plants. The plant information is complemented with chapters filled with ideas about color for butterflies, sun, shade, salt, and wind. The book is a result of decades of plant research by the author to determine which plants and planting strategies give the most color for the least amount of care. The author personally grew most of the plants, giving her practical experience with all aspects of the plants' use and maintenance. It is a companion to the bestselling *Easy Gardens for South Florida*. No information is repeated in either book. The two work together to give you the best garden color for Florida.